THE
BORDER
BOOK

THE
BORDER
BOOK

Anna Pavord

DK Publishing, Inc.

A Dorling Kindersley Book
www.dk.com

To Oenone and her future garden

Project Editor Claire Calman
Project Art Editor Gillian Andrews
Editorial Assistant Melanie Tham
Designer Bob Gordon
US Editor Ray Rogers

Managing Editor Jane Aspden
Managing Art Editor Ina Stradins

Principal Illustrators Sharon Beeden, Martine Collings

FRONT COVER: *A Low-maintenance Scheme pp.82–85*
BACK COVER: *A Tropical Summer Border pp.32–35*

FACING TITLE PAGE:
A shady spring planting with strong foliage interest, the deep purple leaves
of Viola labradorica *contrast with the green-gold ribbons of Bowles' golden*
grass, Milium effusum 'Aureum'. *The soft pink flowers of* Anemone nemorosa
form a foil for the sharper colors of the other plants.

First Paperback Edition, 2000
First American Edition, 1994
2 4 6 8 10 9 7 5 3 1

Published in the United States by Dorling Kindersley Publishing, Inc.,
95 Madison Avenue, New York, New York, 10016

First published in Great Britain 1994
by Dorling Kindersley Publishers Limited,
9 Henrietta Street, London WC2 8PS

Library of Congress Cataloging-in-Publication Data

Pavord, Anna.
    The border book / by Anna Pavord, -- 1st American ed.
        p.   cm.
    Includes index
    ISBN 0–7894–5116–6 Paperback
    ISBN 1–56438–485–2 Hardcover
    1. Garden borders. 2. Gardens--Design.
    3. Garden borders--Pictorial works. I. Title.
SB424.P38 1994
716--dc20   93–28347
                                                                    CIP

Reproduced by Bright Arts (HK) Ltd, Hong Kong
Printed and bound in Singapore by Star Standard Industries (Pte.) Ltd.

PREFACE

WHY DO WE GARDEN? Fortunately, this is a question that psychologists have never tackled. Their findings might put us off for life. Central to the activity is the fact that when you garden you abandon a timetable constructed around dentist appointments, car services, and the possible arrival of trains, to be subsumed into a different one, an immense and inexorable one that is entirely outside your control. This calendar controls the growth of plants, their living, seeding, and dying. In order to garden successfully, we have to respect and become part of that cycle.

But a garden is an artificial construct. It is not usually the same as the natural landscape that may lie over the boundary wall. We garden to provide a setting for ourselves in which we feel comfortable. We garden because we like looking after things. We garden because we want to create but cannot paint or sculpt.

Apprentice gardeners want rules: now is the time to plant the daffodils, this is the way to prune your clematis, here is how to sow your seeds. As with bringing up babies, this information was once absorbed by example rather than simply learned from books. But rules tend to be of limited use in gardening. They act as a kind of life belt when you first start off, but they can be deceptive. In the end, a gardener is better served by his own powers of observation. The vagaries of climate and season and soil constantly force the gardener to rewrite the rule book. In gardening, the learning never stops. The more you know, the more you realize how much there is still to learn.

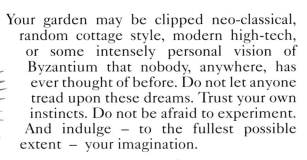

Your garden may be clipped neo-classical, random cottage style, modern high-tech, or some intensely personal vision of Byzantium that nobody, anywhere, has ever thought of before. Do not let anyone tread upon these dreams. Trust your own instincts. Do not be afraid to experiment. And indulge – to the fullest possible extent – your imagination.

ANNA PAVORD

CONTENTS

—— ❧ ——

—— ❧ ——

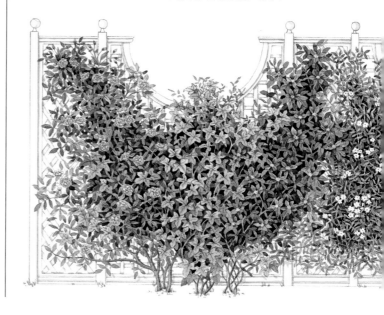

HOW TO USE THIS BOOK

THERE ARE MANY THOUSANDS OF PLANTS available and countless ways of combining them. *The Border Book* demystifies the art of creating effective plant associations and provides a diversity of planting plans for all sorts of sites – from a large, formal border for a hot, sunny garden to a small, informal design for a stony patch of ground. You can use the planting schemes like recipes in a cookbook – follow them precisely or play around with the combination of ingredients to produce your own unique creation. For each scheme, a glorious full-color illustration shows what the design will look like if you reproduce it to the letter. Supplementary plans offer suggestions on ways of introducing alternative plants to suit different growing conditions or different tastes.

THE INTRODUCTION – CREATIVE PLANTING
At the beginning of the book, an introductory chapter on creative planting outlines basic principles of sound design, exploring ways of combining plants to establish pleasing echoes and exciting contrasts of color and form. This chapter also looks at style, foliage interest, texture, and scent, and how to select appropriate plants for the conditions in your garden.

THE PLANTING SCHEMES
The book is divided into five chapters, each comprising a particular type of scheme. *Mixed Borders* includes plans designed to be seen mainly from one side, while *Island and Other Beds* shows schemes that are effective from more than one viewpoint. *Corner Sites* provides designs for awkward corners, and *Vertical Spaces* includes plans for planting up walls, pergolas, and frames. *Forgotten Places* is a collection of schemes for difficult areas – for example, patios and steps. Each scheme is self-contained and includes a complete plant list, clear planting plan, and illustration of the established planting.

PLANTING PLAN KEY
The key below shows the symbols used to denote each type of plant included in the schemes – whether a tree, shrub, perennial, or bulb, for example.

Tree

Shrub

Conifer

Perennial

Annual

Bulb

Succulent   Evergreen

PLANT LIST
Each scheme includes a complete list of all the plants used and the number of plants required. Full botanical names are given, with common names where appropriate. The quantities should be taken only as a rough guide, depending on the area you have available; you can use fewer plants but it will take longer for them to fill the allotted space.

PLANTING PLAN
A clear planting plan shows the type, number, and position of each plant. Numbers around the plan correspond with those on the plant list. The dimensions of the bed as shown are given as a rough guide, but you can easily adapt a scheme for a smaller or larger area, or a site of a different shape, by using the same combination of plants.

DESIGN POINTS
Important design features or characteristics of a scheme, such as distinctive color combinations or strong interest from handsome foliage or architectural plants, are picked out to help you decide whether a scheme will suit you and your garden.

PLANTING SCHEME
A large, full-color artwork, specially commissioned to bring each plan vividly to life, illustrates clearly what a design will look like once it is established. Each planting scheme is shown in the season when it will be at its peak overall, but in order to maintain a long period of interest, some of the plants included will be at their best earlier or later in the year.

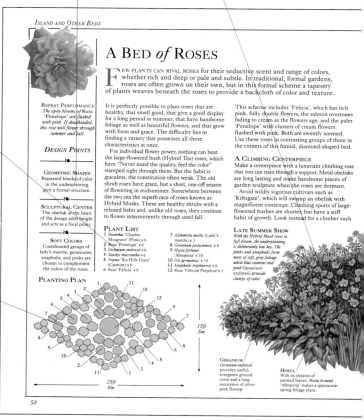

ISLAND AND OTHER BEDS

A BED *of* ROSES

FEW PLANTS CAN RIVAL ROSES for their seductive scent and range of colors, whether rich and deep or pale and subtle. In traditional, formal gardens, roses are often grown on their own, but in this formal scheme a tapestry of plants weaves beneath the roses to provide a backcloth of color and texture.

It is perfectly possible to plant roses that are healthy, that smell good, that give a good display for a long period in summer, that have handsome foliage as well as beautiful flowers, and that grow with form and grace. The difficulty lies in finding a variety that possesses all these characteristics at once.

For individual flower power, nothing can beat the large-flowered bush (Hybrid Tea) roses, which have "Never mind the quality, feel the color" stamped right through them. But the habit is graceless, the constitution often weak. The old shrub roses have grace, but a short, one-off season of flowering in midsummer. Somewhere between the two sits the superb race of roses known as Hybrid Musks. These are healthy shrubs with a relaxed habit and, unlike old roses, they continue to flower intermittently through until fall.

This scheme includes 'Felicia', which has rich pink, fully double flowers, with the salmon overtones fading to cream as the flowers age, and the paler 'Penelope' with clusters of cream flowers flushed with pink. Both are sweetly scented. Use these roses in contrasting groups of three in the corners of this formal, diamond-shaped bed.

A CLIMBING CENTERPIECE
Make a centerpiece with a luxuriant climbing rose that you can train through a support. Metal obelisks are long lasting and make handsome pieces of garden sculpture when the roses are dormant.

Avoid wildly vigorous cultivars such as 'Kiftsgate', which will swamp an obelisk with magnificent contempt. Climbing sports of large-flowered bushes are shorter, but have a stiff habit of growth. Look instead for a climber such

REPEAT PERFORMANCE
The open blooms of Rosa 'Penelope' are flushed with pink. If deadheaded, this rose will flower through summer and fall.

DESIGN POINTS

GEOMETRIC SHAPES
Repeated blocks of color in the underplanting give a formal structure.

SCULPTURAL CENTER
The obelisk at the heart of the design adds height and acts as a focal point.

SOFT COLORS
Coordinated groups of lady's mantle, geraniums, anaphalis, and pinks are chosen to complement the colors of the roses.

PLANT LIST
1 *Dianthus* 'Charles Musgrave' (Pink) x 6
2 *Rosa* 'Penelope' x 6
3 *Geranium endressii* x 6
4 *Stachys macrantha* x 6
5 *Nepeta* 'Six Hills Giant' (Catmint) x 6
6 *Rosa* 'Felicia' x 6
7 *Alchemilla mollis* (Lady's mantle) x 3
8 *Geranium psilostemon* x 6
9 *Hosta fortunei* 'Albopicta' x 10
10 *Iris germanica* x 14
11 *Anaphalis triplinervis* x 6
12 *Rosa* 'Félicité Perpétue' x 1

PLANTING PLAN

25ft
8m

15ft
5m

LATE SUMMER SHOW
With the Hybrid Musk roses in full bloom, the underplanting is deliberately low key. The pinks and anaphalis form mats of soft, gray foliage while blue catmint and pink Geranium endressii provide clumps of color.

GERANIUM
Geranium endressii provides useful, evergreen ground cover and a long succession of silver-pink flowers.

HOSTA
With its sheaves of painted leaves, *Hosta fortunei* 'Albopicta' makes a spectacular spring foliage plant.

58

PLANT GALLERY AND SUPPLEMENTARY SCHEMES

Each scheme includes photographs of all the plants used, while practical tasks needed to maintain the plants are outlined under the Care and Cultivation reminders. Plans that extend to four pages include one or two supplementary artworks that give ideas on substituting alternative plants or adding extra ones. These help you adapt a scheme, either for a different site or to create a different visual effect – by changing the color combination, for example.

SUPPLEMENTARY SCHEME TEXT
This text suggests ways of altering the main plan to suit different growing conditions, change the color balance, or alter the principal season of interest.

SUPPLEMENTARY SCHEME ARTWORKS
Unique artworks graphically show the effect of using the substitute or additional plants. The original scheme is shown in a pale tint, while the new plants are portrayed in full color so that they stand out clearly.

CARE AND CULTIVATION
Brief reminders on the basic care needed for each scheme are given in the left-hand column. The tasks are divided so you can see at a glance what needs to be done in each season.

PLANT PORTRAITS
For every scheme, there is a photographic gallery of all the plants included. Each color photograph is accompanied by a caption that describes the plant and gives its expected height and spread.

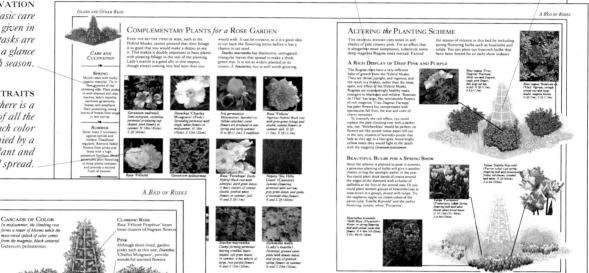

SECOND-SEASON DISPLAY
Schemes that are particularly attractive in another season are illustrated by a second artwork, showing what the design will look like then – in spring, for example, when bulbs that would not show in summer would be in full flower.

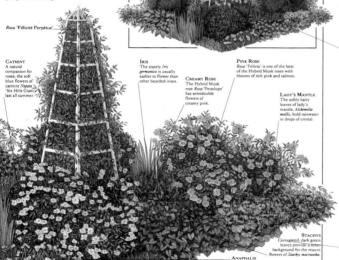

PLANT CHARACTERISTICS
Every plant that is included in a scheme is clearly annotated to point up a particular feature or characteristic.

PRACTICAL ADVICE
All the information you need to recreate and maintain the schemes in this book is included in *Care and Cultivation* (pp.146–153). This section covers basic routine tasks such as planting, staking, mulching, pruning and training, and propagation.

To help adapt a scheme for a particular site, use the *Planter's Guide*; this groups plants according to their tolerance of various growing conditions.

If you want to look up a specific plant, turn to the index, which lists all the plants under both botanical and common names.

CREATIVE PLANTING

Matching plants to positions is the key to good gardening, but in deciding what to put where, you have to consider the plants' needs as well as your own desires. It is no use being determined to have a plant unless you can give it the kind of conditions it would choose for itself, if it had that luxury. Not everything that you fall in love with will necessarily love you in return. Rhododendrons, for instance, demand acidic soil, as do a whole group of other woodland shrubs, such as pieris. It is pigheaded to try to grow them in alkaline soil. If you feel you must have them, but do not have the right soil, grow them in pots in a specially made acidic soil mix.

Space is also an important consideration. A shrub with a ten-foot soul is never going to look happy if it has constantly to be butchered to fit into a four-foot straitjacket. Think ahead when you are planting and, in your schemes, allow some plants the guarantee of living happily ever

▲ **EXPLOITING YOUR SPACE**
An out-of-the-way corner in this graveled yard is transformed by a mass of plants, many of them half hardy, all grown in pots. This suits the spiky agaves, plain and variegated; the waxy aeoniums by the door; the leafy ginger; and the yellow gazanias in the foreground.

▶ **PLANTING TO SUIT THE SITE**
Rich, damp ground, such as you might find beside a pool, is what you need to make Rodgersia podophylla *happy. Its handsomely veined, hand-shaped leaves make a superb foil for the tall, candelabra flowers of* Primula pulverulenta *and the blue-flowered* Iris sibirica.

after in the positions you have chosen for them. A garden that consists only of ephemeral planting will never be truly satisfying.

In the wild, plants are opportunists, adapting themselves to a wide range of conditions. You can exploit this, finding plants that will colonize the least desirable areas of the garden. A gravel path can stand in for an alpine scree; a dark corner by the garbage cans may be brought to life with plants that do not need sun to blossom.

ADAPTING SCHEMES

The dimensions given in this book, both for plants and for schemes, are approximate. Rate of growth depends on climate, soil, and – it must be said – the skill of the gardener. You may need to adjust schemes as they mature, transplanting a shrub to allow its neighbor to spread its wings.

The schemes have been arranged into sections such as beds, borders, and corners, but there is no reason why you should not adapt a bed plan for a corner or a corner planting as part of a border. Do not, however, expect plants such as the rodgersia included in a scheme for a damp poolside to be happy in a dry, hot slope in full sunshine. Remember, too, that vagaries of climate and season will sometimes wreck the most carefully laid plans – or bring you results more magical than in your wildest dreams.

▲ PLANTS FOR A DRY, SUNNY BED
Architectural plants dominate this scheme suitable for a dry, sunny site. The European fan palm, Chamaerops humilis, *is the main focus with* Aeonium arboreum 'Atropurpureum' *in front of it. To the right is spiky* Yucca filamentosa 'Variegata', *its form echoing the leaves of the palm.*

► SPRING COLOR
The Lenten rose, Helleborus orientalis, is at its best in early spring with flowers ranging from deep plum-purple to purest white. The insides of the petals are often freckled with darker color. The leaves are as handsome as the flowers.

►► EXTENDED INTEREST
Ferns are confident enough to dispense with flowers altogether. Form is all and, undistracted by color, you can settle to the engrossing business of finding them suitable partners. They have a long period of interest, at their most dramatic unfurling in late spring, as here.

SEASONAL IMPACT AND CONTINUITY

In spring it is impossible to resist the call of the nursery and garden center. There is a beguiling sensation of making a fresh start. Blinded by an optimism of the most irrational kind, mesmerized by the ranks of plants all bursting into life, you ricochet from magnolia to rhododendron, from ceanothus to chaenomeles, each plant the center of a new dream.

The danger of this spring euphoria is that you may end up with a garden crammed with plants that give their all in spring and early summer and have nothing to show for the rest of the year. Not all areas of the garden will be equally attractive in all seasons – nor do they need to be. You may plan it so that one bed stars in fall and winter, for example, while another is at its best in spring and summer. Your garden must have an underpinning of structural planting, however, shrubs that are the equivalent of the most important pieces of furniture in a room.

In choosing these structural plants, look for ones with a long season of interest; they may be architectural in form or have handsome foliage. Some should be evergreen, so that in winter the garden does not entirely dissolve into a mess of rotting leaves and skeletal branches. The spurge, *Euphorbia characias* subsp. *wulfenii*, is a fine example of a plant that has presence all year, not just when it is flowering.

◄ SEASONAL DISPLAY
Dark-leaved annual dahlias and tumbling nasturtiums are added to more permanent planting for hot summer color. Seasonal displays such as this are a good way of changing a garden's emphasis.

▲ FALL DELIGHTS
Beadlike berries and the changing colors of leaves are a particular pleasure of fall. Sorbus 'Joseph Rock' *bears pale, creamy berries that deepen to yellow as they age. The leaves turn from green to warm orange, red, and purple.*

With these key plants in place, you can start filling in the gaps in between. Foils are as important as features when you are combining plants in the garden. Not everything should be screaming "Look at me!" You need bright pools of summer annuals, but you also need plants that are no more than quietly supportive. After a while, these are the plants that you actually might come to prefer.

It often helps to think of planting as a three-tier affair. Three separate groups of plants can occupy the same piece of ground, though not all will necessarily peak at the same time. High up you have trees and large shrubs, in the middle tier herbaceous perennials, and scrabbling around underneath, low-growing ground cover plants and bulbs. By using the space carefully, you can arrange it so that a spring-flowering tree has summer-flowering perennials under it, interspersed with bulbs, perhaps colchicums, that come spearing through the soil in fall. That patch of ground will be earning its keep over a long period in the garden.

▲ FOLIAGE INTEREST
For long-lasting impact, choose plants with good foliage rather than a brief flush of flowers. The combination of Crocosmia 'Lucifer' *and* Dahlia 'Bishop of Llandaff' *used here provides late summer color, but both plants earn their space twice over with their fine leaves – the upright swords of the crocosmia and the dark bronze foliage of the dahlias make a contribution long before the flowers start to appear.*

◀ SCULPTURAL SEEDHEADS
The flowers of this poppy, Papaver somniferum, *are coming to an end, but the sculptural seedheads will continue to look good until the end of the summer. They also dry well for use later in indoor flower arrangements. Poppies such as this self-seed liberally, making handsome clumps of glaucous foliage among earlier spring flowers.*

PLANTING STYLES

Gardeners are usually told that the first step when laying out a garden is to make a plan, but before you can even begin on this task, you have to decide on the mood of the garden: formal, exotic, wild, cottagey. In a large garden, you can combine several of these styles in different areas, with screens, hedges, and walls dividing one stage set from the next. In a small garden, this is more difficult to arrange. You need more restraint if the design is to cohere well.

The mood of a garden is dictated by its general design and layout, but the right plants are important, too. Particular plants reinforce particular styles. In a formal garden you expect clipped boxwood and yew, or fruit trees trained into espaliers and fans. Single-color borders would be at home here as would borders with bold plants such as red-hot pokers or acanthus used at regular intervals to break up the planting. Although the formal style of gardening grew in the grand manner out of the Italian Renaissance with its balustrades, elaborate stone seats, urns,

▶ **INFORMAL ABUNDANCE**
Bold clumps of Euphorbia characias *subsp.* wulfenii *dominate this informal planting, which relies as much on foliage as flowers for its impact. The central terracotta pot gives a focus to the group, but does not draw too much attention to itself. Gray foliage, used here in quantity, acts as a buffer between plants, softening the effect of color contrasts.*

▼ **FORMAL PATTERNING**
Regularly repeated blocks of plants – alchemilla and mats of acaena in the foreground, bold clumps of rudbeckia behind – emphasize the formal nature of this scheme. The symmetrically placed urns accentuate the formality.

and terraces, it adapts more easily than any other genre to a small town garden. For this sort of style you need symmetry, evergreens, stone, and – if you can stand the expense – water.

In a wild garden, you use glorified versions of wild flowers: papery poppies with petals like colored tissue left in the rain, small-flowered narcissus, foxgloves extravagantly marked at the throat, all planted under apple blossoms. Wild gardening can take many forms: lush planting by a stream, a meadow swaying with long grasses and colorful flowers, an overgrown orchard, or a woodland idyll where azaleas flame lazily over banks of English bluebells. The trick always is not to try too hard – sweet disorder is the key. You can't be tidy and wild at the same time.

Many of the most exciting gardens fit into no category at all. These are the ones fired by a personal vision. They may be eccentric, but their creators show unfailing sympathy for plants and the way that they grow. You too could free yourself from the yoke of conformity.

▲ ON THE WILD SIDE
Borage and dill, both fast-growing culinary herbs, combine here to make an effective informal planting, which will be at its peak in midsummer. Self-seeding plants such as the opium poppy with purple-pink flowers are natural allies in areas where you want a casual, spontaneous effect.

ADAPTABLE PLANTS

Some plants, like the best sort of aunts, get along in any company and can adapt themselves to all styles of planting. Euphorbias immediately come to mind in this context. The flowers, though an extraordinary, wild lime green, tone well with any color you put with them. They are elegant with white, cool with blue, stunning with pink, sophisticated with yellow. Structure is important, too; the plants hold themselves well and have excellent foliage. You soon learn to recognize your best friends when you are planning planting schemes. Whatever the style, include a high proportion of plants that offer more than the color of their flower.

▶ MIXING STYLES
The frame is formal, with the iron bower visually anchored to the ground by two beautifully clipped boxwood balls, but the planting in this large pot is wonderfully exuberant. It peaks in late summer with melianthus, skirts of helichrysum, and a long succession of daisy flowers from the argyranthemum 'Chelsea Girl'.

PLAYING WITH COLOR

Color has dominated theories of garden design for most of this century, ever since the famous plantswoman Gertrude Jekyll laid out her carefully graded borders, working through pale, recessive tones to a crescendo of fiery oranges and reds. But there are no unbreakable rules about using color. In the end, a gardener is best served by his own powers of observation.

Single-color borders are vogueish, but deceptively difficult to do well. And in restricting yourself this way, you deny yourself the pleasures of a wider palette. Use foliage plants as buffers between colors that make you anxious and make a resolution never, ever, ever to plant a white garden. You will not regret it.

Yellow is the color that gardeners appear to be most cautious about, but a certain shade of sugar pink is the only color that it quarrels with noisily. Combined with blue, yellow will give you the authentic Monet effect. Yellow with white and the kind of sharp lime green provided by alchemilla makes an extremely fresh color combination. Create quieter combinations using pastel shades interspersed with gray foliage plants. They should not be so quiet that you fall asleep while looking at them.

► **BENDING THE RULES**
The star plant in this group is the yellow crocosmia which tones beautifully, against all the so-called rules, with the pink Japanese anemones behind it and the richer pink mats of phuopsis in front. Some yellows are easier to work with than others, but it is criminal to ban them altogether from the garden as some highly strung gardeners feel they must. If you are nervous, use them with blue as with the agapanthus here.

► **COOL COLORS**
Blue and white flowers, as with these mixed annual echiums and nemophilas, have an appealing, crisp freshness. This cool combination can be achieved within a single season from spring-sown seed.

◄ **FOLIAGE BUFFER**
The dark foliage of a purple cotinus is used as a buffer between the fiery tones of a red-hot poker and the pink of the foreground phlox. Purple foliage, which absorbs and deadens light, is not always easy to place in the garden but is used well here.

► **LIMITED PALETTE**
The chalky whiteness of the foreground flowers in this delicately controlled color combination is subtly underpinned by the pale pink Alba rose behind and the hints of cream and blue to the right. All benefit by being displayed against the strong shapes of the foliage behind them.

▼ **FRAGRANT ARCHWAY**
Roses scrambling over this simple metal arch bring flower smells just where you need them – right under your nose. Summer gardens are bursting with scents: plant climbing roses, honeysuckle, and moonflowers.

THE PLEASURES OF SCENT

Scent is one of the most dangerously evocative of the senses. In the garden it creates a fourth dimension – a separate, unseen landscape hanging in the air, changing shape with the seasons. Many heavily scented flowers are white – mock orange, summer jasmine, madonna lilies, lily-of-the-valley – and look their best planted against dark backgrounds. Some, such as evening primrose, save their scent for evening, which is thoughtful, since that is when we most often have time to notice them.

Too often plant breeders sacrifice scent in pursuit of other objectives: bigger flowers, a wider range of colors. The loss of natural scent in flowers too highly bred for our own good is ironically paralleled by the rise in aromatherapy. We always knew that smells were good for us, only now we are being asked to pay through the nose for the privilege. Ignore those expensive bottles. Plant some real smells instead.

► **PERFUMED LEAVES**
Plants that have scented foliage, such as many herbs and this pelargonium 'Sweet Mimosa', are a delight – reach out and rub the leaves as you pass by to release their perfume.

SHAPE AND FORM

Shape and form are just as important as color when you are looking for plants to set each other off in the garden. The clever juxtaposition of contrasting shapes may make a less immediate impact than a daring melee of magenta and orange but it is the subtle interplay of height, scale, and substance in a garden that will provide a more sustaining diet. The orange-pink shock will only work once. The contrast of bold rodgersia, say, with a delicate fern such as *Adiantum pedatum*, pierced by the tall stems of a group of white lilies, will draw you back again and again.

Form of one sort or another is vital in a garden; if it is lacking in the overall design, you can reinforce it by patterning the planting. This does not mean restricting the planting to a formula – one of this, two of those and then one of this again – but it does often mean using more of less. In a small garden this requires superhuman restraint, for the urge to cram in as many different plants as possible is strong.

Reinforcing the lines of paths can have a marked effect on the look of a garden. Those that are straight and wide will probably not need this help, but the lines of narrower, curving paths easily become swamped and can look muddled. Think of edging the path with the same plant for its entire length. This immediately makes the path more important. The edging also has a unifying effect on the planting behind it. It all begins to look less random, more cohesive. Of course, you need to use the right kind of

▲ CONTRASTING FORMS
The huge umbrella leaves of gunnera are stunning in their own right but also make a fine backdrop for the different leaf forms in the foreground. The heart-shaped, metallic blue leaves of the hosta form a neat mound, while a pointed contrast is made by the strong verticals of a white Iris sibirica *and tall stems of airy seedheads.*

◄ SCULPTURAL PLANT
Eryngium giganteum *is a biennial sea holly, rising in the second year to make a statuesque plant, the flowers poised like candles in a candelabra.*

plant for the job. Avoid anything that will flop all over the path or anything so tall that it will obscure the plants behind it.

STRUCTURAL PLANTING
Gardens also need landmarks. A landmark plant is the opposite of one that you would use for edging. It must be a bold one-off, strongly architectural, an extrovert, a shark among minnows. Its leaves and general habit of growth will probably be more important than its flower. The variegated aralia is a classic landmark plant, but unfortunately it is not evergreen. Mahonia has all the necessary attributes – and scent, too. How you site landmark plants will influence the way that your eye moves over the garden – and the way *you* move round the garden, too. Use tall crambe as a promontory where you want to create a visual obstacle, masking what lies around the corner, making it more intriguing.

HEIGHT AND SCALE

The scale of a plant in relation to the space that it is sitting in provides endless opportunities to experiment. The tallest plants do not always have to be at the back of a border. A clump of the willowy, tall *Verbena bonariensis* makes a dramatic feature in the foreground of a planting. Nor should you feel that because you have a small garden, you have to fill it with small plants; a plethora of miniature plants can look fussy and lacking in emphasis. A fig tree growing in a small enclosed courtyard has immense drama. So does a yucca. Try it and see.

► FOUNTAIN OF FOLIAGE
The ostrich fern, Matteuccia struthiopteris, *has no need of flowers to impress – its arching fronds spread out like spokes, creating a strong, architectural shape.*

▼ STRENGTHENING INFORMAL PLANTING
A euphorbia adds substance to this unstructured planting and is as handsome in winter as it is in summer. The controlled color combination puts extra emphasis on variations in plant form.

▲ LIVING LANDMARK
The sculptural skeleton of a towering onopordum dominates this section of an informal mixed border, complemented by the shapely spires of purple delphiniums. Architectural plants such as these are ideal for adding structure and substance to a scheme of airy or mound-forming plants.

FINE FOLIAGE

Many useful border plants, such as asters, penstemons, and members of the daisy family, are sadly deficient in the matter of leaves. When they are out of flower there is little else on offer. Although when you first garden you may think always in terms of flowers, the benefits of foliage soon creep up on you. Leaves bring form, bulk, and texture to mixed plantings. They also bring color, though in a more subtle way than flowers: as well as variegated leaves, there are purple, gold, blue, gray, silver, and a thousand different shades of green.

All the most satisfying plant groups include plants with strong foliage – fat bergenia leaves, plumes of artemisia, swords of phormium and yucca. Sword leaves are especially useful in punctuating the low, rounded masses of so many herbaceous plants. You do not want too many of them, in the same way that you do not want to keep tripping over commas in a piece of prose, but if well used, they are invaluable.

SURFACE TEXTURES

When you are combining plants, think about contrasts and echoes of texture as well as form. Some leaves, such as the glaucous, waxy foliage of *Melianthus major*, provide the pleasures of both. Contrast it with a smooth, shiny, purple *Hebe* 'La Séduisante' or with a spiky phormium. Texture is provided both by the surface of a leaf – like the thick, felted covering on lamb's ears, *Stachys byzantina* – and by the effect of leaves *en masse*. Soft, hairy leaves such as those of alchemilla and *Meconopsis regia* hold raindrops in a dazzling way, each one a perfect bead shining like mercury. Foliage such as this will be your true ally in the garden.

▲ BURNING BUSH
The staghorn sumac, Rhus typhina, is ablaze with color when its leaves turn shades of fiery orange and red in fall.

◄ PATTERNED LEAVES
The bright, gold-splashed foliage of euonymus enlivens this planting of pale trilliums. Variegated leaves are as variously patterned as birds' feathers: splashed, striped, and spotted in silver, cream, or gold. The trilliums' lush leaves provide a sober background to offset its pagoda blooms.

► FERN COLLECTION
Ferns are the ultimate foliage plants, their finely fragmented fronds contrasting here with the smooth bulk of the large stones. The gleaming hart's-tongue ferns in front form a foil for the divided foliage of the other ferns behind: Adiantum venustum creeps over the wall, flanked by the shield fern, Dryopteris affinis, on the left and the chain fern, Woodwardia unigemmata, on the right at the rear. They will thrive wherever the ground is cool and damp and are ideal in shady courtyard gardens.

◄ **TEXTURAL CONTRASTS**
A filmy haze of fennel surrounds the newly emerging flowers of Alchemilla mollis, *which, though a rampant and determined self-seeder, is a magnificent plant in foliage as well as flower. The lobed, pleated leaves of the alchemilla have a distinctive shape and downy texture that complements the diaphanous foliage of the fennel.*

▲ **GLOSSY COAT**
Although the leaves of this holly, Ilex aquifolium *'Argentea Marginata', are variegated, the cream markings are hardly more of a pleasure than the surface texture – as shiny as a well-waxed car.*

MIXED BORDERS

◆

*Flexibility is the keynote of the modern border, which
is created on altogether more relaxed lines than
the grand (and difficult to maintain) old-fashioned
borders of carefully staked herbaceous perennials.
Modern borders contain a more eclectic mix
of plants: shrubs to provide structure and extend the
display, bulbs to carpet the ground in spring,
annuals for a burst of summer color. Also, you
do not need acres of garden to create the right effect.*

HYDRANGEA HEADS
On this Hydrangea
aspera *subsp.* aspera,
*compact heads of tiny
flowers are circled by
showy sterile flowers of
palest pink or even white.*

DESIGN POINTS

❧

SERENE SHADE
A tranquil scheme that
makes the most of a
shady situation. Colors
are generally muted apart
from the warm glow of
Bowles' golden sedge,
Carex elata 'Aurea'.

❧

LIVING CARPET
Shade-loving
epimedium, variegated
arum, bugle, and ginger
mint provide an
attractive, weed-
suppressing carpet
under the shrubs.

COOL COLORS *for* DAMP SHADE

THERE IS A SENSE of luxuriance and mystery about plants growing in shade that
you can never match in full sun. In shade, pale colors float like moths at dusk.
In sun, they just look washed out. Despite this, many gardeners treat shade as
a problem. Think of it instead as a heaven-sent opportunity: plenty of plants grow
far better in shade than anywhere else.

Shade brings a change of mood to a garden.
It is contemplative, introverted. It slows
you down, giving you time to notice the
magnificently extravagant diversity of plants
and flowers. From a distance, you may think
that the lacecap flowers of the *Hydrangea
aspera* subsp. *aspera* that features in this border
are rich violet, for example. When you stop
and rub noses with them, however, you can
see that the outside bracts are actually pink
and that the violet effect is created by the
brilliant blue stamens of the small, pink,
knobby flowers in the center of the head.

PLANT LIST

1 *Polygonatum* x *hybridum*
   (Solomon's seal) x 12
2 *Arum italicum* 'Pictum' x 3
3 *Hydrangea quercifolia*
   (Oakleaf hydrangea) x 1
4 *Scilla siberica*
   'Atrocoerulea' x 75
5 *Cotoneaster horizontalis*
   'Variegatus' x 2
6 *Carex elata* 'Aurea'
   (Bowles' golden
   sedge) x 3

7 *Viburnum plicatum*
   'Mariesii' x 1
8 *Epimedium
   perralderianum* x 5
9 *Mentha* x *gentilis* Variegata'
   (Ginger mint) x 3
10 *Hydrangea aspera* subsp.
   aspera syn. *H. villosa* x 1
11 *Ajuga reptans*
   'Atropurpurea'
   (Bugle) x 3
12 *Decaisnea fargesii* x 1

TIERED PLANTING
The large shrubs in this scheme form the
topmost layer of a three-tiered planting plan.
Underneath them, you can fit in a middle tier
of herbaceous plants, such as Solomon's seal
(*Polygonatum* x *hybridum*), with another colony
of low-growing plants at ground level. Some
of the smaller shrubs, such as the cotoneasters
suggested for the foreground of this scheme,
are themselves ground huggers and can only
share their space with miniature bulbs, like the
scillas, which will not crowd them out.

The two hydrangeas are the stars of this
scheme, together with a late spring-flowering
viburnum, a cultivar of *Viburnum plicatum* that is
built up in tiers like a wedding cake. The peak
season of most hydrangeas is late summer when
they are in flower, but the species used here also
have handsome foliage for more lasting pleasure.

Like the hydrangeas, the viburnum has a
long season of interest; this makes these plants
particularly welcome in small gardens, where

A SHOW FOR LATE SUMMER
*In summer, the hydrangeas are at their finest with their
white and misty mauve flowerheads. More dramatic color
comes from the unusual dark pods of the decaisnea
and the bright, beadlike berries of the arums.*

PLANTING PLAN

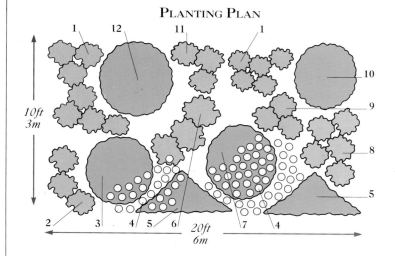

10ft
3m

20ft
6m

OAKLEAF HYDRANGEA
Hydrangea quercifolia is
included as much for its
handsome foliage as for its
heads of white flowers.

SOLOMON'S SEAL
Polygonatum x
hybridum is a
graceful plant
with arching
stems of small
bell flowers.

ARUM
Arum italicum 'Pictum'
has spear-shaped
leaves, marbled in
pale cream, which
are particularly
welcome in
winter.

every inch of space must be used to the full. The overall form of the viburnum, with its branches held out in ascending horizontal layers, is pleasing even when it is not in flower. It needs plenty of space around it, so that its fine form is not spoiled by other plants lurching into its orbit. The flowers are white, and rather like those of a lacecap hydrangea, with a ring of sterile florets around a central cluster of much smaller flowers.

COOL COLORS AND FINE FOLIAGE

White predominates in this scheme, with white flowers hanging from the arching stems of Solomon's seal and greenish white clusters of flowers on *Decaisnea fargesii*, though these are its least important attribute. The real surprise is the fruit: long, navy blue seed pods the size and texture of sausages. The foliage is supremely elegant: each leaf is very long and is made up of pairs of leaflets arranged along a central rib.

LATE SPRING CENTERPIECE
The viburnum hogs the limelight from late spring to summer with its spreading shelves of flowers. Its architectural lines are softened by the hanging flowers of the decaisnea.

VIBURNUM
Each flat head of tiny flowers on *Viburnum plicatum* 'Mariesii' is surrounded by showy, white, sterile flowers.

SCILLA
An easy-to-grow bulb, *Scilla siberica* 'Atrocoerulea' has startlingly blue flowers in early spring. It self-seeds where it is happy.

DECAISNEA
No other shrub bears fruit of such a strange navy blue as *Decaisnea fargesii*.

BOWLES' GOLDEN SEDGE
Strange flowers like fluffy caterpillars climb up the stems of Bowles' golden sedge, *Carex elata* 'Aurea', in spring, but its chief strength is its shining foliage.

BUGLE
Although it can be invasive, the creeping bugle, *Ajuga reptans* 'Atropurpurea', provides shiny mats of foliage topped with spikes of blue, lipped flowers.

HYDRANGEA
Velvet leaves and delicately tinted flowerheads, sometimes a foot across, make *Hydrangea aspera* subsp. *aspera* the queen of hydrangeas.

GINGER MINT
Far more decorative than culinary mints, the ginger mint, *Mentha* x *gentilis* 'Variegata', has brightly variegated leaves.

EPIMEDIUM
The large, glossy leaves of *Epimedium perralderianum* provide excellent ground cover with the bonus of bright yellow flowers.

COTONEASTER
Cotoneaster horizontalis 'Variegatus' is a cream-splashed version of the familiar fishbone cotoneaster.

Viburnum plicatum 'Mariesii'

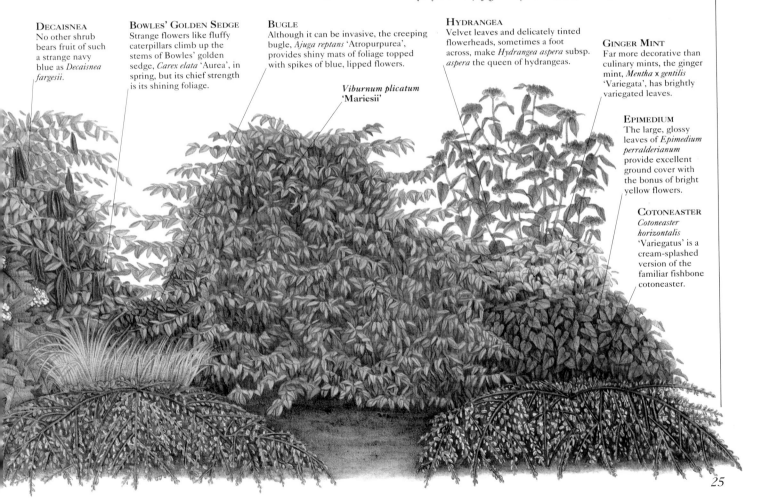

25

PLANTS *for a* SHADY SITE

MANY SUN-LOVING PLANTS flower better when they are half-starved. Shade plants need to be nourished, however, and this scheme is planned for a place that is shady but not starved or dry.

Give the viburnum plenty of space and resist the urge to prune it. This shrub is an object lesson in symmetry: if you cut a branch, you may unbalance the entire form. Keep decaisnea in check by cutting out one or two of the oldest stems entirely each year. Both bugle and ginger mint spread quite rapidly by runners and, if not checked, may squeeze out the scillas. Leave the skeletal heads on the hydrangeas until spring; they look particularly good rimed with frost.

CARE AND CULTIVATION

SPRING
Plant carex, mints, and bugles. Mulch Solomon's seal. Plant hydrangeas now or in fall, and mulch established plants heavily to conserve moisture around the roots. Remove their dead flowerheads. No regular pruning is necessary, but if plants get too big, cut them back now. Shear off old leaves of epimediums and top-dress with fine compost before the flower spikes appear.

SUMMER
If necessary, thin out some of the older stems of the decaisnea after it has finished flowering. Plant arums while dormant.

FALL
Plant the viburnum, Solomon's seal, decaisnea, and cotoneasters. Stop neighboring plants from encroaching on the cotoneasters, because they die back if other plants lie on top of them. Plant epimediums and scilla bulbs, setting the latter 3in (8cm) deep.

WINTER
Clear away old stems of Solomon's seal.

Polygonatum x hybridum (Solomon's seal) *Arching perennial with hanging, greenish white flowers in spring. H 4ft (1.2m), S 3ft (1m).*

Decaisnea fargesii *Deciduous shrub with drooping tassels of light green flowers, followed by large, navy seed pods. H and S 10ft (3m).*

Ajuga reptans 'Atropurpurea' (Bugle) *Low, evergreen perennial with glossy leaves and blue spring flowers. H 6in (15cm), S 3ft (1m).*

Hydrangea aspera subsp. **aspera** syn. **H. villosa** *Deciduous shrub flowering from late summer to midfall. H 10ft (3m), S 9ft (2.5m).*

Hydrangea quercifolia (Oakleaf hydrangea) *Deciduous, mound-forming shrub with fine fall foliage and white flowers from midsummer. H 6ft (2m), S 7ft (2.2m).*

Carex elata 'Aurea' (Bowles' golden sedge) *Evergreen perennial with golden yellow, grassy leaves and small brown flower spikes in summer. H to 16in (40cm), S 6in (15cm).*

Viburnum plicatum 'Mariesii' *Deciduous, bushy shrub with tiered branches and large, rounded flowerheads from late spring to early summer. H 10ft (3m), S 15ft (4m).*

Mentha x gentilis 'Variegata' (Ginger mint) *Spreading perennial with aromatic, gold-splashed leaves and mauve flowers. H 18in (45cm), S 2ft (60cm).*

Arum italicum 'Pictum' *Early spring-flowering perennial with variegated fall foliage followed by spikes of red berries. H to 10in (25cm), S to 12in (30cm).*

Scilla siberica 'Atrocoerulea' *Bulbous perennial with glossy leaves, producing spikes of bell-shaped, blue flowers in early spring. H 6in (15cm), S 2in (5cm).*

Cotoneaster horizontalis 'Variegatus' *Deciduous shrub with herringbone branches covered with cream-variegated leaves, producing red berries in fall. H 2ft (60cm), S 5ft (1.5m).*

Epimedium perralderianum *Semi-evergreen, carpeting perennial with glossy foliage and yellow spring flowers. H 12in (30cm), S 18in (45cm).*

ALTERING *the* PLANTING SCHEME

THERE ARE SEVERAL WAYS to adjust this planting to suit specific conditions. The hydrangeas are easygoing about soil type, provided that it is moist and enriched with good compost, but if you have an acidic soil, you could substitute a pieris for the tall hydrangea and low-growing rhododendrons for the cotoneasters. Another option is to vary the ground cover plants: here, a combination of white, gold, and blue is used.

COLORFUL GROUND COVER

Unrelieved carpets of hypericum have given ground cover a bad name, but at its best it can be as rich and intricate as a Turkish rug. Try to combine plants with modest territorial ambitions and complementary characters that provide interest over a long season.

Choose a hosta with warmth in the leaves. For this scheme, the white-flowered variety of lily-of-the-valley, with its startling, marble purity, is preferable to the pink.

Omphalodes cappadocica
Perennial with bright blue flowers carried in spring–summer above crinkled leaves. H 6–8in (15–20cm), S 10in (25cm) or more.

Hosta 'Gold Standard'
Perennial with pale green leaves that turn to gold from midsummer and are margined with dark green. H 2½ft (75cm), S 3ft (1m).

Tiarella wherryi (Foamflower) *Perennial with feathery flowers. H 4in (10cm), S 6in (15cm).*

Convallaria majalis (Lily-of-the-valley)
Low-growing perennial with matte, dark green leaves and sprays of fragrant, bell-shaped flowers. H to 12in (30cm), S indefinite.

A BORDER WITH SPRING INTEREST FOR ACIDIC SOIL

Certain shrubs such as rhododendrons, camellias, and pieris thrive only on acidic soils. In the wild, these plants are most often found in woodland habitats and, similarly, in the garden they prefer some shade. Choose rhododendrons with pale flowers to blend with the rest of the planting. Offset the beefy effect of the rhododendrons by using ground cover plants with filigree or divided leaves.

Pieris is a distinguished evergreen shrub, at its showiest in spring when the young foliage is suffused with a rich copper-red. The small, scented, cream flowers hang in drooping spikes.

Rhododendron 'Snow'
Low, mound-forming shrub that is covered with pure white flowers in early spring. H and S to 2ft (60cm).

Pieris 'Forest Flame'
Shrub with glossy leaves that turn from red when young to pink, cream, and then dark green. H 12ft (4m), S 6ft (2m).

PRETTY PASTELS

MELIANTHUS, THE STAR of this border, is the most sumptuous foliage plant that a gardener could imagine. It has magnificent leaves of a strange, glaucous sea green. In bud, they are tightly pleated, but they shake themselves open to display neatly crimped edges, each leaf a masterpiece.

The melianthus is a native of South Africa and will need to be nursed through cold winters and icy winds. Like all stars, it is accustomed to a life of luxury and ease. Treat it right and it will out-perform any other plant in the garden.

COLOR MIXING WITH HAZY TONES

Pale, misty mauves and blues are the keynotes of this border, drifting around the pools of gray and cool sea green made by foliage plants such as the melianthus and amiable lamb's ears, *Stachys byzantina*. Even the yellow broom used here is a muted, creamy shade, rather than the brilliant, custard yellow of many of the family.

Plants of strong, bold form prevent the border from being too sleepy in tone. The spherical seedheads of the alliums last as stiff skeletons long after the flowers have faded. The sea

hollies, too, look as though they have been forged by a sculptor working in spun metal.

If you want to expand this scheme, include more plants with soft tones: penstemons, blue Canterbury bells (*Campanula medium*), lavender (*Lavandula*), abutilon, and cranesbills (*Geranium*).

Silver-leaved plants such as lamb's ears are excellent foils for pale flowers whose own foliage is nothing special. Interplant them with bulbs such as tulips, lilies, and alliums. Do not include too many silver-foliaged plants in the same bed, however, or you will lose contrasts of color and texture. Either gray or lime-colored helichrysum could be used in this border; the lime will give the more interesting effect. Both types grow prodigiously, but they will thread attractively through other plants rather than steamroller over them.

STRIKING SHAPES
The distinctive, jagged-edged leaves of Eryngium x oliverianum *make a bold backdrop to the lavender-blue flowerheads in late summer.*

DESIGN POINTS

— ❧ —

LONG-LASTING DISPLAY
Creamy broom and pink and white tulips bring interest in spring, while the seedheads of the sea hollies last well into winter.

— ❧ —

CALMING COLORS
Soft-colored pastel flowers and cool foliage combine to create a serene, restful scheme.

— ❧ —

CHANGING SPECTRUM
If you include tulips, which are not always great stayers, you can change the balance of the color scheme slightly each year. Dark purple parrot tulips will provide a contrast with the surrounding pale foliage.

PLANT LIST

1 *Eryngium x oliverianum* (Sea holly) x 10
2 *Lilium regale* (Regal lily) x 25
3 *Aster x frikartii* 'Mönch' (Michaelmas daisy) x 8
4 *Melianthus major* (Honeybush) x 2
5 *Viola cornuta* (Horned violet) x 15
6 *Stachys byzantina* (Lamb's ears) x 3

7 *Tulipa* 'Angélique' and 'White Triumphator' x 50
8 *Helichrysum petiolare* 'Limelight' x 8
9 *Astrantia major* 'Shaggy' (Masterwort) x 4
10 *Cytisus x praecox* (Warminster broom) x 1
11 *Allium giganteum* x 16
12 *Eupatorium ligustrinum* x 1

PLANTING PLAN

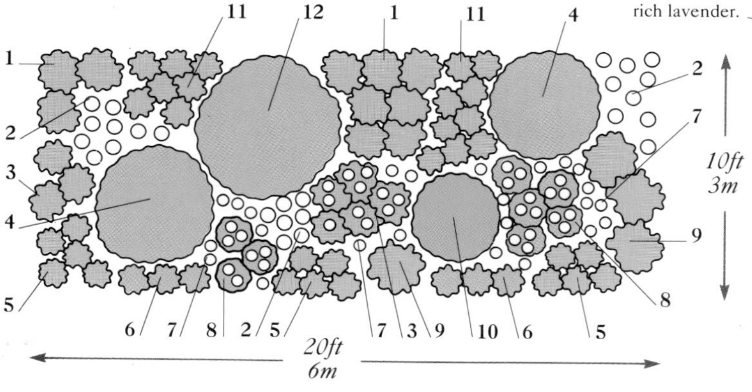

[Planting plan diagram with numbered sections. Labels around the diagram: 11, 12, 1, 11, 4 across the top; 1, 2, 3, 4, 5 down the left side; 2, 7, 9, 8 on the right side; 6 / 7 / 8 / 2 / 5, 7 / 3 / 9 / 10 / 6, 5 across the bottom. Dimensions: 10ft / 3m vertical, 20ft / 6m horizontal]

A SEA OF FOLIAGE AND FLOWERS
By late summer, the melianthus has built up to maximum effect, providing a sea green background to the skeleton heads of the alliums and the sea hollies' striking, metallic, thistlelike heads.

SEA HOLLY
In a family noted for its good looks, this sea holly, *Eryngium x oliverianum*, is one of the most handsome.

MICHAELMAS DAISY
Far less disease-prone than normal Michaelmas daisies, *Aster x frikartii* 'Mönch' has shaggy daisy flowers of rich lavender.

HONEYBUSH
Although tender, the supreme foliage plant *Melianthus major* is worth fussing over for the sake of its glorious leaves.

HORNED VIOLET
The flower power of violas is astonishing, given their miniature size. Here, the pale *Viola cornuta* is used.

SHRUBS FOR SUBSTANCE AND SHOW

The shrubs are there to give bulk and height to the border. The broom, *Cytisus x praecox*, will enjoy the same growing conditions as the gray foliage plants. In late spring, the flowers drip down the branches like melting ice cream.

The evergreen eupatorium is an antidote to the grays, which look their worst in winter. To call it a useful shrub is demeaning. It is a low-key shrub certainly, its dark leaves exactly like the privet's from which it takes its name. But in late summer it sheds its sobriety, covering itself with a mass of flattish flowerheads, each made up of hundreds of tiny, white, spidery flowers. The effect is charming: a banker surprised at his own frippery.

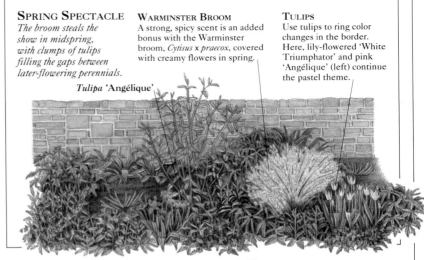

SPRING SPECTACLE
The broom steals the show in midspring, with clumps of tulips filling the gaps between later-flowering perennials.

Tulipa 'Angélique'

WARMINSTER BROOM
A strong, spicy scent is an added bonus with the Warminster broom, *Cytisus x praecox*, covered with creamy flowers in spring.

TULIPS
Use tulips to ring color changes in the border. Here, lily-flowered 'White Triumphator' and pink 'Angélique' (left) continue the pastel theme.

LAMB'S EARS
A favorite garden plant, lamb's ears, *Stachys byzantina*, makes excellent ground cover under taller plants.

ALLIUM
The purple globe flowers of *Allium giganteum* become buff seedheads that remain an important feature.

EUPATORIUM
In mild areas, *Eupatorium ligustrinum* may still be in flower in winter, white flowerheads contrasting with the sober foliage.

Cytisus x praecox

HELICHRYSUM
The foliage of *Helichrysum petiolare* 'Limelight' weaves its way between other plants, knitting them together.

MASTERWORT
'Shaggy', this particular form of the masterwort, *Astrantia major*, has an extra-large collar around the flower.

REGAL LILY
One of the most popular of garden lilies, *Lilium regale* has long, trumpet flowers of purest white.

PLANTS *for a* WELL-DRAINED SITE

ALL THE PLANTS IN THIS BORDER need an open, sunny situation. In cold areas, think of the half-hardy melianthus as a pelargonium. Take cuttings in fall and overwinter them inside ready for the following season, or buy fresh plants each year. They will not cost much more than a bottle of wine, and the effect will be twice as intoxicating. Once established, melianthus will survive temperatures just above freezing. The problem lies in getting it through its first few winters. It may help if you protect the crowns with straw. Where it is not butchered by cold, it will grow up to 10ft (3m), but if it has to start from scratch each spring, it will not reach half that. Winter dampness is as much an enemy of plants such as melianthus as is winter cold. This is true of a whole family of silver-leaved plants such as lamb's ears; they all grow best in light, well-drained soil.

Allium giganteum
Summer-flowering bulb with a stout stem and dense purple flowerheads 5in (12cm) across. H 4ft (1.2m), S 14in (35cm).

Eupatorium ligustrinum syn. **E. micranthum**
Evergreen, rounded shrub with fragrant flowers. H and S 6ft (2m).

Eryngium x **oliverianum (Sea holly)** *Upright perennial with thistlelike, lavender-blue flowerheads in late summer. H 3ft (1m), S 2ft (60cm).*

Lilium regale (Regal lily) *Summer-flowering bulb with fragrant, outward-facing, funnel-shaped blooms. H to 6ft (2m), S to 12in (30cm).*

Aster x **frikartii 'Mönch' (Michaelmas daisy)** *Bushy perennial bearing daisylike flowers in fall. H 2½ft (75cm), S 18in (45cm).*

Melianthus major (Honeybush)
Evergreen shrub with brownish red flowers from spring to summer. H and S 6–10ft (2–3m).

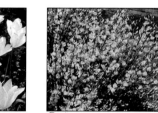

Tulipa 'White Triumphator' *Bulb that flowers in late spring, bearing white blooms with reflexed petals. H 26in (65cm), S to 8in (20cm).*

Cytisus x **praecox (Warminster broom)** *Deciduous, densely branched shrub flowering from mid- to late spring. H and S 5ft (1.5m).*

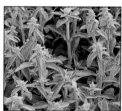

Viola cornuta (Horned violet)
Perennial with toothed leaves and purplish blue flowers in spring–summer. H 5–8in (12–20cm), S 8in (20cm) or more.

Stachys byzantina syn. **S. lanata (Lamb's ears)**
Evergreen perennial with mauve-pink flowers in summer. H 15in (38cm), S 2ft (60cm).

Helichrysum petiolare syn. **H. petiolatum**
Evergreen, mound-forming shrub with gray, felted leaves. It produces creamy yellow flowers in summer. H 12in (30cm), S 5ft (1.5m).

Astrantia major 'Shaggy' (Masterwort)
Clump-forming perennial that bears small, white flowers veined with green from summer to fall. H 2ft (60cm), S 18in (45cm).

ALTERING *the* PLANTING SCHEME

ANY SUBSTITUTE PLANTS must be suited to dry, well-drained soil, although you can heavily mulch areas that you want to make more nourishing. For a dramatic foliage contrast, include a purple-leaved shrub instead of the eupatorium. To complement the melianthus at its opulent best, substitute late summer-flowering plants for some of the bulbs.

COLOR FOR ALL SEASONS

For richly colored foliage, choose the smoke tree *Cotinus coggygria*, a purple-leaved hebe such as 'La Séduisante', or a purple berberis (although the flowers can be a particularly savage orange). Use a spring-flowering clematis to twine through the smoke tree, and blowsy pink poppies to contrast with its summer foliage.

For a late summer show, replace some of the tulips and lilies with pink nerines and blue agapanthus.

Cotinus coggygria **'Notcutt's Variety' (Smoke tree)** *Deciduous shrub with rich reddish purple leaves. To encourage foliage growth rather than flowers, cut the shrub back hard in fall. H and S to 15ft (5m).*

***Agapanthus* Headbourne Hybrids** *Perennial with arching leaves and large heads of deep purple-blue flowers on erect stems. H 3ft (1m), S 20in (50cm).*

Clematis alpina 'Frances Rivis' *Deciduous climber that produces nodding, mid-blue flowers in spring followed in summer by fluffy, silvery seedheads. H 10ft (3m), S 5ft (1.5m).*

Papaver orientale **(Oriental poppy)** *Hardy, spreading perennial that forms mounds of coarse, hairy, deeply cut leaves. Large, showy blooms are borne singly on straight stems during early summer. These may be salmon-pink, white, orange, or a rich mahogany-red, usually with an inky blotch at the base of each petal. H 2½ft (75cm), S 12in (30cm).*

Nerine bowdenii Bulb with *strap-shaped, basal leaves. In fall, each stem carries a head of pretty, glistening, pink flowers that curl back at the tips of the petals. H 18–24in (45–60cm), S 5–6in (12–15cm).*

A TROPICAL SUMMER BORDER

T HINK OF THE JUNGLE as your inspiration for this border. The effect should be leafy, luxuriant, strange, exotic. It is not a style that is worth considering in any place where summer comes late and winter early. Nor does it have any pretension to be low maintenance, but for anyone prepared to put in the extra effort it requires, this sumptuous border is a star attraction.

A BORDER WITH BRAVADO
This is a border that throws caution to the wind. Strong shapes, lush foliage, and hot colors combine to create a dazzling display.

KALEIDOSCOPE OF COLOR
The cannas and castor beans are particularly effective seen against the light, the bronze of the leaves fractured into a hundred different colors. In late summer, the plants are set alight by flame-colored flowers.

PRIME POSITION
The border is designed to be viewed head on. It would be ideal, for instance, sited at the end of a sheltered courtyard where you could look on to it from the windows of the house, but it will be bare in winter.

COLORFUL CLEOME
Long, leggy stamens protrude from the flowers of Cleome hassleriana *'Colour Fountain', giving it its common name, spider flower. It flowers generously, flourishing especially well in hot summers.*

DESIGN POINTS

In the grand gardens of Edwardian England where there was never a shortage of labor, borders such as this were commonplace. Landowners competed with each other to produce ever more outrageous effects, and head gardeners were as familiar with the needs of a tropical banana palm as they were with the homegrown cabbage. The style lives on in the famous red borders at Hidcote Manor in Gloucestershire, England, where in summer tender cannas and cordylines, rich red lobelias, and luscious dahlias are bedded out among the more hardy inhabitants of the border.

FORMAL PATTERNING
An unashamedly theatrical border such as this looks its best if the artifice is stressed, not squashed. Plant in a formal fashion, with groups of plants repeated at regular intervals like the pattern on a roll of wallpaper. Once the pattern is established, you can extend the border to the length you need. Vary the positions of some of the foreground plants, however, so that the overall effect is not too mechanical.

The heavyweights in this border are the banana palms, the castor beans, and the cannas. For the full *fortissimo* effect, you need all three. The bananas give height

and importance: few other plants provide their kind of bulk and beefiness. You are growing them for their huge leaves, which unfurl with all the drama of the best conjuring trick. Outside the tropics, bananas will not produce edible fruit and, during winter, they will need a warm berth

CASTOR BEAN
Ricinus communis is included for its lush, deeply lobed leaves.

COSMOS
Cosmos 'Sensation' forms a bushy mound of fine, feathery leaves and hovering pink flowers.

A SHOW-STOPPING SCHEME
Plants with bold foliage – bananas, castor beans, cannas – set the tone for this tropical-looking border, while cleomes, cosmos, and tobacco plants contribute color and scent.

ARGYRANTHEMUM
Argyranthemum frutescens 'Jamaica Primrose' provides yellow flowers throughout summer.

AEONIUM
Aeonium arboreum 'Schwarzkopf' has neat, wine-dark, fleshy rosettes.

(such as a heated conservatory) where they can dream of the tropics between their summer performances. The castor beans and cannas also provide the leafiness and succulence essential in a tropical border, as does the tall tobacco plant, *Nicotiana sylvestris*. Other exotics such as phormium, tetrapanax, yucca, and the Japanese cartwheel tree, *Trochodendron araloides*, would also be at home in this border.

ADDING SCENT AND COLOR

Cosmos, cleomes, and tobacco plants provide scent as well as color. All these annuals are available in shades of pink, mauve, and white. Decide whether you prefer single colors or a mixture. Too much white could be counterproductive because it would dilute the boldness of the scheme.

PLANTING PLAN

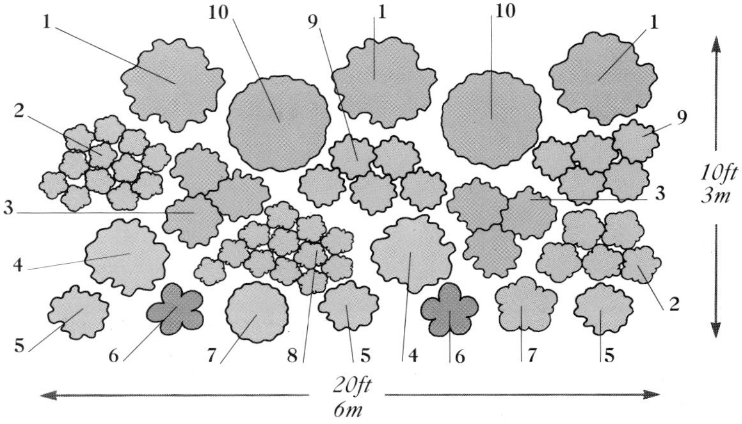

10ft
3m

20ft
6m

PLANT LIST

1 *Ensete ventricosum* (Banana palm) x 3
2 *Cleome hassleriana* 'Colour Fountain' x 17
3 *Canna indica* x 6
4 *Argyranthemum frutescens* 'Jamaica Primrose' x 2
5 *Pelargonium* 'Royal Oak' x 3
6 *Aeonium arboreum* 'Schwarzkopf' x 2
7 *Felicia amelloides* 'Santa Anita' x 2
8 *Cosmos* 'Sensation' x 12
9 *Nicotiana sylvestris* (Tobacco plant) x 10
10 *Ricinus communis* (Castor bean) x 1 and *R.c.* 'Carmencita' x 1

BRONZE CASTOR BEAN
Ricinus communis 'Carmencita' is just one of a number of forms of the castor bean that has bronze or reddish leaves.

BANANA PALM
The arching, quill-like leaves of banana palms – *Ensete ventricosum* – add height and dramatic sculptural interest.

TOBACCO PLANT
These tall tobacco plants, *Nicotiana sylvestris*, provide scent and cool touches of pure white.

CANNA
Broad, bronze leaves and fiery flowers of *Canna indica* add an exotic look.

CLEOME
Cleome hassleriana 'Colour Fountain' adds tall spires of pink, purple, and white flowerheads.

FELICIA
The blue heads of *Felicia amelloides* 'Santa Anita' add a cool note to offset the scheme's hot colors.

PELARGONIUM
Use *Pelargonium* 'Royal Oak' for its spicy-scented leaves splashed at the center with deep brown.

33

PLANTS *for a* HOT SPOT

In cool or temperate regions, tender plants such as the bananas and aeoniums grown here must be overwintered in a heated greenhouse or conservatory. The easiest way to deal with the bananas is to keep them permanently in pots, which you can plunge in the border for the summer display once all danger of frost has passed. As winter approaches, lift the pots, hose them down, and then bring them in under cover for the cooler months. The other two stars of this exotic border, the castor beans and the cannas, are equally tender. In fall, lift and store the cannas under cover for the winter. The castor bean comes from tropical Africa. Although by nature an evergreen shrub, in temperate climates this fast-growing plant is usually treated as a half-hardy annual, raised each year from seed.

Cleome hassleriana 'Colour Fountain'
Bushy annual with divided leaves, flowering in summer. H 4ft (1.2m), S 2ft (60cm).

Argyranthemum frutescens 'Jamaica Primrose' *Bushy, evergreen perennial with fernlike leaves and yellow flowers throughout summer. H and S to 3ft (1m).*

Pelargonium 'Royal Oak' *Bushy evergreen with compact, scented leaves and small, mauve-pink flowers. H 15in (38cm), S 12in (30cm).*

Ensete ventricosum (Banana palm)
Evergreen, upright, palmlike perennial with huge leaves that have a reddish midrib. H to 20ft (6m), S to 10ft (3m).

Aeonium arboreum 'Schwarzkopf'
Perennial succulent with distinctive rosettes of stiff, dark purple leaves. H to 2ft (60cm), S 3ft (1m).

Ricinus communis (Castor bean)
Fast-growing, evergreen shrub with heads of green and red flowers in summer. H 5ft (1.5m), S 3ft (90cm).

Nicotiana sylvestris (Tobacco plant)
Branching perennial with panicles of fragrant, tubular, white flowers in late summer. H 5ft (1.5m), S 2½ft (75cm).

Cosmos 'Sensation'
Bushy annual that has feathery leaves and daisylike flowers from early summer to early fall. H 3ft (90cm), S 2ft (60cm).

Canna indica
Perennial with broad, branching leaves, sometimes tinged red-purple, and red or orange flowers in summer. H 4ft (1.2m), S 18in (45cm).

Felicia amelloides 'Santa Anita'
Evergreen shrub with daisylike flowers in late spring–fall. H and S 12in (30cm).

ALTERING *the* PLANTING SCHEME

IN AREAS WHERE SUMMERS ARE SHORT, you could substitute hardier species for some of the more tender plants. This will help to make the scheme less labor intensive, although the dramatic effect will diminish along with the man-hours. The bananas, which need special care in winter, are the most obvious candidates for replacement.

PLUMES OF PAMPAS FOR A COOL CLIMATE

In cool climates, pampas grass will make the border easier to manage since it can stay in the ground all year. Choose an early type that puts on its plumes before the rest of the plants have died back.

Cordylines may be plunged in their pots, then lifted and brought into a frost-free place for winter. Tie the leaves together in a bundle for extra protection. Dahlia tubers should be lifted after the first frosts.

Cordyline australis **'Atropurpurea'** *Slow-growing tree with arching leaves. H 4ft (1.2m), S to 3ft (1m).*

Cortaderia selloana **'Sunningdale Silver' (Pampas grass)** *Grass with feathery plumes from late summer on. H 7ft (2.1m), S 4ft (1.2m).*

Dahlia **'Bishop of Llandaff'** *Tuberous perennial with bronze-green leaves that complement the border's color scheme. In summer–fall, it produces showy, bright red flowers. H and S 3ft (1m).*

RICH COLOR COMBINATIONS

Choose rich purple *Verbena patagonica* and gladioli in magenta, crimson, and purple against a backcloth of variegated aralia and the shining bronze castor beans. Use the silver-variegated aralia, rather than the gold: it is a finer foil for the vibrant flowers. The gladioli have splendid flower spikes that enhance the scheme's exotic effect.

Aralia elata **'Variegata'** *Deciduous tree or shrub with white-edged leaves. In late summer–fall, it produces large, flat heads of tiny, creamy white flowers. H and S to 8ft (2.5m).*

Verbena patagonica Tall perennial with upright stems topped by pinkish purple flowers in summer–fall. It self-seeds happily, and never needs support. H 5ft (1.5m), S 20in (50cm).

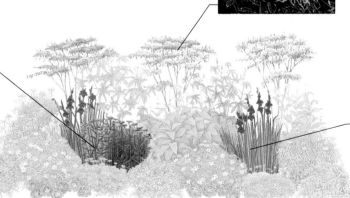

Gladiolus **'Robin'** *Corm that produces erect spires of flowers in late summer. The stems need discreet staking. H 4ft (1.2m), S 8in (20cm).*

A LUSH POOLSIDE

LEAFINESS IS THE KEYNOTE of this border with plenty of plants that do not depend solely on flowers for their effect. Foliage and water are as naturally compatible as Laurel and Hardy, but for the best effect you must make sure that the scale of the planting is in keeping with the size of the pool or stream.

HANDSOME FOLIAGE
The distinctively veined leaves of Rodgersia podophylla *are washed over with bronze. In summer, they form a good foil for airy sprays of creamy white flowers.*

DESIGN POINTS

— 🐌 —

SEASONAL CONTINUITY
This border has a long season of interest. The first flowers appear on the irises and primulas in late spring. The lobelias and the hostas will still be blooming in early fall. The flowers of the hostas are also finely scented.

— 🐌 —

SHIFTING PATTERNS
The reflection of light on water can have a dramatic effect on a planting such as this. On a sunny day, ripples of green and bronze make endlessly changing patterns on the undersides of the leaves.

— 🐌 —

REGAL BEAUTY
The royal fern, *Osmunda regalis*, may take time to settle, but it is worth persevering with. It is an exceptionally handsome, tall fern with bright green fronds, and has flowering spikes covered in dark spores, which look like the dried heads of the astilbes.

This scheme is designed with a smallish pool in mind. If you are planting beside large stretches of water, you need correspondingly larger plants: giant gunnera with leaves large enough to picnic under in a rainstorm, big stands of willow.

FINE FOLIAGE COLLECTION
The permanently damp conditions of a poolside border encourage lush leaf growth, and here there is a rich interplay of foliage shapes, too: solid swords of the variegated water iris, *Iris pseudacorus* 'Variegata', the hand-shaped leaves of rodgersias, the intricate parallel fronds of ferns. The leaves of the rodgersias are made up from a series of leaflets arranged like the spokes of a wheel, radiating out at right angles to the central stalk. When they emerge in spring, they are richly suffused with bronze. Their warm foliage provides an excellent backdrop for grassy clumps of Bowles' golden sedge, *Carex elata* 'Aurea'. In a strict botanical sense, the sedges are not grasses, but they look and behave like ornamental grasses, and they have the added advantage of doing best in damp soils. They are ideal for a boggy poolside area. They are evergreen, or rather evergold, a bonus in this scheme where most of the plants dive underground for the winter.

ACCENTS OF YELLOW AND RED
The brightest color comes from the magenta-red heads of *Primula japonica* and the yellow flowers of the iris. The flowers seem almost to suck their yellow from the leaves, for after the plant blooms in early summer, the foliage loses much of its striped green-yellow variegation.

PLANT LIST
1 *Primula florindae* (Giant cowslip) x 16
2 *Astilbe* x *arendsii* x 3
3 *Hosta plantaginea* x 6
4 *Osmunda regalis* (Royal fern) x 3
5 *Lobelia syphilitica* x 3
6 *Rodgersia aesculifolia* x 3
7 *Primula japonica* (Japanese primrose) x 16
8 *Carex elata* 'Aurea' (Bowles' golden sedge) x 2
9 *Ligularia przewalskii* x 3
10 *Eupatorium rugosum* x 3
11 *Rodgersia podophylla* x 3
12 *Iris pseudacorus* 'Variegata' x 9

You will need to be careful in your choice of astilbes: some are a particularly vicious shade of pink. Because this scheme contains a good deal of clear yellow and bronze, choose astilbes in brick colors or play safe with white.

THE SCHEME IN HIGH SUMMER
As the primulas fade, the ligularias and eupatoriums come into bloom. Rodgersia aesculifolia is in flower now with thick, buff-pink sprays the texture of plush.

GIANT COWSLIP
Primula florindae produces several stems of yellow flowers arising from each leafy clump.

LOBELIA
Flourishing in damp, heavy soils, *Lobelia syphilitica* has erect stems set with clear blue flowers.

PLANTING PLAN

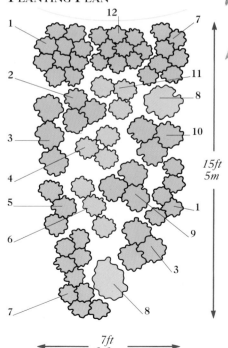

15ft
5m

7ft
2.2m

ASTILBE
Crimson-bronze and amber cover the spring shoots of *Astilbe* x *arendsii*, the color echoed in the dried mahogany stems of winter.

Iris pseudacorus 'Variegata'

ROYAL FERN
The royal fern, *Osmunda regalis*, is the largest fern that can be grown outdoors in temperate regions.

LATE SPRING
Clumps of Iris pseudacorus 'Variegata' *and* Primula japonica *add bright touches of color to a tapestry of different leaf shapes and textures.*

IRIS
Iris pseudacorus 'Variegata' contributes cheerful splashes of bright yellow.

JAPANESE PRIMROSE
Candelabra primulas such as *Primula japonica* hold their heads high above rosettes of leaves.

Primula japonica

JAGGED RODGERSIA
Big, jagged leaves are the trademark of *Rodgersia podophylla*, bronze when young, turning green as they mature.

EUPATORIUM
Flat, fluffy heads of white flowers are produced in late summer on the slender, branching stems of *Eupatorium rugosum*.

LIGULARIA
Elegant, deeply fingered leaves provide the underpinning for narrow spires of clear yellow flowers in *Ligularia przewalskii*.

HORSE-CHESTNUT RODGERSIA
Broad, crinkled leaves, similar to those of a horse chestnut tree, characterize the foliage plant *Rodgersia aesculifolia*.

HOSTA
Showy white flowers that smell of lilies are the surprise that *Hosta plantaginea* provides in early fall.

BOWLES' GOLDEN SEDGE
Although not always easy to establish, Bowles' golden sedge, *Carex elata* 'Aurea', is worth including for the arresting color of its leaves.

PLANTS *for a* POOLSIDE BORDER

BEFORE YOU EMBARK on this kind of planting, make sure that your bog has the right kind of underpinning. Flood water must be able to escape without dislodging the plants. In a long, dry summer, will the bog retain the right level of bogginess? An underlay of thick plastic, similar to a pool liner, may be necessary.

    The iris can be planted in the water, if need be, or at the water's edge in the boggiest part of the ground. If you are planting in the water, you will need to sink the roots in a plastic basket, weighted down with a stone.

Iris pseudacorus 'Variegata' *Rhizomatous perennial with striped foliage and yellow flowers. H to 6ft (2m), S indefinite.*

Primula japonica (Japanese primrose) *Perennial with reddish pink flowers. H 2ft (60cm), S 12in (30cm).*

CARE AND CULTIVATION

SPRING
Plant irises in full sun – if in water, no more than 6in (15cm) deep. Plant rodgersias with crowns just below the soil surface, osmundas with crowns at soil level, and lobelias in the shade of a neighboring plant. Remove dead stems from carex. Protect emerging hostas against slugs. Top-dress all plants with humus-rich material.

SUMMER
Deadhead irises after flowering. Divide and replant clumps every three years, immediately after flowering. Remove faded flower stems of rodgersias in late summer.

FALL
Plant astilbes now, and carex, ligularias, eupatoriums, hostas, and primulas now or in spring. Cut established astilbes down to ground level, and lift and divide clumps once every three years. Cut down stems of eupatoriums after flowering, and cut back osmunda foliage, leaving the brown flowering spikes.

WINTER
Cut ligularias down to ground level.

Primula florindae (Giant cowslip) *Perennial with heads of bell-shaped, yellow flowers. H 3ft (1m), S 2ft (60cm).*

Astilbe x arendsii *Perennial with fernlike foliage and feathery flower plumes. H 3ft (90cm), S 18in (45cm).*

Rodgersia podophylla *Clump-forming perennial with large leaves and cream flowers in summer. H 4ft (1.2m), S 3ft (1m).*

Eupatorium rugosum *Perennial that bears flat heads of white flowers in late summer. H 4ft (1.2m), S 18in (45cm).*

Hosta plantaginea *Perennial with glossy leaves and fragrant flowers in late summer–fall. H 2ft (60cm), S 4ft (1.2m).*

Rodgersia aesculifolia *Perennial with bronze-green foliage, and plumes of flowers in midsummer. H and S 3ft (1m).*

Lobelia syphilitica *Perennial with blue flowers on tall spikes in late summer and fall. H 3ft (1m), S 9in (23cm).*

Osmunda regalis (Royal fern) *Deciduous fern with broad fronds, and rusty flower spikes when mature. H 6ft (2m), S 3ft (1m).*

Ligularia przewalskii *Perennial with deeply cut leaves and yellow flower spikes from midsummer. H 6ft (2m), S 3ft (1m).*

Carex elata 'Aurea' (Bowles' golden sedge) *Evergreen perennial with grasslike leaves. H 16in (40cm), S 6in (15cm).*

ALTERING *the* PLANTING SCHEME

THERE ARE MANY WAYS to change the emphasis of your planting plan. You can alter the color scheme, for example, perhaps cooling down the warm colors of the original plan by introducing more white-flowered plants. If the pool is in a prominent position, you may want to extend the season of the border's interest with plants that star in winter and early spring.

CREATING A COOLER MOOD

Some gardeners are particularly fastidious in the matter of yellow flowers. Diehards of the anti-yellow brigade may prefer to omit the offending color and cool down this planting by using white and silvery plants instead. Substitute pale silver-variegated *Iris laevigata* for the carex, waxy white calla lilies for the flag irises, and white bugbane for the ligularias. This combination of plants will be less cheerful but more serene. It looks particularly effective at dusk.

Zantedeschia aethiopica **'Crowborough' (Calla lily)** *Early to midsummer flowering tuber with white, gobletlike spathes and deep green leaves. H 3ft (1m), S 18in (45cm).*

Cimicifuga simplex **(Bugbane)** *Upright perennial with glossy, divided leaves. In fall, arching flower spikes wave above the foliage. Each spike is made up of tiny, star-shaped flowers. H 5ft (1.5m), S 2ft (60cm).*

Iris laevigata **'Variegata'** *Perennial with striped leaves. It often flowers a second time in fall after its first show in early to midsummer. H 10in (25cm), S indefinite.*

PLANTING FOR WINTER AND SPRING

To extend the season of this border, choose a dogwood such as *Cornus alba* 'Elegantissima' for its bare red winter stems, later clothed in variegated foliage. For the best color, cut it back hard in late winter and feed it to stimulate new, young growth. Use yellow skunk cabbage for its brilliant yellow spathes. The angelica adds height and drama, with its large, divided leaves and its tall, proud stems crowned with domed, greenish flowerheads.

Cornus alba **'Elegantissima' (Dogwood)** *Variegated shrub with creamy white flowers in late spring followed by white fruits. H and S 5ft (1.5m).*

Lysichiton americanus **(Yellow skunk cabbage)** *Vigorous, deciduous perennial with fascinating, stiff, bright yellow spathes in early spring followed by cabbagey, fresh green leaves. H to 3ft (1m), S 2½ft (75cm).*

Angelica archangelica *Statuesque perennial, usually grown as a biennial, with lush, divided leaves, and heads of white or green flowers in late summer. H 6ft (2m), S 3ft (1m).*

BRIGHT BERRIES *for* FALL

PLANT THIS CURVING BORDER along the driveway to your house for a warm welcome home in fall and winter, or along a boundary to provide shelter or block out an unwanted view. It needs little in the way of maintenance and is packed with plants that generously pay their rent twice a year – with a mass of spring flowers and a colorful display of fall fruits.

The rose, crabapple, mountain ash, and spindletree all provide a rich crop of berries and hips, while shiny sealing-wax berries hang from the viburnum. In spring, the same plants froth with blossoms: creamy white heads on the viburnum, clusters of china pink and white petals along the branches of the crabapple, and wide, heavy heads on the mountain ash. The rose comes later with single flowers of clear, paintbox red.

FRUITS AND BERRIES FOR COLOR

The crabapple *Malus* 'John Downie' makes a neat, well-balanced tree, covered in brilliant fruits. In regions where fire blight is a problem, choose *M. floribunda*. Where space is tight, try 'Golden Hornet' or 'Red Sentinel' instead.

Spindletrees, *Euonymus europaeus*, have striking fall fruit – pink seed capsules that split open to show orange berries, an astonishing color combination. 'Red Cascade' has arching branches thickly covered with red seed capsules. The leaves also turn scarlet in a dramatic last display before the onset of winter.

The mountain ash *Sorbus* 'Joseph Rock' grows in an upright, compact way. It has bunches of cream flowers in late spring and glossy green, toothed leaves that turn russet red in fall. In fall, too, there are pale yellow berries that darken to amber as they age. If you want this scheme to fit a larger area, choose the taller Korean mountain ash *S. alnifolia*, which has attractive, egg-shaped, orange fruits.

The holly used here is a female and will produce berries only if there is a male holly somewhere within reach of pollinating insects. This does not have to be in your own garden.

ROSY BLUSH
The conical fruits of Malus *'John Downie' are a deep yellow, flushed with red. They can be made into an excellent translucent jelly.*

DESIGN POINTS

❧

COLOR REVIVAL
This border provides interest when much of the garden may be at a low ebb.

❧

SUBSTANTIAL SHRUBS
Trees and shrubs provide height and substance as well as contributing shelter and screening.

❧

MELLOW SHADES
Rich, russet tones from fall leaves and fruits add warmth and vitality.

❧

SPLASH OF WHITE
Snowdrops and daffodils add a cheering dash of light and color in late winter.

PLANT LIST

1 *Lunaria annua* 'Variegata' (Honesty) x 16
2 *Euonymus europaeus* 'Red Cascade' (Spindletree) x 1
3 *Galanthus nivalis* (Snowdrop) x 170
4 *Helleborus foetidus* (Stinking hellebore) x10
5 *Rosa moyesii* 'Geranium' x 2
6 *Narcissus* 'Thalia' (Daffodil) x 55
7 *Callicarpa bodinieri* x 2
8 *Ilex aquifolium* 'Argentea Marginata' (Holly) x 1
9 *Iris foetidissima* (Stinking iris) x 15
10 *Viburnum opulus* 'Compactum' x 1
11 *Sorbus* 'Joseph Rock' (Mountain ash) x 1
12 *Malus* 'John Downie' (Crabapple) x 1

PLANTING PLAN

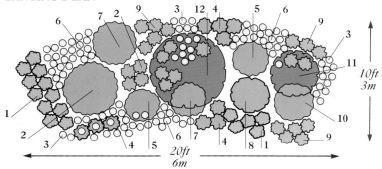

10ft 3m

20ft 6m

A BLAZE OF BRILLANT COLOR
In fall, many of the plants are encrusted with beadlike berries or colorful hips. The fiery combination of reds, oranges, and yellows is complemented by the changing fall colors of the leaves.

SPINDLETREE
Particularly good on alkaline soils, the spindletree, *Euonymus europaeus* 'Red Cascade', is weighed down by its abundant fall fruits.

HONESTY
Once established, honesty, including this variegated one, *Lunaria annua* 'Variegata', will seed itself about the border.

Helleborus foetidus

WINTER AND SPRING BEAUTY

This border provides a long season of interest. The snowdrops are first on the scene, set off by the brilliant seed pods of the iris and the handsome foliage of the hellebore. By the time the snowdrops are fading, the hellebores are in flower, followed by the daffodils. After these, the honesty will take over the scene until it is time for the explosion of blossoms in the trees above it.

LATE SPRING DISPLAY
Although planned for fall interest, this border offers treats at other times, too. In late spring, the hellebores will still be flowering when the pale, creamy bells of the daffodils open, creating a flower show in green and white.

SNOWDROP
Always eagerly awaited in early spring, snowdrops – *Galanthus nivalis* – slowly spread to make carpets beneath trees and shrubs.

DAFFODIL
Narcissus 'Thalia' carries three or more milk-white flowers on each stem.

STINKING HELLEBORE
Handsome, black-green leaves provide a foil for the pale spring flowers of *Helleborus foetidus*.

CALLICARPA
An entirely new color is introduced into this scheme with the purple berries of *Callicarpa bodinieri*.

CRABAPPLE
All the crabapples make excellent small trees, but *Malus* 'John Downie' has the largest and showiest fruits.

ROSE
The flowers of this rose, *Rosa moyesii* 'Geranium', tell you what to expect in its hips: both are a clear, singing red.

MOUNTAIN ASH
At their best in moist climates, mountain ashes, like this *Sorbus* 'Joseph Rock', provide an excellent display of fall fruit.

HOLLY
The broad-leaved silver-variegated holly, *Ilex aquifolium* 'Argentea Marginata', grows very slowly but makes a stately contribution to any garden.

VIBURNUM
Viburnum opulus 'Compactum' is the best cultivar of this species; it is very free with both its flowers and its berries.

STINKING IRIS
The flowers of *Iris foetidissima* are not at all showy, but the bright red seed pods compensate.

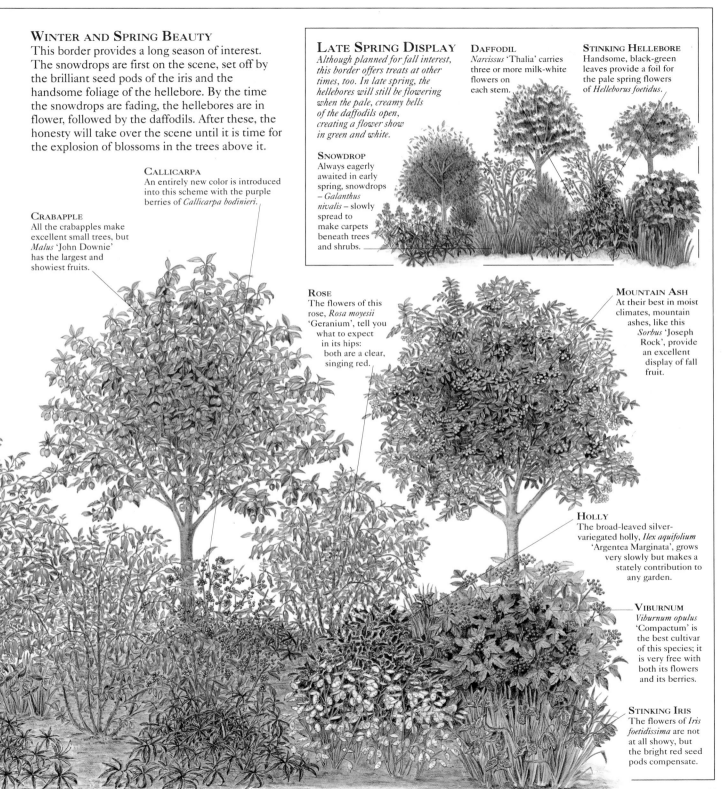

PLANTS *for a* FALL BORDER

THE KEY PLANTS IN THIS SCHEME are the trees and shrubs, and it is vital to give them a good start in life. Enrich the soil with compost or well-rotted manure before planting. Deciduous species such as the mountain ash and the crabapple are best planted in fall or early winter so they can settle their roots well before having to produce leaves in spring.

Select bare-root trees, if possible, since they usually have better-developed root systems than those grown in containers. If choosing a container-grown tree, slide it out of the pot before buying to check that the roots are not tightly coiled.

CARE AND CULTIVATION

SPRING
Plant snowdrops, preferably "in the green" just after they have finished flowering. Plant the holly. Mulch the crabapple and roses with well-rotted manure. Prune roses hard the first spring after planting, thereafter remove only dead or diseased branches. Deadhead daffodils, and remove dead leaves and seed pods on irises.

SUMMER
Sow honesty in early summer. Water newly established trees and shrubs, if necessary, and mulch around them to conserve moisture.

FALL
Plant the deciduous trees and shrubs. Plant irises about 12in (30cm) apart, and daffodils 6in (15cm) deep. Site hellebores in shade when planting them. Transplant the honesty to flowering positions in early fall.

WINTER
Cut previous year's growth of callicarpas back to young wood in late winter and, in exposed areas, protect the base of young plants with bracken or straw.

Helleborus foetidus (Stinking hellebore) *Evergreen, clump-forming perennial with green flowers. H and S 18in (45cm).*

Iris foetidissima (Stinking iris) *Rhizomatous perennial with seed pods of scarlet fruits. H 3ft (1m), S indefinite.*

Euonymus europaeus 'Red Cascade' (Spindletree) *Deciduous shrub or tree with red fruits. H and S 8ft (2.5m).*

Malus 'John Downie' (Crabapple) *Deciduous tree with white flowers borne amid bright green foliage in late spring, and attractive fruits in fall. H 28ft (9m), S 15ft (5m).*

Sorbus 'Joseph Rock' (Mountain ash) *Deciduous tree with clusters of yellow berries in fall. H and S to 50ft (15m).*

Lunaria annua 'Variegata' (Honesty) *Biennial with round, silvery seed pods. H 2½ft (75cm), S 12in (30cm).*

Rosa moyesii 'Geranium' *Vigorous rose with large, red hips in fall. H to 10ft (3m), S 8ft (2.5m).*

Ilex aquifolium 'Argentea Marginata' (Holly) *Evergreen tree with cream-edged, dark leaves. H to 45ft (14m), S 15ft (5m).*

Galanthus nivalis (Snowdrop) *Bulb with green-tipped, white flowers and strap-shaped leaves. H 6in (15cm), S 3in (8cm).*

Narcissus 'Thalia' (Daffodil) *Bulb bearing graceful, milky white flowers in midspring. H to 15in (38cm), S to 8in (20cm).*

Callicarpa bodinieri *Deciduous shrub with small, lilac flowers in midsummer, then violet berries. H 10ft (3m), S 8ft (2.5m).*

Viburnum opulus 'Compactum' *Dense, deciduous shrub with white flowers in spring, then red berries. H and S 5ft (1.5m).*

ALTERING *the* PLANTING SCHEME

IF YOU WANT TO BEEF UP THE SUMMER DISPLAY, include more shrub roses in the scheme. Choose those with attractive hips and colorful fall foliage for an extended period of interest.

If you have an acidic soil, your choice of plants is widened considerably. You can grow all sorts of heathers, and lime-hating shrubs such as pernettya, hamamelis, and various maples.

ROSES FOR SUMMER GLORY

All the Rugosa roses are first-class shrubs that never suffer from rust or blackspot. *Rosa rugosa* 'Frau Dagmar Hartopp' has single flowers of pale pink that continue over a long season. The last flowers appear with the first hips: showy red fruits, the size of small tomatoes, finished off with a flurry of elegant sepals. *R. virginiana* is a smaller, suckering shrub rose with orange hips.

Rosa virginiana Wild rose with glossy foliage and open, pink flowers. The leaves color well in fall. H to 5ft (1.5m), S 3ft (1m).

Rosa rugosa 'Frau Dagmar Hartopp' Vigorous rose with flowers followed by large, red hips. H and S 6ft (2m).

Clematis macropetala *Hardy climber with divided leaves, and small, bell-shaped flowers produced in spring. H 10ft (3m), S 5ft (1.5m).*

ACID-LOVING SHRUBS

On acidic soil, replace the irises with pink heather as winter-flowering ground cover. While the callicarpa in the original scheme provides only purple berries, pernettya gives you a choice of colors from white through pink to deep purple, and it is evergreen. The witch hazel has flowers like drunken spiders, but they come when they are most welcome in the dark days of late winter. They smell wonderful, too.

Pernettya mucronata 'Mulberry Wine' *Bushy, evergreen shrub with white flowers in spring–summer, and magenta to purple berries. H and S 4½ft (1.35m).*

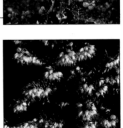

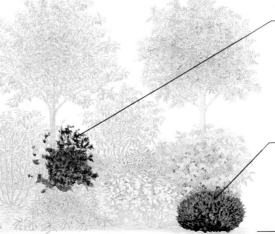

Hamamelis x intermedia 'Arnold Promise' (Witch hazel) *Deciduous shrub with yellow flowers in winter. H 12ft (4m), S 10ft (3m).*

Erica x darleyensis 'Ghost Hills' (Heather) *Shrub with needlelike foliage, cream-tipped in spring, and pink flowers in winter. H 18in (45cm), S 3ft (1m).*

COTTAGE-GARDEN BORDER

DREAMS OF THE COUNTRY are usually more comfortable than the reality. The idea of a cottage garden conjures up an idealized image of gentle disorder, with roses tumbling around the door – and no mud. But unchecked charm can easily turn into unfettered chaos. A gardener's skill lies in balancing on the tightrope between the two.

It is one of the ironies of gardening that the old-fashioned, cottage style is so in vogue with affluent, urban thirty-somethings. The style is based not on historical accuracy but on artifice – a contemporary, romantic view of country gardens of the past. It should have an air of spontaneity, but you will have to act as referee, to make sure that hefty plants, such as the peonies, do not knock out more delicate ones, such as the columbines.

PLANTS WITH OLD-FASHIONED STYLE
Peonies, columbines, and double English daisies are classic ingredients of an old-fashioned country border. *Paeonia* 'Sarah Bernhardt' has outrageous powder-puff blooms, appleblossom pink and scented. The deeply divided foliage sometimes turns a warm, foxy red in fall.

The columbines, for preference, should be the stubby kind sometimes called granny's bonnets, rather than those with long spurs. Any kind of double English daisy will be charming and, although the plants are short-lived, they will perpetuate themselves by self-seeding. The columbines will self-seed too, often putting themselves in places that you would never have thought of yourself. You can learn from that. Sometimes, you may even find a new color strain arising in a seedling, which is a great thrill. And, by nurturing the novelty, you will be carrying on in the best traditions of the cottage garden.

Use a scented daphne, such as the semi-evergreen *Daphne* x *burkwoodii*, which flowers in spring, or the evergreen *D. bholua*, which brightens up the dull days of winter.

PERFECTLY PLUMP
A key plant in this scheme is an exquisite peony – Paeonia 'Sarah Bernhardt'. *It produces wonderfully plump blooms, packed with soft tissue petals of pale pink.*

DESIGN POINTS

❧

A TOUCH OF TRADITION
An unfussy border with a nostalgic air that includes traditional cottage-garden plants.

❧

OLD HABITS
Old-fashioned varieties are included rather than modern cultivars because their habit, color, and form is most in keeping with the relaxed air of the scheme.

❧

INFORMAL DESIGN
There is no centerpiece in this scheme; that would be too neat, too contrived. An amiable disorder is what you are trying to achieve.

PLANT LIST
1 *Viola labradorica* 'Purpurea' (Purple-leaved violet) x 12
2 *Bellis perennis* 'Pomponette' (Double English daisy) x 23
3 *Camassia leichtlinii* (Quamash) x 16
4 *Aquilegia vulgaris* (Columbine) x 12
5 *Daphne* x *burkwoodii* 'Somerset' x 1
6 *Geranium pratense* 'Flore-pleno' x 3
7 *Paeonia* 'Sarah Bernhardt' (Peony) x 3
8 *Salvia sclarea* var. *turkestanica* (Vatican sage) x 5
9 *Thalictrum delavayi* (Meadow rue) x 5
10 *Campanula lactiflora* 'Prichard's Variety' x 5
11 *Gypsophila paniculata* 'Bristol Fairy' (Baby's breath) x 3
12 *Lychnis coronaria* x 7

PLANTING PLAN

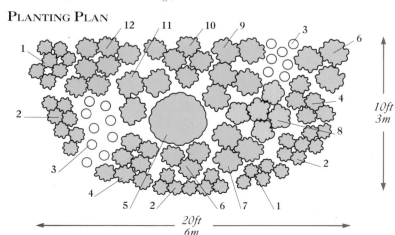

10ft
3m

20ft
6m

LYCHNIS
Gray leaves the texture of flannel make a clump from which rise the magenta flowers of *Lychnis coronaria*.

QUAMASH
A native American plant, *Camassia leichtlinii* bears slender stems of starry flowers in summer.

DOUBLE ENGLISH DAISY
The fat, double English daisy, *Bellis perennis* 'Pomponette', flowers generously.

A Relaxed Approach

The original creators of this style could not afford the luxury of agonizing over the exact shade of blue for their campanulas. Nor should you. If you try too hard, you will have lost the point. Borders such as this work as often as not because of something you didn't do rather than something you did.

Color Harmonies

At the height of summer, the border froths with flowers – soft mounds of blues, mauves, and pinks, given an edge by the sharp, clear magenta of the Lychnis coronaria.

Late Spring Display
In late spring, the peonies are the main focal point, backed by the pink daphne and complemented by the airy columbines.

Columbine
Pretty, nodding, purple flowers hang from the upright stems of *Aquilegia vulgaris.*

Daphne
Daphne x *burkwoodii* 'Somerset' brings fragrance to the border in late spring.

Peony
The peony, *Paeonia* 'Sarah Bernhardt', has splendid flowers of pale blush pink.

Campanula
Campanula lactiflora 'Prichard's Variety' is one of the taller campanulas with spires of violet-blue flowers.

Daphne x *burkwoodii* 'Somerset'

Baby's Breath
Tiny, starry flowers make a cloud of white over the gray leaves of *Gypsophila paniculata* 'Bristol Fairy'.

Meadow Rue
The wide, pyramidal heads of *Thalictrum delavayi* make a fine summer display.

Vatican Sage
Salvia sclarea var. *turkestanica* adds textural interest with its hairy, gray-green leaves.

Geranium
Geranium pratense 'Flore-pleno' has fine foliage and double, blue flowers.

Aquilegia vulgaris

Paeonia 'Sarah Bernhardt'

Purple-leaved Violet
Viola labradorica 'Purpurea' makes excellent ground cover under larger plants.

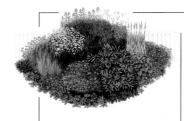

FREE PLANTING *for an* UNPLANNED EFFECT

BECAUSE SEVERAL OF THESE PLANTS – the Vatican sage, the columbines, and the double English daisies – are enthusiastic self-seeders, they will soon make nonsense of any preordained planting plan. Let them. This is not a border that prides itself on its neatness. In any case, the sage needs to self-seed to survive because it is a biennial.

You will have to be decisive about the position of the peonies, though. They resent being transplanted, and as a result may refuse to flower again for several years, so it is important to site them carefully at the outset. Planting them too deeply also prevents them from flowering: a little soil – about 1in (2.5cm) – on top of the crown is enough.

Campanula lactiflora 'Prichard's Variety' *Perennial flowering in early summer–late fall. H 4ft (1.2m), S 2ft (60cm).*

Thalictrum delavayi (Meadow rue) *Perennial that flowers in midsummer. H 5–6ft (1.5–2m), S 2ft (60cm).*

Lychnis coronaria *Perennial, often grown as a biennial, bearing bright magenta flowers on branched, felted, gray stems from mid- to late summer. H 18–24in (45–60cm), S 18in (45cm).*

Gypsophila paniculata 'Bristol Fairy' (Baby's breath) *Perennial with small, dark green leaves and wiry, branching stems covered with a froth of tiny, double, white flowers in summer. H 2–2½ft (60–75cm), S 3ft (1m).*

Daphne x burkwoodii 'Somerset' *Semi-evergreen shrub bearing scented flowers in late spring. H 5ft (1.5m), S 4ft (1.2m).*

Salvia sclarea var. **turkestanica (Vatican sage)** *Erect biennial with aromatic leaves. H 2½ft (75cm), S 12in (30cm).*

Geranium pratense 'Flore-pleno' *Blue-flowered perennial with bronze fall leaves. H to 30in (75cm), S 24in (60cm).*

Paeonia 'Sarah Bernhardt' (Peony) *Clump-forming perennial that bears large, fragrant flowers. H and S to 3ft (1m).*

Camassia leichtlinii (Quamash) *Bulb that has star-shaped, white or violet-blue flowers. H 5ft (1.5m), S 12in (30cm).*

Aquilegia vulgaris (Columbine) *Perennial with divided leaves and nodding flowers. H 2½ft (75cm), S 20in (50cm).*

Bellis perennis 'Pomponette' (Double English daisy) *Perennial with double spring flowers. H and S to 8in (20cm).*

Viola labradorica 'Purpurea' (Purple-leaved violet) *Spring-flowering perennial. H 2in (5cm), S indefinite.*

Altering *the* Planting Scheme

There are many ways of shifting the balance of color in the scheme. If you choose deep red peonies, purple columbines, and red lychnis, the effect will be far richer than if you use the same flowers in pink, blue, and white. Here, the alternative planting concentrates on other priorities: scaling up the plan for a larger area, and making it more fit for heavy, damp soils.

A Substantial Design for a Larger Plot

If you are adapting the plan for a larger area, add different varieties and colors of the same plants or include other old-fashioned plants such as pinks (*Dianthus*), poppies (*Papaver rhoeas*), biennial stocks (*Matthiola*), and sweet williams (*Dianthus barbatus*). Or introduce some shrubs to give bulk and height to the scheme. Choose those with an upright habit, or they will tangle with the plants around them. By using fragrant philadelphus and honeysuckle, you can also intensify the degree of scent in the border.

In soils that are heavy and damp, both the gypsophila and the Vatican sage will sulk and possibly rot away altogether. In these conditions, substitute Japanese anemones – in tones of pink and white – with a scattering of gently colored primulas.

Clematis 'Perle d'Azur' *Deciduous climber that bears a profusion of large, open, azure blue flowers during summer. H 10ft (3m), S 3ft (1m).*

Lonicera periclymenum 'Belgica' (Early Dutch honeysuckle) *Bushy climber with richly perfumed blooms in late spring–early summer. H to 22ft (7m).*

Philadelphus 'Belle Etoile' (Mock orange) *Deciduous, arching shrub smothered with scented, white blooms in late spring–early summer. H and S to 10ft (3m).*

Anemone x hybrida, syn. **A. japonica, 'Honorine Jobert'** *Vigorous perennial that has open, pure white flowers in late summer– fall. These are carried on wiry stems above deeply divided, dark green leaves. H 5ft (1.5m), S 2ft (60cm).*

Primula vulgaris 'Gigha White' *Low-growing primrose with yellow-eyed white flowers. H and S 6–8in (15–20cm).*

A Display *for* Fall *and* Winter

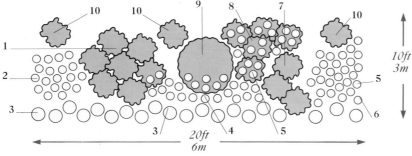

WINTER IS USUALLY THE ORPHAN of the garden scene. Spring and summer get all the best clothes, while winter has to make do with secondhand castoffs from other seasons. But the garden does not disappear with the first dark days of winter. It is still there outside the windows, and not all winter days are so miserable that we want to spend them entirely inside.

WINTER WELCOME
In the depths of winter, the delicate, cup-shaped flowers of Helleborus lividus subsp. corsicus are a welcome sight.

DESIGN POINTS

CONTINUITY OF INTEREST
A low-maintenance border with evergreen plants continuing to provide good form and foliage through the whole year.

FOLIAGE FEATURES
Handsome leaves are a strong feature of the mahonia, the cyclamen, the ivy, and both hellebores.

SHADE LOVERS
Suitable for a site shadowed by overhanging trees, since all the plants in this scheme thrive in shade.

One of the main attractions of this winter border is its display of evergreen foliage, which provides an altogether more sustaining diet in the garden than flowers. The whole purpose of a flower is instant seduction; foliage, however, works in a more subtle way, continuing to give quiet pleasure long after the accompanying flowers have withdrawn their offers.

SCENTED SHRUBS
Many winter-flowering shrubs, such as viburnum, daphne, chimonanthus, corylopsis, hamamelis, osmanthus, as well as the mahonia that forms the focal point of this winter planting, have the added advantage of scent. This is one of the most elusive of pleasures in the garden. A single waft of perfume from a particular flower can open up a whole Pandora's box of emotions. And in winter, when there is less in the garden to distract the senses, a scented flower seems much more precious than it would in summer.

PLANT LIST
1 *Helleborus orientalis* (Lenten rose) x 7
2 *Cyclamen coum* subsp. *coum* x 20
3 *Cyclamen hederifolium* x 20
4 *Erythronium dens-canis* (Dog's-tooth violet) x 24
5 *Galanthus nivalis* (Snowdrop) x 100
6 *Hyacinthoides hispanica* (Spanish bluebell) x 30
7 *Helleborus lividus* subsp. *corsicus* (Hellebore) x 3
8 *Phyllitis scolopendrium* (Hart's-tongue fern) x 5
9 *Mahonia* x *media* 'Charity' x 1
10 *Hedera helix* 'Adam' (Ivy) x 3

FINE FOLIAGE AND FLOWERS
The advantage of using the mahonia, rather than any other of the scented shrubs of winter, is its form. Tall and craggily handsome, evergreen, uncompromising, it never falters. The leaves are pinnate, each one made up of a series of leaflets arranged in matching pairs along the leaf's rib, with a terminal flourish of a leaflet at the end. Some species have as many as twenty pairs of leaflets arranged along the midrib. If you choose *Mahonia* x *media* 'Charity', the peak season will be early winter when the shrub bears its upright, terminal spikes of lemon yellow flowers, smelling of lily-of-the-valley.

The two groups of hellebores flower in succession. The pale green-white clusters of *Helleborus lividus* subsp. *corsicus* often appear by Christmas. The Lenten rose, *H. orientalis*, with flowers in a wide range of colors from freckled white to rich plum-black, follows on in late winter and early spring. Both have excellent foliage, new leaves emerging before the old have quite given up, so there is never a bare patch.

WINTER CYCLAMEN
Snub-nosed flowers, either pink or white, appear among the shiny leaves of *Cyclamen coum* subsp. *coum* in late winter.

FALL CYCLAMEN
Long-lasting, marbled foliage is as much of an asset of *Cyclamen hederifolium* as its fall flowers.

LENTEN ROSE
The flowers of *Helleborus orientalis* vary widely in color, dark or pale, plain or freckled.

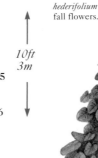

PLANTING PLAN

10ft
3m

20ft
6m

COLORFUL GROUND COVER

The rest of the planting fills in at ground level, creating a continuity of color and texture for many months. The bright fronds of the evergreen fern, the marbled leaves of *Cyclamen hederifolium*, and the variegated ivy continue to provide interest in this border long after winter has given way to spring. The cyclamen rest, leafless, in early summer before producing masses of tiny shuttlecock flowers, miniature versions of *C. persicum*, the popular houseplant. *C. hederifolium* is followed by *C. coum* subsp. *coum*, which carries flowers from midwinter to early spring. Pink is the usual color, but both species also produce white flowers.

Snowdrops will flower with the first of the Lenten hellebores. Other bulbs such as dog's-tooth violets and Spanish bluebells add color and extend the season through into late spring.

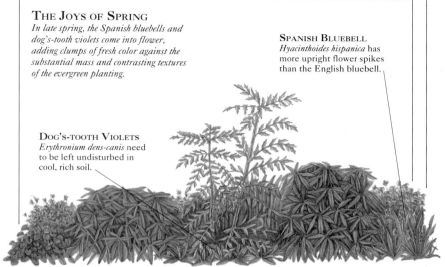

THE JOYS OF SPRING
In late spring, the Spanish bluebells and dog's-tooth violets come into flower, adding clumps of fresh color against the substantial mass and contrasting textures of the evergreen planting.

SPANISH BLUEBELL
Hyacinthoides hispanica has more upright flower spikes than the English bluebell.

DOG'S-TOOTH VIOLETS
Erythronium dens-canis need to be left undisturbed in cool, rich soil.

SCHEME FOR A COOL SEASON
In late winter, both hellebores are at their best, with elegant flowers offset by a backcloth of dark leaves. The mahonia makes a striking centerpiece all year.

IVY
Hedera helix 'Adam' has neat, variegated leaves and can easily be controlled.

MAHONIA
A shrub with magnificent foliage, *Mahonia* x *media* 'Charity' also has scented, umbrella-like spikes of flowers in winter.

HART'S-TONGUE FERN
Broad, undulating, strap-shaped fronds are the trademark of the evergreen hart's-tongue fern, *Phyllitis scolopendrium.*

HELLEBORE
Helleborus lividus subsp. *corsicus* has the most beautiful leaf of any hellebore, veined and edged with fine prickles.

SNOWDROP
With its flowers of purest white, the snowdrop, *Galanthus nivalis*, is a welcome sight at the beginning of the year.

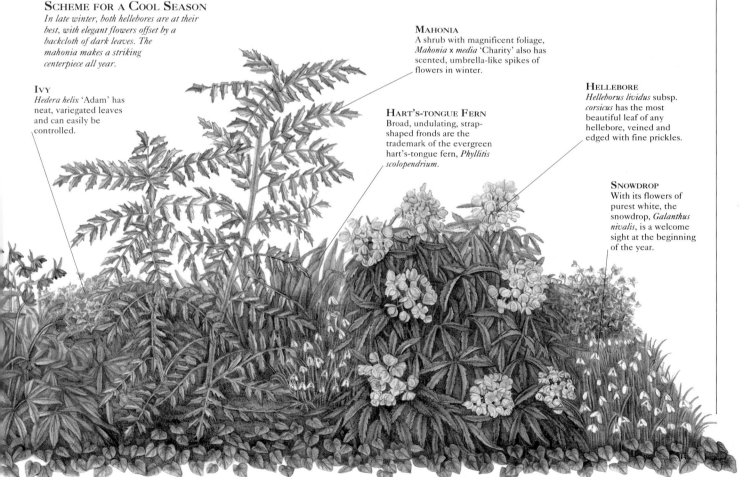

LOW-MAINTENANCE PLANTS *for* WINTER INTEREST

LEFT TO ITSELF, the mahonia will reach for the sky until its terminal spikes of flowers are far beyond nose level. Curb this tendency by cutting a few of its stems back by half each winter. The habit of the mahonia is sternly upright, so you can easily grow other plants beneath it. The mahonia, as well as the other plants used here, will cope in a position shaded by overhanging trees. This kind of shade is often slightly dry, and you need to compensate for this by feeding all the plants liberally with compost or by mulching around them with a bulky manure.

The ground cover plants in this scheme need very little attention, but encourage the ivies to spread in the direction you want by pegging down long growths with wire hoops. The cyclamen seed themselves about with magnificent abandon. Fortunately, this is one of the few plants you can never have too many of, so let them spread where they will.

CARE AND CULTIVATION

SPRING
Plant the mahonia and ivies now or in fall. Once established, the mahonia needs little attention, apart from a regular, deep mulch. Plant snowdrops "in the green" as soon as they have finished flowering. Cut out old, flowered stems of *Helleborus lividus* subsp. *corsicus* and mulch around new growth.

SUMMER
Plant dog's-tooth violets as soon as available in late summer, also ferns, keeping them well watered until established. Before cyclamen start to flower, feed them with a scattering of bone meal and a layer of leaf mold about 1in (2.5cm) thick.

FALL
Plant hellebores. They resent disturbance, so once they are settled leave them alone. Plant cyclamen in early fall, barely covering the corms with soil. Plant Spanish bluebells, setting them about 4in (10cm) deep.

WINTER
Cut back old leaves of *Helleborus orientalis* when new flower stems start to show through. Cut out dying fronds of ferns.

Hedera helix 'Adam' (Ivy) *Spreading, evergreen creeper with small, light green leaves edged with creamy yellow. H 4ft (1.2m), S 3ft (1m).*

Helleborus orientalis (Lenten rose) *Evergreen perennial with white, pink, or purple flowers in winter–spring. H and S 18in (45cm).*

Mahonia x media 'Charity' *Evergreen shrub with dark green leaves and slender, yellow flower spikes. H 10ft (3m), S 8ft (2.5m).*

Phyllitis scolopendrium (Hart's-tongue fern) *Fully hardy, evergreen fern with bright green, slightly frilled, tongue-shaped fronds. H 18–30in (45–75cm), S to 18in (45cm).*

Helleborus lividus subsp. **corsicus (Hellebore)** *Evergreen perennial with greenish white flowers in winter–spring. H and S to 2ft (60cm).*

Hyacinthoides hispanica (Spanish bluebell) *Bulb with blue, white, or pink, bell-like flowers in spring. H to 12in (30cm), S 4–6in (10–15cm).*

Galanthus nivalis (Snowdrop) *Bulb with pendent, white flowers in winter–spring, and strappy leaves. H 4–6in (10–15cm), S 2–3in (5–8cm).*

Cyclamen coum subsp. **coum** *Tuber with bright pink flowers in winter. H to 4in (10cm), S 2–4in (5–10cm).*

Erythronium dens-canis (Dog's-tooth violet) *Tuberous perennial with attractively mottled, pointed leaves and nodding, pink, purple, or white flowers in spring. H 6–10in (15–25cm), S 3–4in (8–10cm).*

Cyclamen hederifolium *Tuber with patterned leaves, and pink flowers in fall. H to 4in (10cm), S 4–6in (10–15cm).*

ALTERING *the* PLANTING SCHEME

FEW OTHER WINTER-FLOWERING shrubs can match the mahonia for year-round interest, but in areas where there are doubts about its hardiness, another shrub, such as viburnum, could be used instead. There is plenty of room to experiment with the ground cover plants, too. Try other ferns and other bulbs, although you must avoid those that need full sun.

SHADES OF PINK

To create a scheme dominated by shades of pink, substitute a winter-flowering viburnum for the mahonia. The growth of *Viburnum* x *bodnantense* 'Dawn' is stiff and upright, the stems covered in midwinter with clusters of scented, pink-flushed flowers. Disguise its summer dullness with a cloak of clematis, choosing a pale variety such as the pink 'Comtesse de Bouchaud', which flowers in late summer. Choose a clematis that you can cut back each year, so that the viburnum has a chance each season to flex its muscles. Both viburnum and clematis will need a slightly more open situation than the mahonia if they are to flower well.

There are plenty of plants that enjoy life snuffling around at ground level in dappled shade. Use periwinkles in place of the ivies to introduce more flowers, and crinkly-edged hart's-tongue ferns instead of the plain ones. Or use the ostrich fern, *Matteuccia struthiopteris*; it is not evergreen, but the drama of its eruption in late spring makes up for that.

Viburnum x *bodnantense* **'Dawn'** *Deciduous shrub carrying clusters of deep pink buds that open to fragrant, pink flowers from late fall to early spring. H 10ft (3m), S 8ft (2.5m).*

Phyllitis scolopendrium **'Marginatum'** *Fully hardy, evergreen fern with long, upright, bright green, slender fronds that are attractively frilled at the edges. H and S 12–16in (30–40cm).*

Vinca minor **'Argenteovariegata'** (Lesser periwinkle) *Evergreen ground cover with white-margined leaves and lilac-blue flowers. H 6in (15cm), S indefinite.*

Clematis **'Comtesse de Bouchaud'** *Hardy, strong-growing, deciduous climber. In late summer, it is covered with masses of single, large, mauve-pink flowers with yellow anthers. H 6–10ft (2–3m), S 3ft (1m).*

CLUMPS OF COLOR
The distinctive rosettes of
Sempervivum tectorum
are suffused with deep red.

DESIGN POINTS

❧

SMALL IS BEAUTIFUL
A miniature garden,
perfect for a very narrow
border, is created using
alpines and other
compact plants.

❧

FORM AND CONTRAST
Delicate flowers and
bulbs contrast with the
robust, architectural
shapes of dwarf conifers
and the rough texture of
gravel and tufa rocks.

BORDER *of* MINIATURES

Provided you always keep in mind the sort of conditions that alpine plants thrive in, you can grow them in many different places in the garden: in the cracks between paving stones on a terrace or a patio, in a lawn or scree bed, in shallow troughs and pans, in a cool greenhouse, or, as here, in a raised border.

Abandon any attempts to recreate the Alps in your back garden. Nothing you can do to builder's rubble will ever make it look like an alpine scree. Grow the plants in a raised bed instead and you will be able to enjoy them at close quarters. You could plant the border in a low retaining wall, perhaps marking the boundary between terrace and lawn, or arrange it to fill in one end of a patio. As well as making it easier for you to admire the plants, siting them in a raised border provides the sharply drained conditions they need to flourish. They will also need sun and an open situation.

COLORFUL ALPINES AND BULBS
Spring is the peak of the year for alpine plants and the kinds of bulb that fit in well with them, for example fritillaries, scillas, dwarf narcissus, and species tulips and crocuses. Fortunately, many of the spring-flowering plants, such as the saxifrages, are pleasing enough in form and leaf to pay their way all year.

The saxifrages are a huge and diverse family and, indeed, you could make a whole border using nothing else. But here, with heroic restraint, you will have to restrict yourself to two. One should be a mossy type that will form neat hummocks of green foliage, scattered in spring with short-stemmed flowers. For the other saxifrage, choose *Saxifraga* 'Southside Seedling', which has enormously showy, arching plumes of flowers, a mass of white, blotched and spotted with crimson. The rosette of 'Southside Seedling' dies after it has flowered, leaving several satellite rosettes that take a season or

PUTTING ON A SHOW FOR SPRING
In late spring, the hebe, pulsatillas, and mossy saxifrages are covered in flowers, while a dwarf pine and a group of columnar dwarf junipers add strong shapes and contrasting textures.

CONVOLVULUS
Convolvulus cneorum
is a pretty silver-
leaved plant
but not
reliably
hardy.

PLANT LIST
1 *Convolvulus cneorum* x 1
2 *Sempervivum tectorum* (Houseleek) x 14
3 *Pulsatilla vulgaris* (Pasque flower) x 6
4 *Dianthus gratianopolitanus* (Cheddar pink) x 6
5 *Saxifraga* 'Southside Seedling' (Saxifrage) x 10
6 *Sisyrinchium graminoides* x 5
7 *Campanula carpatica* (Dwarf bellflower) x 6
8 *Saxifraga* 'Sanguinea Superba' (Mossy saxifrage) x 3
9 *Lithodora diffusa* 'Heavenly Blue' x 6
10 *Pinus mugo* 'Humpy' (Dwarf pine) x 1
11 *Hebe pinguifolia* 'Pagei' x 1
12 *Juniperus communis* 'Compressa' (Dwarf juniper) x 3

PLANTING PLAN

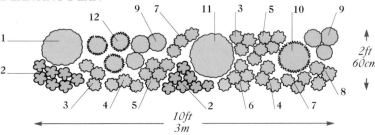

2ft
60cm

10ft
3m

more to build up to flowering size again. Buy half the plants you need one year, half the next. That way, they will not all die out at the same time, and you should always have some in flower.

Include at least one plant to flop over the edge of the retaining wall and soften its hard lines. Some campanulas and dianthus will do this and will extend the flowering season into summer.

STRUCTURAL FRAMEWORK

Include a selection of plants of greater substance and stature to help balance the display. Dwarf conifers are traditional companions for rock plants and provide evergreen bulk all year. There are many upright junipers that will add height and solidity. A pine such as *Pinus mugo* 'Humpy' or *P. pumila* 'Globe' makes a compact, rounded dome, the needles arranged like bottle brushes in whorls round the stubby branches. *P. leucodermis* 'Schmidtii' is another dwarf conifer of character. Before buying, check that the conifers you choose are truly dwarf rather than young plants of larger trees.

THE BORDER IN LATE SUMMER

In summer, the convolvulus, sisyrinchiums, lithodoras, and campanulas come to the fore, displaying a wealth of colorful blooms.

LITHODORA
The spreading, prostrate stems of *Lithodora diffusa* 'Heavenly Blue' are covered in summer with deep blue flowers.

SISYRINCHIUM
Sisyrinchium graminoides has star-shaped flowers held on stiff stems.

DWARF BELLFLOWER
Neat, low mounds of bright green leaves are studded in summer with the blue or white flowers of the dwarf bellflower, *Campanula carpatica*.

DWARF JUNIPER
Juniperus communis 'Compressa' is an excellent dwarf juniper to use with low-growing alpines.

HOUSELEEK
All the houseleeks, varieties of *Sempervivum tectorum*, share the same form, making compact rosettes of fleshy leaves.

HEBE
A low, dense shrub, *Hebe pinguifolia* 'Pagei' has foliage of an intense, glaucous gray.

PASQUE FLOWER
Pulsatilla vulgaris, the Pasque flower, has silky leaves topped with purple flowers.

Sisyrinchium graminoides

SAXIFRAGE
Saxifraga 'Southside Seedling' has a froth of showy, pink and white flowers on foot-long stems.

CHEDDAR PINK
The long-lived Cheddar pink, *Dianthus gratianopolitanus*, fills the air with its sweet scent in early summer.

DWARF PINE
The most compact form of the mountain pine, *Pinus mugo* 'Humpy' grows slowly into a dense, rounded bush.

Campanula carpatica

MOSSY SAXIFRAGE
Saxifraga 'Sanguinea Superba' is a mossy saxifrage with red flowers in spring.

Lithodora diffusa 'Heavenly Blue'

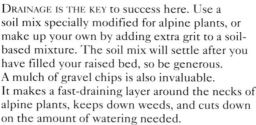

A WELL-DRAINED BORDER *for* MINIATURE PLANTS

DRAINAGE IS THE KEY to success here. Use a soil mix specially modified for alpine plants, or make up your own by adding extra grit to a soil-based mixture. The soil mix will settle after you have filled your raised bed, so be generous. A mulch of gravel chips is also invaluable. It makes a fast-draining layer around the necks of alpine plants, keeps down weeds, and cuts down on the amount of watering needed.

Vary the horizontal plane with lumps of natural tufa. Bury it to at least one-third of its depth so that it is stable and looks settled.

CARE AND CULTIVATION

SPRING
Plant junipers and pinks, adding bone meal to the soil for the latter. Plant campanulas, convolvulus, lithodoras, sempervivums, and sisyrinchiums. Protect campanulas against slugs, and add leaf mold to the soil for lithodoras. Split and reset congested clumps of sempervivums. Cut back leggy growth of hebes if necessary.

SUMMER
Shear off dead flowers of mossy saxifrages. Cut out flowered stems of *Saxifraga* 'Southside Seedling', pinks, and campanulas. Remove dead, flowered rosettes of sempervivums. Deadhead hebes after flowering.

FALL
Plant saxifrages now or in spring, working plenty of grit into the hole, and position pulsatillas in a sunny spot. Cut out dead, flowered stems and leaves of sisyrinchiums. Cut back lithodoras if they encroach on neighboring plants.

WINTER
Plant the pine in a sunny position now or in spring. Remove fallen leaves from pinks and saxifrages. In cold, wet areas, protect convolvulus with panes of glass or a cloche.

Saxifraga 'Southside Seedling' (Saxifrage)
Evergreen perennial, flowering in late spring–early summer. H and S 12in (30cm).

Lithodora diffusa 'Heavenly Blue'
Evergreen subshrub with summer flowers. H 12in (30cm), S 18in (45cm).

Convolvulus cneorum
Evergreen shrub with silvery leaves, and white flowers in late spring–summer. H and S 2½ft (75cm).

Hebe pinguifolia 'Pagei'
Evergreen, spreading shrub with small, glaucous leaves, flowering profusely in early summer. H and S 3ft (90cm).

Pinus mugo 'Humpy' (Dwarf pine) *Dwarf conifer with needlelike, dark green leaves. H and S 10–12in (25–30cm).*

Sempervivum tectorum (Houseleek) *Evergreen succulent with neat, fleshy rosettes. H 6in (15cm), S 8in (20cm).*

Juniperus communis 'Compressa' (Dwarf juniper) *Conifer with aromatic leaves. H 2½ft (75cm), S 6in (15cm).*

Campanula carpatica (Dwarf bellflower)
Perennial with blue or white summer flowers. H 4in (10cm), S 12in (30cm).

Pulsatilla vulgaris (Pasque flower)
Perennial with red, pink, purple, or white flowers in spring. H and S 9in (23cm).

Dianthus gratianopolitanus (Cheddar pink)
Evergreen perennial. H 6in (15cm), S 12in (30cm).

Saxifraga 'Sanguinea Superba' (Mossy saxifrage) *Perennial with reddish pink flowers. H 4in (10cm), S indefinite.*

Sisyrinchium graminoides *Semi-evergreen perennial with blue summer flowers. H 12in (30cm), S 3in (8cm).*

ALTERING *the* PLANTING SCHEME

DWARF BULBS OF MANY KINDS will complement the other plants in this border, and will also help to extend its season of interest. Growing bulbs in pots to plunge into the bed temporarily makes it easy to change the scheme each season. Choose varieties that are in scale with the rest of the plants; some daffodils look as if they spend their rest time at body-building classes.

BULBS FOR A LONGER DISPLAY

Include cyclamen for a breath of life when many plants are lying low: *Cyclamen coum* subsp. *coum* may produce its flowers in early winter. Colchicums carry the torch at the other end of the season, pushing up sheaves of checkered pink flowers. In spring the choice is enormous: species crocus, scillas, chionodoxas, puschkinias, and *Anemone blanda* all make fine displays. Plant tulips and narcissus in pots, then lift them after flowering and allow the leaves to die down before storing the bulbs until next year.

Colchicum agrippinum *Early fall-flowering bulb bearing erect, funnel-shaped, pink flowers. H 4–6in (10–15cm), S 4in (10cm).*

Cyclamen coum subsp. ***coum*** *Winter-flowering tuber with rounded, silver-splashed or plain green leaves and pink flowers. H and S 4in (10cm).*

***Narcissus* 'Hawera'** *Bulb that bears delicate, nodding, lemon yellow blooms in midspring. H and S to 8in (20cm).*

***Iris reticulata* 'Cantab'** *Bulb with pale blue flowers, each fall marked with a blaze of bright yellow. H 4–6in (10–15cm), S 2in (5cm).*

***Tulipa linifolia* (Species tulip)** *Early spring-flowering bulb with gray-green leaves and red flowers that have blackish purple centers, usually ringed with cream or yellow. H and S to 20cm (8in).*

Crocus tommasinianus *Spring-flowering bulb that produces long, slender, goblet-shaped flowers that may be lilac, deep purple, or violet, occasionally silver outside. It naturalizes well. H to 4in (10cm), S to 3in (8cm).*

ISLAND AND OTHER BEDS

*Beds in a garden need to work from more
than one viewpoint. Island beds are particularly
demanding in this respect because there is such
a large proportion of foreground to background.
The shape of the bed may suggest the style of
planting: symmetrical or geometric-shaped
beds lend themselves to formal schemes, while
informal planting is appropriate for
curving or irregular beds.*

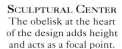

A BED *of* ROSES

FEW PLANTS CAN RIVAL ROSES for their seductive scent and range of colors, whether rich and deep or pale and subtle. In traditional, formal gardens, roses are often grown on their own, but in this formal scheme a tapestry of plants weaves beneath the roses to provide a backcloth of color and texture.

REPEAT PERFORMANCE
The open blooms of Rosa *'Penelope' are flushed with pink. If deadheaded, this rose will flower through summer and fall.*

DESIGN POINTS

GEOMETRIC SHAPES
Repeated blocks of color in the underplanting give a formal structure.

SCULPTURAL CENTER
The obelisk at the heart of the design adds height and acts as a focal point.

SOFT COLORS
Coordinated groups of lady's mantle, geraniums, anaphalis, and pinks are chosen to complement the colors of the roses.

It is perfectly possible to plant roses that are healthy, that smell good, that give a good display for a long period in summer, that have handsome foliage as well as beautiful flowers, and that grow with form and grace. The difficulty lies in finding a variety that possesses all these characteristics at once.

For individual flower power, nothing can beat the large-flowered bush (Hybrid Tea) roses, which have "Never mind the quality, feel the color" stamped right through them. But the habit is graceless, the constitution often weak. The old shrub roses have grace, but a short, one-off season of flowering in midsummer. Somewhere between the two sits the superb race of roses known as Hybrid Musks. These are healthy shrubs with a relaxed habit and, unlike old roses, they continue to flower intermittently through until fall.

This scheme includes 'Felicia', which has rich pink, fully double flowers, the salmon overtones fading to cream as the flowers age, and the paler 'Penelope' with clusters of cream flowers flushed with pink. Both are sweetly scented. Use these roses in contrasting groups of three in the corners of this formal, diamond-shaped bed.

A CLIMBING CENTERPIECE
Make a centerpiece with a luxuriant climbing rose that you can train through a support. Metal obelisks are long lasting and make handsome pieces of garden sculpture when the roses are dormant.

Avoid wildly vigorous cultivars such as 'Kiftsgate', which will swamp an obelisk with magnificent contempt. Climbing sports of large-flowered bushes are shorter, but have a stiff habit of growth. Look instead for a climber such

PLANT LIST
1 *Dianthus* 'Charles Musgrave' (Pink) x 6
2 *Rosa* 'Penelope' x 6
3 *Geranium endressii* x 6
4 *Stachys macrantha* x 6
5 *Nepeta* 'Six Hills Giant' (Catmint) x 6
6 *Rosa* 'Felicia' x 6
7 *Alchemilla mollis* (Lady's mantle) x 3
8 *Geranium psilostemon* x 6
9 *Hosta fortunei* 'Albopicta' x 10
10 *Iris germanica* x 14
11 *Anaphalis triplinervis* x 6
12 *Rosa* 'Félicité Perpétue' x 1

PLANTING PLAN

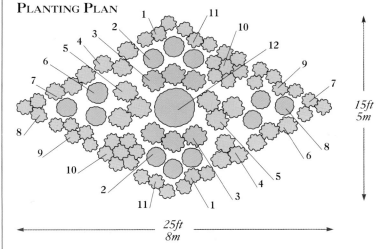

15ft
5m

25ft
8m

LATE SUMMER SHOW
With the Hybrid Musk roses in full bloom, the underplanting is deliberately low key. The pinks and anaphalis form mats of soft, gray foliage while blue catmint and pink Geranium endressii *provide clumps of color.*

GERANIUM
Geranium endressii provides useful, evergreen ground cover and a long succession of silver-pink flowers.

HOSTA
With its sheaves of painted leaves, *Hosta fortunei* 'Albopicta' makes a spectacular spring foliage plant.

as 'Félicité Perpétue', which has no ambitions beyond the 15ft (5m) level. In mild areas, its foliage should be evergreen – an added bonus. The flowers are small, but borne in big clusters, creamy white, sometimes flushed with pink, and beautifully scented.

If even this seems too much to keep under control, try 'The Garland', one of Gertrude Jekyll's favorite roses, which rarely reaches beyond 10ft (3m). It flowers profusely and the scent is sweetly pungent, like oranges.

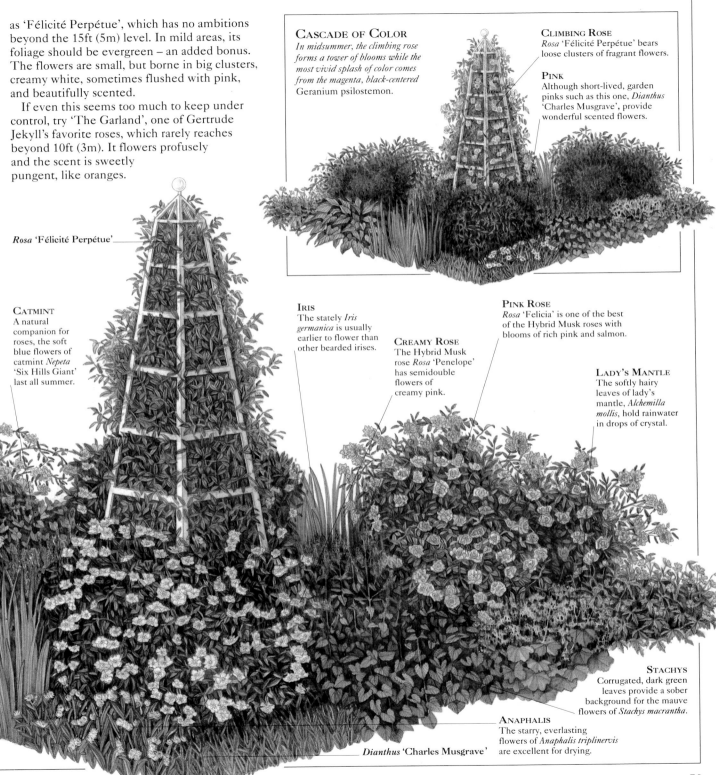

CASCADE OF COLOR
In midsummer, the climbing rose forms a tower of blooms while the most vivid splash of color comes from the magenta, black-centered Geranium psilostemon.

CLIMBING ROSE
Rosa 'Félicité Perpétue' bears loose clusters of fragrant flowers.

PINK
Although short-lived, garden pinks such as this one, *Dianthus* 'Charles Musgrave', provide wonderful scented flowers.

Rosa 'Félicité Perpétue'

CATMINT
A natural companion for roses, the soft blue flowers of catmint *Nepeta* 'Six Hills Giant' last all summer.

IRIS
The stately *Iris germanica* is usually earlier to flower than other bearded irises.

CREAMY ROSE
The Hybrid Musk rose *Rosa* 'Penelope' has semidouble flowers of creamy pink.

PINK ROSE
Rosa 'Felicia' is one of the best of the Hybrid Musk roses with blooms of rich pink and salmon.

LADY'S MANTLE
The softly hairy leaves of lady's mantle, *Alchemilla mollis*, hold rainwater in drops of crystal.

STACHYS
Corrugated, dark green leaves provide a sober background for the mauve flowers of *Stachys macrantha*.

ANAPHALIS
The starry, everlasting flowers of *Anaphalis triplinervis* are excellent for drying.

Dianthus 'Charles Musgrave'

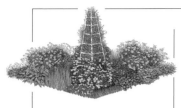

CARE AND CULTIVATION

SPRING

Mulch roses with bulky organic material. Tie in new growths of the climbing rose. Plant pinks in well-drained soil, also stachys, lady's mantles, catmints, geraniums, hostas, and anaphalis. Start protecting young leaves of hostas from slugs in late spring.

SUMMER

Spray roses if necessary against aphids and mildew. Deadhead regularly. Remove faded flowers from pinks and dress with a high-potassium fertilizer. Shear geraniums after flowering to keep plants compact and provide a second flush of blooms.

FALL

Plant irises in early fall, incorporating plenty of bone meal and setting the rhizomes with the upper surface exposed. Trim the leaves to half their length. Remove dead leaves from established clumps. Cut back anaphalis hard if necessary. Cut down catmints.

WINTER

Plant roses, incorporating bone meal and compost. Prune established climbers. If a wilder, more natural look is preferred, Hybrid Musks may be left unpruned.

EVEN THE BETTER TYPES OF ROSE, such as the Hybrid Musks, cannot pretend that their foliage is so good that you would make a detour to see it. This makes it doubly important to have plants with pleasing foliage in the rest of the planting. Lady's mantle is a good ally in this respect, though always coming into leaf later than you would wish. It can be invasive, so it is a good idea to cut back the flowering stems before it has a chance to set seed.

Stachys macrantha has distinctive, corrugated, triangular leaves that spread to make a thick, green mat. It is not as widely planted as its cousin, *S. byzantina*, but is well worth growing.

Geranium endressii
Semi-evergreen, carpeting perennial producing cup-shaped, pink flowers in summer. H 18in (45cm), S 2ft (60cm).

Dianthus 'Charles Musgrave' (Pink)
Spreading perennial with single, white flowers in midsummer. H 18in (45cm), S 12in (30cm).

Iris germanica
Rhizomatous, bearded iris. Yellow-splashed, violet flowers are produced in late spring and early summer. H to 4ft (1.2m), S indefinite.

Rosa 'Felicia'
Vigorous Hybrid Musk rose with gray-green foliage and double, scented flowers in summer–fall. H 5ft (1.5m), S 7ft (2.2m).

Rosa 'Félicité Perpétue' *Semi-evergreen, climbing rose bearing clusters of fully double, blush pink to white flowers in midsummer. H 15ft (5m), S 12ft (4m).*

Geranium psilostemon
Clump-forming perennial bearing pink flowers with black centers in midsummer. The deeply cut leaves have good fall color. H and S 4ft (1.2m).

Rosa 'Penelope' *Bushy Hybrid Musk rose with plentiful, dark green leaves. It bears clusters of scented, double, pinkish white flowers in summer–fall. H and S 3ft (1m).*

Nepeta 'Six Hills Giant' (Catmint)
Summer-flowering perennial with narrow, gray-green leaves and spikes of lavender-blue flowers. H and S 2ft (60cm).

Hosta fortunei 'Albopicta' *Clump-forming perennial grown mainly for its cream-splashed foliage. It has pale violet flowers in early summer. H and S 3ft (1m).*

Anaphalis triplinervis
Dwarf, leafy perennial with gray-green foliage and silvery stems. The white flowerheads appear in late summer. H 8–12in (20–30cm), S 6in (15cm).

Stachys macrantha
Clump-forming perennial bearing crinkled, heart-shaped, soft green leaves. In summer, it has whorls of large, rose-purple flowers. H and S 12in (30cm).

Alchemilla mollis (Lady's mantle)
Perennial, ground cover plant with downy leaves and sprays of greenish yellow flowers in summer. H and S 20in (50cm).

ALTERING *the* PLANTING SCHEME

THE ORIGINAL SCHEME USES ROSES in soft shades of pale creamy pink. For an effect that is altogether more sumptuous, substitute some deep magenta Rugosa roses instead. Extend the season of interest in this bed by including spring-flowering bulbs such as hyacinths and tulips. You can plant out hyacinth bulbs that have been forced for an early show indoors.

A RICH DISPLAY OF DEEP PINK AND PURPLE

The Rugosa roses have a very different habit of growth from the Hybrid Musks. They are dense, upright, and vigorous, and the result is a thicket, rather than the loose, open, airy effect of the Hybrid Musks. Rugosas are outstandingly healthy roses, strangers to blackspot and mildew. 'Roseraie de l'Haÿ' has large, flat, semidouble flowers of rich magenta. 'Frau Dagmar Hartopp' has paler flowers but compensates with spectacular fall fruit, the size and color of cherry tomatoes.

To intensify the rich effect, you could replace the pale climbing rose with a darker one, too. 'Veilchenblau' would be perfect: its flowers are like purple tissue paper left out in the rain, clusters of lavender-purple that fade as they age to a lilac-gray. Avoid bright yellow roses; they would fight to the death with the magenta *Geranium psilostemon*.

Rosa rugosa 'Frau Dagmar Hartopp' *Shrub rose with fragrant, single, pink flowers, then large red hips in fall. H 5ft (1.5m), S 4 ft (1.2m).*

Rosa rugosa 'Roseraie de l'Haÿ' *Vigorous, strongly scented rose with large, double, magenta blooms. H 6ft (2m), S 5ft (1.5m).*

BEAUTIFUL BULBS FOR A SPRING SHOW

Since the scheme is planned to peak in summer, a generous planting of bulbs will give it another chance to hog the spotlight earlier in the year. You could plant thick bands of crocus around the edges of the diamond with a cluster of daffodils at the feet of the central rose. Or you could plant random groups of hyacinths (use at least seven in a group), mixed with tulips. Try the raspberry ripple ice cream colors of the parrot tulip 'Estella Rijnveld' and the earlier flowering, simple, white 'Purissima'.

Tulipa 'Purissima' (Fosteriana tulip) *Spring-flowering bulb with white blooms above broad leaves. H 14–16in (35–40cm), S to 8in (20cm).*

Tulipa 'Estella Rijnveld' (Parrot tulip) *Late spring-flowering bulb with fantastically frilled, red blooms, streaked with white. H 2ft (60cm), S to 8in (20cm).*

Hyacinthus orientalis 'Delft Blue' (Hyacinth) *Winter- or spring-flowering bulb with scented, violet-blue flowers. H 4–8in (10–20cm), S 2½–4in (6–10cm).*

A BOLD DESERT BED

HANDSOME EXOTICS such as yucca, agave, kniphofia, and phormium need to be displayed like pieces of sculpture in a gallery, with plenty of room all around them. This bed would work well in a modern setting alongside a patio, planted in a courtyard with plain, whitewashed walls, or adapted to fit around two sides of a terrace. You could also modify it to suit a conservatory; then, even in cold regions, the scheme would work for twelve months of the year instead of four.

STEELY SUCCULENT
The fleshy, succulent leaves of Agave parryi *form a compact, spiky, steely blue rosette and help the plant to tolerate long periods of drought.*

DESIGN POINTS

— ❧ —

CONTEMPORARY STYLE
Bold, architectural plants complement an unfussy, contemporary setting.

— ❧ —

DRY SITE
An ideal scheme for a very dry, well-drained, sunny spot or a bed in a frost-free conservatory.

— ❧ —

AFTER-DARK DISPLAY
Plants of sculptural form such as those used here look particularly striking if lit up at night.

COLOR AND FORM

Foliage carries much of the color in this group: blue-gray and variegated gold in the agave, glaucous gray in the eucalyptus, deep purple in the phormium. The aeoniums look as if they are made of wax, toy trees with succulent rosettes of leaves arranged in perfect symmetry. The surface of the leaves is glossy and slippery, a fine contrast to the dull sheen of the phormium. Even the fuchsia, which is from a family not generally noted for its foliage, has lustrous leaves, darker and silkier than those on ordinary fuchsias.

This scheme uses the alpine snow gum, *Eucalyptus niphophila*, which is smaller and slower growing than the widely planted *E. gunnii*

though it is equally hardy and wind resistant. The young leaves are a light mahogany, and this color spreads in winter to the twigs which glow glossy red. In spring, they are covered in a blue-white bloom, the same color as the bark on young trees. Older trees shed their bark, which changes through cream to gray and reddish brown.

The phormium makes a strong upright feature in the center of the group, its evergreen sword leaves very much more important than its flowers. Only the bright yellow gazania (which will grow as a perennial in mild areas) is here chiefly on account of its flowers, which are models of symmetry – yet even the gazania has foliage that is attractively backed with silver.

PLANT LIST

1 *Datura* x *candida* (Angels' trumpets) x 1
2 *Gazania uniflora* x 16
3 *Agave americana* 'Variegata' x 1 and *Agave parryi* x 2
4 *Fuchsia* 'Thalia' x 1
5 *Begonia rex* 'Helen Lewis' x 4
6 *Phormium tenax* 'Purpureum' (New Zealand flax) x 1
7 *Aeonium arboreum* 'Schwarzkopf' x 3
8 *Kniphofia caulescens* (Red-hot poker) x 3
9 *Eucalyptus niphophila* (Alpine snow gum) x 1
10 *Crassula falcata* (Propeller plant) x 1
11 *Echeveria gibbiflora* var. *metallica* x 1
12 *Yucca whipplei* x 1

PLANTING PLAN

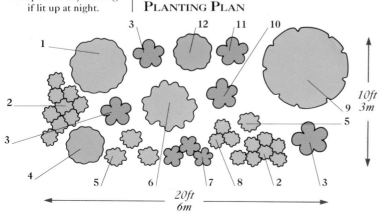

3 12 11 10
1
2
3
4
5 6 7 8 2 3
9 5
5
10ft
3m
20ft
6m

SCULPTURAL TABLEAU
The strength of this scheme is its simplicity – plants with strong silhouettes, limited colors, and echoing forms and habits are seen against a textured plane of gravel or pebbles.

ANGELS' TRUMPETS
The heavily scented flowers of angels' trumpets, *Datura* x *candida*, are produced over a long period in late summer and fall.

FUCHSIA
The green leaves of *Fuchsia* 'Thalia' are red beneath and make an excellent foil for the tubular, orange-red flowers.

GAZANIA
Each one a miniature sun, the brilliant flowers of *Gazania uniflora* shine out against the dark foliage.

A SCHEME OF SUN-LOVERS

Few of these plants make any pretense at being hardy. They are sybarites, built for sun and pleasure, not frost and torment. In warm areas around the Mediterranean, in Australia, and the southern United States, all the plants could stay out permanently. In regions where winters are cold and winds harsh, they should only be left out in the garden for a temporary summer display. The smaller plants such as the crassula and aeoniums may be grown in clay pots to stand out on the gravel during the summer months. The begonias will also look good in pots, and both can then be shifted easily if necessary to overwinter in a frost-free greenhouse.

In favorable mild areas, the eucalyptus, the spiky yucca, the phormium, and the kniphofia can stay as permanent features. These four on their own will provide effective contrasts of foliage and form.

ALPINE SNOW GUM
Grow *Eucalyptus niphophila*, the Alpine snow gum, as a single-trunk tree or coppice it to provide the most handsome foliage.

VARIEGATED AGAVE
Although dangerously sharp, the pointed leaves of this *Agave americana* 'Variegata' add drama in a planting scheme.

BLUE AGAVE
Agave parryi is a scaled-down version of the big American agaves, but its rosettes are no less arresting.

PROPELLER PLANT
Handle *Crassula falcata* carefully since the bloom easily rubs off its succulent leaves.

YUCCA
Vast panicles of cream bells rise from the gray foliage of *Yucca whipplei* in summer.

BEGONIA
Good-looking leaves rather than flowers are the chief glory of *Begonia rex* 'Helen Lewis'.

AEONIUM
The whorls of leaves on *Aeonium arboreum* 'Schwarzkopf' are wonderfully dark and gleaming.

NEW ZEALAND FLAX
Phormium tenax 'Purpureum' forms a fountain of arching leaves.

RED-HOT POKER
Beautiful gray leaves set off the soft coral-red flowers of *Kniphofia caulescens*, the red-hot poker.

ECHEVERIA
The succulent leaves of *Echeveria gibbiflora* var. *metallica* are suffused with pink.

PLANTS *for a* DRY, WELL-DRAINED SITE

A DESERT SCHEME such as this needs an open position in full sun. Most of the plants used here need dry, well-drained conditions, particularly the succulents such as the echeveria and aeoniums, which will rot if they are too damp. Cover the ground around the plants with gravel or small pebbles. This will set them off well and make them look more natural than if they are surrounded by bare soil. Using gravel has practical advantages, too: it acts as a weed suppressant and also slows down the rate at which water evaporates from the soil.

CARE AND CULTIVATION

SPRING
Plant the yucca, kniphofias, gazanias, and phormium. Repot agaves in a gritty, free-draining soil mix. Pot on begonias, and the echeveria and crassula if necessary, using a soil mix with coarse sand added. Set out the fuchsia once all danger of frost has passed.

SUMMER
Plant the eucalyptus in well-drained soil; water well until the tree is fully established and stake if necessary. Set out agaves. Syringe foliage of begonias with water to maintain a humid atmosphere, and give them a liquid feed every two weeks. Plunge datura in its pot, or plant out, depending on conditions. Set out pots of aeoniums.

FALL
Lift and overwinter mature fuchsia plants or propagate fresh plants from cuttings. Cut down stems of remaining plants after first frosts.

WINTER
Keep the crassula and agaves under cover on the dry side: they rot if they are too damp. In late winter, cut down growths of the datura to within 6in (15cm) of the base.

Eucalyptus niphophila (Alpine snow gum) *Evergreen tree with red-edged, gray-green leaves. H to 30ft (10m), S 20ft (6m).*

Echeveria gibbiflora var. **metallica** *Succulent with gray-green, fleshy leaves tinged with pink. H 3ft (1m), S 6in (15cm).*

Gazania uniflora *Mat-forming perennial bearing yellow flowers in early summer. H 18–24in (45–60cm), S 18in (45cm).*

Kniphofia caulescens (Red-hot poker) *Fall-flowering, evergreen perennial. H 4ft (1.2m), S 2ft (60cm).*

Begonia rex 'Helen Lewis' *Evergreen perennial with cream flowers in early summer. H and S to 2ft (60cm).*

Yucca whipplei *Evergreen shrub with slender, blue-green leaves and a tall flower spike. H 5ft (1.5m), S 3ft (1m).*

Aeonium arboreum 'Schwarzkopf' *Perennial succulent with narrow, purple leaves. H to 2ft (60cm), S 3ft (1m).*

Agave americana 'Variegata' *Perennial succulent with stiff, pointed leaves edged with yellow. H and S to 6ft (2m).*

Fuchsia 'Thalia' *Tender, deciduous shrub with long, slender flowers and dark foliage. H and S 3ft (1m).*

Phormium tenax 'Purpureum' (New Zealand Flax) *Evergreen perennial with bold leaves. H 6ft (2m), S 3ft (1m).*

Crassula falcata (Propeller plant) *Perennial succulent that has fleshy, twisted, gray leaves. H and S 3ft (1m).*

Datura x candida (Angels' trumpets) *Semi-evergreen shrub with scented flowers in summer–fall. H and S to 9ft (3m).*

ALTERING *the* PLANTING SCHEME

THE EFFECT OF THE PURPLE FOLIAGE and the brilliantly colored flowers in the original scheme is rich and sumptuous, but where a lighter, airier effect is required, this can easily be achieved by altering some of the planting.

Use the feathery-leaved albizia instead of the more architectural phormium. Substitute plants with pale flowers of cream, white, and pink for the bright red and yellow flowers of the fuchsia, the kniphofia, and the gazania.

COOLER COLOR COMBINATIONS

Albizia, the silk tree, is airiness incarnate, a shimmering mirage of gray-green leaflets and, in late summer, preposterous small, pink powder-puff flowers. It is not fully hardy but fortunately will grow in a large pot and can be put under cover if necessary.

Other plants have to be toned down to fit the new mood of this scheme. Use only the steely blue-gray agaves, rather than the variegated one, and switch the red kniphofia for a creamy white one. Plant patches of pink and white impatiens instead of the bright gazanias.

Albizia julibrissin **(Silk tree)** *Deciduous tree with large, divided leaves and clusters of frothy, pink flowers in late summer. H and S to 30ft (10m).*

Impatiens 'Accent Pink' *Tender perennial, usually grown as an annual, that is covered with pink flowers in summer–fall. H and S to 38cm (15in).*

Begonia fuchsioides Evergreen, shrublike begonia with oval, toothed, dark green leaves and single, red, hanging flowers. H to 4ft (1.2m), S 12in (30cm).

Echeveria elegans Clump-forming, perennial succulent with rosettes of pale silvery blue leaves and a pink flower that shoots above the leaves in summer. H 2in (5cm), S 20in (50cm).

Kniphofia 'Percy's Pride' *Upright perennial with large, cream-colored flower spikes tinged with green, borne on erect stems in autumn. H 3ft (1m), S to 20in (50cm).*

Agave parryi Perennial succulent with stiff, blue-gray leaves radiating from a basal rosette. Mature plants may produce a tall stem bearing creamy yellow flowers. H 20in (50cm), S 3ft (1m).

INSTANT FLOWERS

ALL GARDENS NEED SHORT-TERM as well as long-term plantings. This bed shows how you can have the best of both worlds. The centerpiece is a magnolia, which will take many years to acquire distinction. While you are waiting, you can use the space around the tree to grow colorful, summer-flowering, short-lived plants.

The principle of creating an instant display around a long-term plant can be adapted to any other tree or shrub that takes a long time to grow into its adult clothes. Where this scheme suggests a magnolia, you could equally well use a mulberry (*Morus*), a tulip tree (*Liriodendron tulipifera*), or a standard wisteria. Choose whatever is most likely to thrive in your own particular situation.

Magnolias grow best on soil that is rich, fertile, moisture retentive, and slightly on the acid side; the finest magnolias grow in areas that receive at least 28in (70cm) of rain a year, and do not have prolonged droughts in summer. They will grow on alkaline soils, but should not be wasted on poor, thin ground.

A SILVERY CARPET
The flowery bed under the magnolia includes four big bushes of daisy-flowered argyranthemums. Try to get hold of the fine gray-leaved cultivar with white flowers, known as *Argyranthemum gracile* 'Chelsea Girl'. It flowers nonstop throughout the summer until the first frosts. Few annuals have attractive, bulky foliage and this is what you gain from the argyranthemums as well as the tireless show from its flowers.

Add more body to the scheme by including plants of dusty miller, *Senecio maritima* 'Silver Dust'. The leaves and stems are covered with white, woolly hairs; the whole thing looks as though it has been cut from felt. In mild areas, it will overwinter, since it is by nature a shrubby plant, but it is often used like an annual, raised each spring from seed.

ARGYRANTHEMUM
All the argyranthemums are attractive, but 'Chelsea Girl' has intensely blue-gray, needle-fine foliage to set off the white daisy flowers.

FINE ORIGINS
Named after the famous English garden where it was raised, Verbena 'Sissinghurst' *is prized for its hot pink flowers and finely divided foliage.*

DESIGN POINTS

LIVING FRAME
A colorful frame of flowers for a slow-growing specimen tree or shrub.

SHORT-TERM PLEASURES
Instant effect from a combination of fast-growing plants.

LONG-TERM EFFECT
Long-term promise in the centerpiece, here the well-known *Magnolia* x *soulangeana*.

OLD AND NEW
A scheme that can be adapted to fit almost any existing specimen tree or shrub in your garden.

A SPECTACLE FOR SUMMER
In summer, the bed is at its best, with gloriously colorful flowers repeated in patches to create a patterned yet luxuriant effect.

SALVIA
The purple-blue flowers of *Salvia farinacea* 'Victoria' are held high on upright stems of the same color.

TOADFLAX
The neat toadflax, *Linaria maroccana* 'Fairy Lights', bears pretty little flowers, each with a contrasting white throat.

VERBENA
Intense pink flowers appear all through summer on *Verbena* 'Sissinghurst'.

Splashes of Color

When this gray background is in place, you can start adding color. Edge the bed with the toadflax, *Linaria maroccana* 'Fairy Lights', mixed with some brightly colored verbena such as the deep pink 'Sissinghurst'. Fill in behind this border and between the argyranthemums with pale pink diascia and the tall, purplish blue *Salvia farinacea* 'Victoria'. This is often late in working up to its display, but do not let this prejudice you against it. It is agreeable to have something fresh to look forward to in the garden and once the salvia has got going, only frost will stop it. Into this mix of pink, blue, gray, and white, throw an unexpected surprise: a few clumps of acid yellow snapdragons. Choose the shade carefully: the best color will be a yellow with green rather than red overtones.

Planting Plan

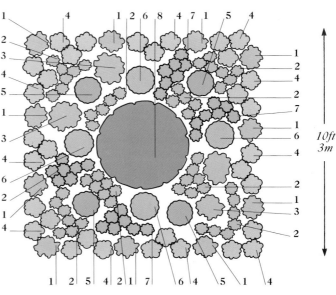

10ft
3m

10ft
3m

Magnolia
Though susceptible to late frosts, the fragrant flowers of *Magnolia* x *soulangeana*, which appear in late spring, are undeniably showy.

Snapdragon
Use a rust-resistant, acid yellow snapdragon, *Antirrhinum majus*, for a striking color contrast in this scheme.

Plant List

1 *Verbena* 'Sissinghurst' x 11
2 *Antirrhinum majus*, rust-resistant yellow (Snapdragon) x 40
3 *Diascia rigescens* x 3
4 *Linaria maroccana* 'Fairy Lights' (Toadflax) x 27
5 *Argyranthemum gracile* 'Chelsea Girl' x 4
6 *Senecio maritima* 'Silver Dust' (Dusty miller) x 4
7 *Salvia farinacea* 'Victoria' x 24
8 *Magnolia* x *soulangeana* x 1

Dusty Miller
By midsummer, *Senecio maritima* 'Silver Dust' makes low mounds of fern!like, silver-white foliage.

Diascia
A plant of low, almost shrubby growth, *Diascia rigescens* has copper-pink flowers that last all summer.

PLANTS *for an* INSTANT DISPLAY

THIS SCHEME MAKES MUCH USE of flowering plants that, although technically classified as perennials or even subshrubs, can be used and cultivated as annuals to create an instant effect. The argyranthemums, the verbenas, the diascias, and the salvias all share the cheerful characteristic of flowering continuously right through the season until fall.

Argyranthemums are not hardy, but you can plunge them in the bed in pots or pot them up before the first frosts and keep them under cover through winter; alternatively, take cuttings in late summer and raise new plants from these to plant out in late spring. The trick with tender plants such as these, as with the true annuals, is to make sure that they do not get such a shock when they are planted out that their growth is checked. If this happens, you will have to wait longer than you need for them to produce flowers. For an early display, make sure that plants reared indoors are properly hardened off before they have to face the harsh world outside. Help them get over the shock of the new by providing plentiful rations of food and water as well.

CARE AND CULTIVATION

SPRING
Plant the magnolia in a sheltered site. In mid-spring, give young magnolias a fertilizer rich in potassium, and top-dress the soil each year with leaf mold or compost. Damaged branches can be removed in late spring. Once all danger of frost has passed, plant out verbenas, linarias, snapdragons, diascias, argyranthemums, and senecios.

SUMMER
Deadhead all plants regularly. Give occasional liquid feeds and water during dry spells; in very dry summers, diascias will stop flowering unless well watered. Pinch out leading shoots of verbenas to encourage bushy growth and, in early summer, tips of snapdragons to promote the formation of side shoots. Spray against rust if necessary.

FALL
Lift and pot up argyranthemums if necessary to overwinter in a frost-free place.

WINTER
Protect argyranthemums against frost. Water them sparingly.

Salvia farinacea 'Victoria' *Perennial with violet flower spikes in summer–fall. H 18in (45cm), S 12in (30cm).*

Argyranthemum gracile 'Chelsea Girl' *Subshrub with deeply divided leaves and daisy flowers. H and S to 2½ft (75cm).*

Antirrhinum majus, rust-resistant yellow (Snapdragon) *Bushy, summer-flowering perennial. H and S 18in (45cm).*

Linaria maroccana 'Fairy Lights' (Toadflax) *Annual with snapdragon-like flowers in summer. H 8in (20cm), S 6in (15cm).*

Diascia rigescens *Perennial bearing salmon-pink flowers in summer and early fall. H 9in (23cm), S 12in (30cm).*

Verbena 'Sissinghurst' *Mat-forming perennial with brilliant pink flowers in summer. H 8in (20cm), S 18in (45cm).*

Magnolia x soulangeana *Deciduous shrub or tree bearing large, pink-flushed, white flowers in midspring. H and S 20ft (6m).*

Senecio maritima 'Silver Dust' (Dusty miller) *Evergreen, bushy subshrub, usually grown as an annual, with finely divided, matte, silver leaves. Small, daisylike, yellow flowerheads appear in summer but are best removed. H and S 12in (30cm).*

ALTERING *the* PLANTING SCHEME

SHIFT THE BALANCE of color in this scheme by substituting a different selection of annuals and tender perennials. Replace the pinks and purples of the verbenas, diascias, and linarias with a crisp, white and blue combination of Swan River daisies, lobelias, and *Osteospermum* 'Whirlygig'. The osteospermum has superbly lunatic daisy flowers, each petal neatly pinched in near the center so that it makes a spoon shape. The flowers are white, washed with dark blue on their backs. The centers are rich, deep blue. Replace the acid yellow snapdragons with rich butter-colored gloriosa daisies; these will match the centers of the Swan River daisies.

FRESH BLUES AND YELLOWS FOR A SUNNY EFFECT

Use lobelias to edge the bed in the same way as the linarias in the original scheme. 'Crystal Palace' has lustrous, dark foliage that is a perfect foil for its flowers and, like all lobelias, is tolerant and free-flowering. The spider plants replace the senecios, warming up the foliage element of the scheme. They are fast growing, and their fountains of foliage will make a pleasing contrast with the dumpy annuals. Use the Swan River daisies and the gloriosa daisies in groups around the center of the bed. The gloriosa daisies will be later into flower than the Swan River daisies since their timetable matches that of the salvias.

Chlorophytum comosum 'Vittatum' (Spider plant) *Tufted, tender perennial with distinctive, green and white-striped leaves. H and S 12in (30cm).*

Rudbeckia hirta 'Marmalade' (Gloriosa daisy) *Erect perennial bearing golden orange flowers with black centers in summer and early fall. H 18in (45cm), S 12in (30cm).*

Brachycome iberidifolia (Swan River daisy) *Bushy annual with small, fragrant, daisylike flowers in summer and early fall. H and S 18in (45cm).*

Osteospermum 'Whirlygig' *Clump-forming, tender, evergreen perennial with gray-green foliage and a lax habit. During summer, it is covered with a mass of bluish white flowers with deep blue centers. H 2ft (60cm), S 12–18in (30–45cm).*

Lobelia erinus 'Crystal Palace' *Compact annual with bronze leaves and deep blue flowers throughout summer. H 8in (20cm), S 6in (15cm).*

A YEAR-ROUND DISPLAY

ALL-YEAR INTEREST in a garden is a concept that should be carefully appraised. A dozen dwarf conifers in a bed will certainly furnish the space for twelve months of the year, but will your spirits lift when you look at them? Will the plants have sufficient contrast in foliage and form? Will you feel that this is the most exciting, imaginative way to fill the space available?

SPRING BLOSSOMS
Prunus 'Tai Haku' *is a*
stunning sight in spring,
covered with clusters of
white flowers. The blossoms
contrast strongly with the
young foliage, which is
suffused with bronze.

DESIGN POINTS

CONTINUITY AND CHANGE
Evergreens provide
continuity and substance
throughout the year,
while other plants shift
the focus of the scheme
as the seasons change.

FRESH FLOWERS
Different lilies can be
used each year to alter
the color balance and
add extra variety.

You certainly need a fair proportion of evergreens in any bed that is planted for winter as well as summer interest, but they need not be dull. There are plenty of plants that will give you abundant opportunity to play with contrasts of shape and texture. Imagine the blood red stems of a dogwood, *Cornus alba*, set against the upright, glossy foliage of *Choisya ternata*, the Mexican orange blossom. Imagine the sculptural, whorled stems of the massive spurge, *Euphorbia characias* subsp. *wulfenii*, soaring above the fine, evergreen foliage of epimediums snuffling around its feet.

PLANT LIST
1 *Epimedium pubigerum* x 6
2 *Cornus alba* 'Elegantissima' (Dogwood) x 1
3 *Bergenia ciliata* x 8
4 *Polystichum setiferum* 'Densum' x 3
5 *Lilium* 'Black Beauty' (Lily) x 16
6 *Cyclamen hederifolium* x 14
7 *Choisya ternata* (Mexican orange blossom) x 1
8 *Tellima grandiflora* 'Purpurea' x 5
9 *Pennisetum villosum* (Feather top) x 3
10 *Prunus* 'Tai Haku' (Great white cherry) x 1
11 *Polystichum setiferum* (Soft shield fern) x 5
12 *Euphorbia characias* subsp. *wulfenii* (Spurge) x 1

PLANTING PLAN

SEASONAL SPLENDORS
Even a bed with pretensions to a nonstop show should include some plants that peak strongly in one particular season. These accents change the flavor of the bed, as spring moves into summer, fall into winter. You need this flow of special events in a garden. A bed planted with too many rigid, static plants becomes as tedious as a video stuck on freeze-frame. In spring you need blossoms. The choice is enormous: crabapples, amelanchier, hawthorn, and, of course, cherries. This scheme uses the great white cherry 'Tai Haku', but in a small garden you might go for a more compact variety. Make sure that it contributes another special effect in fall. 'Tai Haku' has leaves that turn a clear, buttery shade of yellow before they fall.

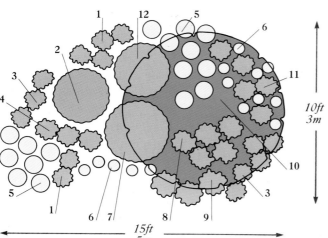

10ft
3m

15ft
5m

THE SCENE IN SPRING
In spring, statuesque, lime green
flowers of the euphorbia rise from
mounds of foliage, while abundant,
white blossoms come from the
cherry and the choisya.

Cornus alba
'Elegantissima'

POLYSTICHUM
Polystichum setiferum
'Densum' is one of the
most elegant of the
family with finely
divided fronds.

EPIMEDIUM
Although the least
ornamental in flower,
Epimedium pubigerum
has excellent, smooth,
evergreen foliage.

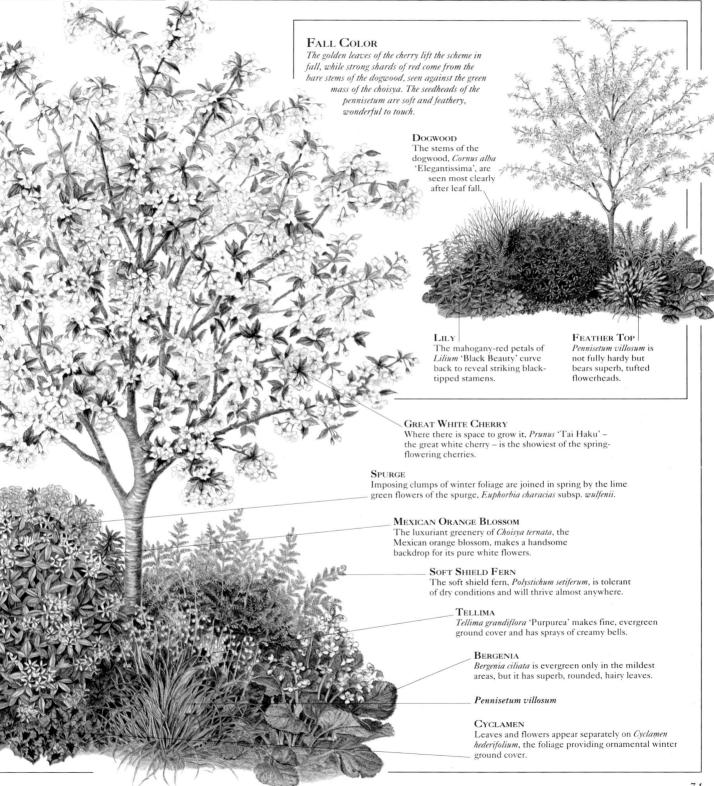

FALL COLOR
The golden leaves of the cherry lift the scheme in fall, while strong shards of red come from the bare stems of the dogwood, seen against the green mass of the choisya. The seedheads of the pennisetum are soft and feathery, wonderful to touch.

DOGWOOD
The stems of the dogwood, *Cornus alba* 'Elegantissima', are seen most clearly after leaf fall.

LILY
The mahogany-red petals of *Lilium* 'Black Beauty' curve back to reveal striking black-tipped stamens.

FEATHER TOP
Pennisetum villosum is not fully hardy but bears superb, tufted flowerheads.

GREAT WHITE CHERRY
Where there is space to grow it, *Prunus* 'Tai Haku' – the great white cherry – is the showiest of the spring-flowering cherries.

SPURGE
Imposing clumps of winter foliage are joined in spring by the lime green flowers of the spurge, *Euphorbia characias* subsp. *wulfenii*.

MEXICAN ORANGE BLOSSOM
The luxuriant greenery of *Choisya ternata*, the Mexican orange blossom, makes a handsome backdrop for its pure white flowers.

SOFT SHIELD FERN
The soft shield fern, *Polystichum setiferum*, is tolerant of dry conditions and will thrive almost anywhere.

TELLIMA
Tellima grandiflora 'Purpurea' makes fine, evergreen ground cover and has sprays of creamy bells.

BERGENIA
Bergenia ciliata is evergreen only in the mildest areas, but it has superb, rounded, hairy leaves.

Pennisetum villosum

CYCLAMEN
Leaves and flowers appear separately on *Cyclamen hederifolium*, the foliage providing ornamental winter ground cover.

71

PLANTS *for* ALL-YEAR INTEREST

THE CORE PLANTS in this scheme provide structure and substance over a long period and need little maintenance. The ferns' elegant new fronds start to unfurl in late spring, ready to replace the previous season's foliage; by now this may be rather battered and can be cut away. The choisya needs no regular pruning, but you can cut back any straggly growth after flowering.

In winter, the brightest splash of color comes from the stems of the dogwood. The fresh, young growth has the strongest color, so cut it back hard each spring to stimulate a new flush of stems. Give the bed a fresh image each year by changing the variety of lily. You can raise lilies in pots, then simply plunge them in the bed for the summer season.

Epimedium pubigerum *Evergreen, carpeting perennial grown for its heart-shaped foliage and creamy white or pink flowers in spring. H and S 18in (45cm).*

Euphorbia characias subsp. **wulfenii (Spurge)** *Evergreen, upright shrub with gray-green leaves and fat spikes of acid green flowers. H to 5ft (1.5m), S 2½ft (75cm).*

Prunus 'Tai Haku' (Great white cherry) *Deciduous, spreading tree with large, single, white flowers in midspring. H 25ft (8m), S 30ft (10m).*

Lilium 'Black Beauty' (Lily) *Summer-flowering bulb bearing green-centered, very deep red flowers with curved-back petals. H 5–6ft (1.5–2m).*

Cornus alba 'Elegantissima' (Dogwood) *Vigorous, deciduous shrub. Young stems are bright red in winter. H and S 6ft (2m).*

Choisya ternata (Mexican orange blossom) *Evergreen shrub with fragrant, white blooms in late spring. H 8ft (2.5m), S 7ft (2.2m).*

Tellima grandiflora 'Purpurea' *Semi-evergreen perennial with reddish purple leaves and pinkish cream flowers in late spring. H and S 2ft (60cm).*

Bergenia ciliata *Clump-forming perennial with large, rounded leaves. In spring, it bears white flowers that age to pink. H 12in (30cm), S 20in (50cm).*

Polystichum setiferum 'Densum' *Evergreen fern with soft-textured, spreading fronds, clothed with white scales as they unfurl. H 2ft (60cm), S 18in (45cm).*

Cyclamen hederifolium syn. *C. neapolitanum Tuber with pale to deep pink flowers in fall and silvery green, ivy-shaped leaves. H to 4in (10cm), S 4–6in (10–15cm).*

Pennisetum villosum (Feather top) *Herbaceous, tuft-forming, perennial grass covered in fluffy, creamy pink plumes that fade to pale brown in fall. H to 3ft (1m), S 20in (50cm).*

Polystichum setiferum (Soft shield fern) *Evergreen fern with finely divided, mosslike fronds that are covered with white scales as they open. H 2ft (60cm), S 18in (45cm).*

ALTERING *the* PLANTING SCHEME

IN AREAS THAT HAVE LONG WINTERS with hard frosts and cutting winds, several plants in the scheme will freeze to death. The choisya, euphorbia, bergenias, cyclamen, and pennisetums will need to be replaced with plants of a more rugged disposition.

PLANTS FOR COLD AREAS

The biggest loss will be the euphorbia, a child of the balmy Mediterranean. The hellebore used in its place is hardier, but not as dramatic. Its deeply divided foliage eventually makes a handsome, but sober, dome. Like many quiet plants, it grows on you. Another hardier euphorbia is used to replace the bergenia. Its foliage is less appealing than the bergenia's, but it is crowned with flowers of an intense acid green.

The pyracantha will provide white blossoms a little later than the choisya, with the added benefit of brilliant red berries in winter. Grow a late summer-flowering clematis over it to bridge the gap between flowers and fruit.

Low mats of cool color come from the textured mass of a blue juniper and the silver leaves of a creeping deadnettle.

Pyracantha x wateri
Glossy-leaved, evergreen shrub bearing white flowers in summer and bright red berries in fall.
H and S 8ft (2.5m).

Euphorbia cyparissias
(Spurge) *Leafy perennial with gray-green foliage, and lime green flowers in late spring. H and S 12in (30cm).*

Clematis viticella
'Purpurea Plena Elegans'
Climber with rose-purple flowers in summer–fall. H to 12ft (4m), S 5ft (1.5m).

Juniperus squamata 'Blue Star' (Juniper) *Clump-forming, dwarf conifer with dense, gray-blue foliage. H 20in (50cm), S 2ft (60cm).*

Lamium maculatum 'White Nancy' (Deadnettle)
Silver-leaved perennial with white flowers in spring–summer. H 6in (15cm), S 3ft (1m).

Helleborus foetidus
(Stinking hellebore)
Evergreen perennial with pale green flowers in late winter– spring. H and S 18in (45cm).

A FORMAL HERB DESIGN

THERE IS AN IRRESISTIBLE URGE in an herb garden to classify, sort, and arrange: all mints here; all sages there; all culinary herbs in one corner; all medicinal herbs in another. This may suit the neat-minded but will not necessarily result in a good-looking display. You must decide how much you are prepared to bend the rules.

CONSTANT DISPLAY
The glossy, aromatic foliage of bay, Laurus nobilis, *is a constant feature of the herb garden, staying green all year. Bay may be clipped to shape.*

DESIGN POINTS

FORMAL LINES
Geometric shapes and a strong, simple pattern create a well-ordered, formal effect.

COLOR CONTRASTS
Foliage plants such as purple sage and golden hop provide distinctive blocks of color.

STYLISH SUPPORTS
The climbers can be supported by smart trellis obelisks or simple wigwams of poles. Let the style be dictated by the wider garden setting.

Herb gardens are popular because they can be fitted into the tiniest of spaces. Formality suits them, but the design should not be too intricate. Some herbs flop about a good deal and may upset the finer points of your well-planned symmetry.

Four pyramids of bay mark the inside corners of these herb beds, echoing the tall pyramids of hop on the outside edges. Borders of parsley and chives, invaluable in cooking, surround patches of purple sage, sweet cicely with ferny foliage and edible seeds, and sweet woodruff with leaves that smell of new-mown hay when dried. An herb garden is usually at its peak for just a month in midsummer. If you want your patch to work harder than that, plant tulips for an early

display among the emerging herbs, and include colorful plants such as nasturtiums or heliotropes to keep the show going in late summer.

PLANT PYRAMIDS FOR HEIGHT
Unless you want a low, Persian carpet effect of thyme, marjoram, chervil, parsley, and mint, you will also need to add some plants to give height. The golden hop, *Humulus lupulus* 'Aureus', is a climber that you can train up tall pyramids in the

PLANT LIST

1 *Tulipa* 'Orange Favourite' (Parrot tulip) x 60
2 *Laurus nobilis* (Bay) x 4
3 *Eschscholzia californica* (California poppy) x 60
4 *Petroselinum crispum* (Parsley) x 48
5 *Allium christophii* x 60
6 *Salvia officinalis* 'Purpurascens' (Purple sage) x 4
7 *Galium odoratum* syn. *Asperula odorata* (Sweet woodruff) x 12
8 *Clematis* 'Jackmanii Superba' x 4
9 *Humulus lupulus* 'Aureus' (Golden hop) x 4
10 *Myrrhis odorata* (Sweet cicely) x 12
11 *Tanacetum parthenium* 'Aureum' (Golden feverfew) x 28
12 *Allium schoenoprasum* (Chives) x 48

GOLDEN HOP
Less vigorous than the plain green hop, this golden variety, *Humulus lupulus* 'Aureus', is easier to contain on a support.

PLANTING PLAN

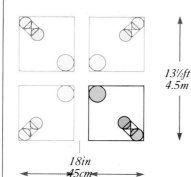

18in
45cm

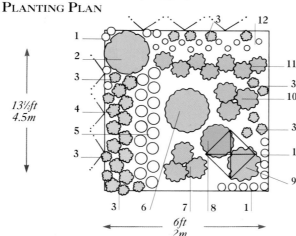

13½ft
4.5m

6ft
2m

6ft
2m

outside corner of each bed. Add some early and late-flowering clematis to make up for the hops' own lack of flowers. For a more formal effect, use standard roses instead of the hop pyramids.

COLOR CONTRASTS AND HARMONIES

The greenish yellow of the hops is echoed in the finely cut foliage of the ground-hugging feverfew. Contrasting in color is the dull purple foliage of the aromatic sage, which grows in a low, sprawling mound. If you think the orange of the parrot tulip, *Tulipa* 'Orange Favourite', makes too violent a contrast with this, choose a dark purple cultivar such as 'Queen of the Night' instead. Add extra color for summer by scattering seeds of bright annuals such as California poppies over any bare patches.

GOLDEN DAYS OF SUMMER
At the height of summer, the golden hops seem to reflect the sunlight back onto the California poppies and daisylike feverfews about their feet. But the whole scheme is not dominated by yellows: the purple clematis, the blue-flowered sage, and the mauve pompom heads of the chives make a cool contrast.

SPRING SURPRISE
Tulips are not the first thing you would expect to see in an herb bed, but when space needs to be filled in spring, they do the job admirably. The foliage of some herbs tends to be slow coming through, so a blast of color from the bulbs helps to prevent the bed from looking bare.

PARROT TULIP
Tulipa 'Orange Favourite' is a showy parrot tulip, orange-red feathered with apple green.

CALIFORNIA POPPY
Eschscholzia californica has tissue-paper flowers of orange, red, yellow, and cream.

BAY
Laurus nobilis makes a dense, evergreen pyramid, and responds well to being clipped into geometric forms.

CLEMATIS
Few clematis are as generous with their flowers as 'Jackmanii Superba', an old cultivar raised in the middle of the 19th century.

SWEET CICELY
Myrrhis odorata is a charming self-sower that thrives in sun or shade.

GOLDEN FEVERFEW
The foliage of golden feverfew, *Tanacetum parthenium* 'Aureum', makes bright splashes of color early in the year, and it is a useful self-seeder.

CHIVES
The grassy leaves of chives, *Allium schoenoprasum*, have a more delicate flavor than onions, and the pretty, edible flowers may be added to salads.

PURPLE SAGE
The grayish purple leaves of *Salvia officinalis* 'Purpurascens' combine well with a wide variety of other plants.

PARSLEY
Petroselinum crispum, either curled or flat-leaved parsley, is one of the most useful of all culinary herbs.

ALLIUM
A blown-up version of common chives, *Allium christophii* has showy, explosive heads of purple flowers.

SWEET WOODRUFF
In the wild, sweet woodruff, *Galium odoratum*, is found in dappled, wooded areas but adapts easily to most places in the garden.

EDIBLE EDGING *for an* HERB BED

TRADITIONAL HERB GARDENS have beds edged with boxwood. In design terms, this is an advantage: the lines are clearly marked out. But boxwood is unproductive and greedy.

Chives and parsley are both good, edible alternatives; in this scheme, the edging plants follow the lines of the paths, chives in one direction, parsley in the other. Unfortunately, chives dive underground in the winter, but do not hold that against them. The pinkish purple lollipop flowers on the green stems in summer make up for that. Parsley is a biennial and will need renewing every couple of years. The curly-leaved parsley makes the prettiest edging, but the flat-leaved type has the best flavor.

If necessary, paths in the herb garden can be very narrow, just wide enough to shuffle along for picking and weeding. Bricks, laid on edge, have a more interesting texture than concrete slabs. If the ground is not too sticky, leave the paths as plain compacted soil.

CARE AND CULTIVATION

SPRING
Plant hops and mulch liberally each year. Train shoots up supports as they grow. Plant bay trees, feverfews, sweet woodruffs, sages, and chives. Top-dress chives each year. Plant clematis and train shoots as they grow; mulch regularly. Cut back sages if necessary to stop them becoming leggy. Sow parsley seed. Guard alliums against slugs. Sow California poppies, covering seed with a fine sifting of compost.

SUMMER
Trim bay trees to shape if necessary and treat any infestation of scale insects. Water chives in dry periods. Cut out old, flowered stems of sweet cicely. Deadhead tulips.

FALL
Plant sweet cicely. Plant tulips, setting them at least 6in (15cm) deep, and alliums at three times their own depth. Remove dead leaves and stems. Cut down parsley to encourage fresh growth.

WINTER
Cut down hops in late winter or early spring. Cut down clematis to about 18in (45cm) in late winter.

Humulus lupulus **'Aureus' (Golden hop)** *Twining climber with greenish yellow, divided foliage. H to 20ft (6m).*

Galium odoratum syn. ***Asperula odorata*** **(Sweet woodruff)** *Perennial with white flowers in summer. H 6in (15cm), S 12in (30cm).*

***Clematis* 'Jackmanii Superba'** *Vigorous climber producing single, purple flowers in midsummer. H 10ft (3m), S 3ft (1m).*

Salvia officinalis **'Purpurascens' (Purple sage)** *Semi-evergreen shrub with purple, aromatic foliage. H 2ft (60cm), S 3ft (1m).*

Allium christophii *Summer-flowering bulb with spherical, purplish violet flowerheads. H 16in (40cm), S 8in (20cm).*

Petroselinum crispum **(Parsley)** *Biennial with ornamental, curly-edged, bright green leaves. H and S 12in (30cm).*

Myrrhis odorata **(Sweet cicely)** *Perennial with fragrant, white flowers in early summer. H 3ft (1m), S 2ft (60cm).*

Eschscholzia californica **(California poppy)** *Annual with red, orange, or yellow flowers in summer. H 12in (30cm), S 6in (15cm).*

***Tulipa* 'Orange Favourite' (Parrot tulip)** *Spring-flowering bulb with orange-red blooms. H to 2ft (60cm), S to 8in (20cm).*

Tanacetum parthenium **'Aureum' (Golden feverfew)** *Perennial with greenish gold foliage. H and S 8–18in (20–45cm).*

Allium schoenoprasum **(Chives)** *Clump-forming bulb with pink or mauve flowers in summer. H 10in (25cm), S 4in (10cm).*

Laurus nobilis **(Bay)** *Dense, evergreen tree with glossy, tough, aromatic leaves. H to 40ft (12m), S to 30ft (10m).*

ALTERING *the* PLANTING SCHEME

EVERYONE HAS THEIR OWN FAVORITE HERBS, and the plan below shows how you can substitute other herbs of your choice in the bed; those used here are good for cooking. You could also add a large, decorative terracotta pot to the scheme, placing it as a centerpiece where the two paths cross. Scented-leaved pelargoniums would fit in well with the theme of the bed;

the aromatic leaves borrow their scents from other plants like peppermint, lemon, pine, and even roses. Surround the pelargoniums with *Convolvulus sabatius*, planted to tumble over the side of the pot. For a hotter effect, use trailing nasturtiums; as well as being attractive, their colorful flowers and peppery leaves make an unusual, edible addition to salads.

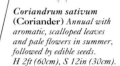

Coriandrum sativum (Coriander) *Annual with aromatic, scalloped leaves and pale flowers in summer, followed by edible seeds. H 2ft (60cm), S 12in (30cm).*

CULINARY HERBS WITH A FOCAL POINT

Instead of the hops, use bronze fennel to give height at each corner of bed. Its fine, filigree foliage is topped with flat heads of flowers. Substitute coriander for the sweet cicely: its leaves are essential for cooking Indian-style. It is easy to grow from seed, but some varieties quickly leap up into flower without much leaf. The flowers eventually turn into seeds, which are also useful in cooking, but if it is leaves you want, choose your variety with care.

For extra color, add scented-leaved pelargoniums in a large pot. In very mild areas, they may overwinter outside. In cool regions, take cuttings or move the plants under cover until spring.

Pelargonium tomentosum (Peppermint-scented geranium) *Tender, evergreen, bushy perennial with strongly scented, velvety, gray-green leaves and clusters of small, white flowers. H 12–24in (30–60cm), S to 3ft (1m).*

Convolvulus sabatius *Trailing perennial with purplish blue, flat trumpet flowers throughout summer. It is not hardy and should be overwintered in a greenhouse. H 6–8in (15–20cm), S 12in (30cm).*

Foeniculum vulgare 'Purpureum' (Bronze fennel) *Tall, upright perennial with finely divided, feathery, bronze leaves, which have an aniseed fragrance, and heads of golden flowers. H 6ft (2m), S 18in (45cm).*

ROSY CHEEKS
The fruits of the pear
Pyrus communis
'Marguerite Marillat'
*are flushed with warm
coppery red.*

DESIGN POINTS

ADDING HEIGHT
The upright form of the
pear tree allows planting
beneath it and lends
height and structure to
the scheme.

REPEAT PATTERNS
Using the same plant
several times, such as the
London pride here,
creates a degree of
patterning that pulls
mixed plantings together.

FLOWERS *and* FRUITS

A SINGLE FRUIT TREE can scarcely be called an orchard, but in a small garden where every plant has to work hard for its living, one is better than none. A fruit tree is as beautiful to look at in spring as any purely ornamental tree and twice as useful in fall when you can gather in your own home-grown fruit.

A PEAR OF GRACEFUL STATURE

This scheme is built around a pear, but you could adapt the planting to fit around a tree that you already have in your garden. If buying a tree, choose a half-standard – one that has 4–5ft (1.2–1.5m) of clean, straight trunk below its branches. This will make a far more graceful and long-lived tree than a dwarf type and will also give a pleasant feeling of permanence to a new and perhaps rather bare garden.

Your pear will need a partner to help it set fruit, a pollinator not more than a bee's hop away. Bees hop surprisingly long distances, so the pollinator need not be in your own garden. Check with a specialist fruit nursery regarding the varieties compatible with your chosen pear before you buy.

AN ISLAND PLANTING

Use the pear as the off-centerpiece of an island planting with a crambe to take over the starring role in summer. When the pear blossoms in spring, the crambe will be nothing more than a low mound of leaves. Then in early summer it erupts, with huge clouds of tiny, white flowers held on towering stems. The crambe has large, heavy leaves; do not be tempted to plant other perennials too close to it. In spring there may seem to be spare space. Fill it with bulbs that can get their act over before the crambe gets into its stride.

Beneath the pear, gray-leaved senecio provides bulk and winter furnishing. For this scheme, dominated by pinks and mauves, you should cut off its yellow flowers as they open. Wherever you can find room, push in a few alpine strawberry plants. The leaves are decorative, and the small, succulent fruits provide a welcome reward during summer weeding sessions.

PLANTING PLAN

8ft
2.5m

12ft
4m

PLANT LIST

1 *Fragaria vesca* (Alpine strawberry) x 5
2 *Saxifraga* x *urbium* (London pride) x 15
3 *Viola* 'Nellie Britton' and 'Primrose Dame' x 14
4 *Pyrus communis* 'Marguerite Marillat' (Pear) x 1
5 *Geranium* 'Johnson's Blue' x 3
6 *Senecio* 'Sunshine' x 1
7 *Helianthemum* 'Wisley Pink' (Rock rose) x 3
8 *Crambe cordifolia* x 1
9 *Geranium psilostemon* x 3
10 *Digitalis purpurea* 'Suttons Apricot' (Foxglove) x 7 and *Cleome hassleriana* 'Colour Fountain' (Spider flower) x 7
11 *Sedum spectabile* 'Brilliant' (Stonecrop) x 3
12 *Pulmonaria saccharata* (Lungwort) x 5

ALPINE STRAWBERRY
As well as delicious fruits, *Fragaria vesca* has attractive, rounded leaves.

Saxifraga x *urbium*

YELLOW VIOLA
Viola 'Primrose Dame' flowers from midspring through until early fall.

BLUE GERANIUM
Elegant, divided leaves make dense ground cover over which *Geranium* 'Johnson's Blue' sends up stems of fine china blue flowers.

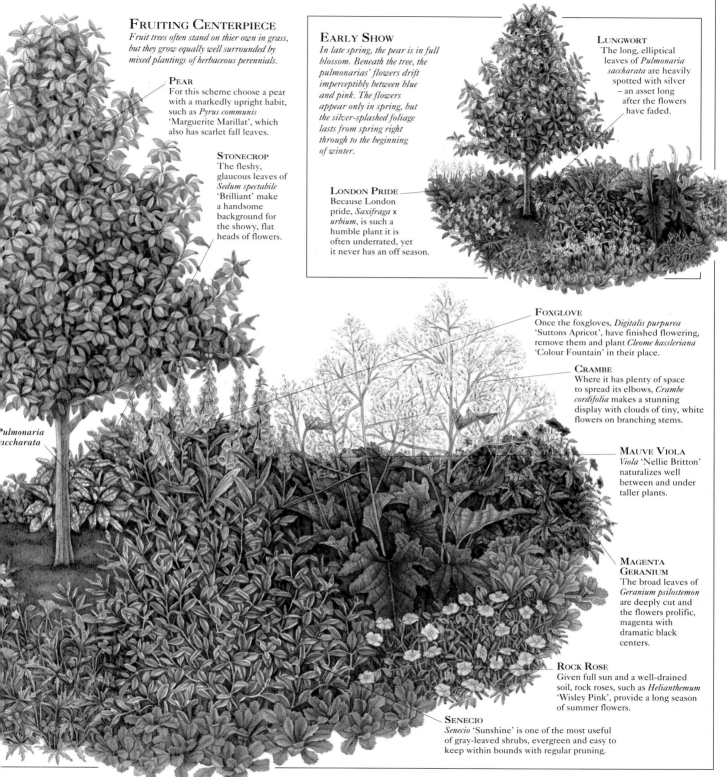

FRUITING CENTERPIECE

Fruit trees often stand on thier own in grass, but they grow equally well surrounded by mixed plantings of herbaceous perennials.

PEAR
For this scheme choose a pear with a markedly upright habit, such as *Pyrus communis* 'Marguerite Marillat', which also has scarlet fall leaves.

STONECROP
The fleshy, glaucous leaves of *Sedum spectabile* 'Brilliant' make a handsome background for the showy, flat heads of flowers.

EARLY SHOW

In late spring, the pear is in full blossom. Beneath the tree, the pulmonarias' flowers drift imperceptibly between blue and pink. The flowers appear only in spring, but the silver-splashed foliage lasts from spring right through to the beginning of winter.

LONDON PRIDE
Because London pride, *Saxifraga x urbium*, is such a humble plant it is often underrated, yet it never has an off season.

LUNGWORT
The long, elliptical leaves of *Pulmonaria saccharata* are heavily spotted with silver – an asset long after the flowers have faded.

Pulmonaria saccharata

FOXGLOVE
Once the foxgloves, *Digitalis purpurea* 'Suttons Apricot', have finished flowering, remove them and plant *Cleome hassleriana* 'Colour Fountain' in their place.

CRAMBE
Where it has plenty of space to spread its elbows, *Crambe cordifolia* makes a stunning display with clouds of tiny, white flowers on branching stems.

MAUVE VIOLA
Viola 'Nellie Britton' naturalizes well between and under taller plants.

MAGENTA GERANIUM
The broad leaves of *Geranium psilostemon* are deeply cut and the flowers prolific, magenta with dramatic black centers.

ROCK ROSE
Given full sun and a well-drained soil, rock roses, such as *Helianthemum* 'Wisley Pink', provide a long season of summer flowers.

SENECIO
Senecio 'Sunshine' is one of the most useful of gray-leaved shrubs, evergreen and easy to keep within bounds with regular pruning.

FLOWER FILLERS *for* LATE SUMMER

TO KEEP THIS BORDER going through the second half of summer, you will need to replace the foxgloves with later-flowering annuals. Cleomes have the necessary height and will flower with large heads of pink and white until the first frosts. Pull up the foxgloves when they have finished but leave one to set and ripen seed. Shake the stem over the soil where you want the next batch of plants to grow and save yourself the bother of raising fresh plants in seed trays. Alternatively, buy plants in early spring which will flower at the beginning of summer.

Sedum spectabile **'Brilliant' (Stonecrop)** *Perennial with pink flowers in late summer–fall. H and S to 18in (45cm).*

Geranium psilostemon *Summer-flowering perennial with black-centered, magenta flowers. H and S 2½ft (75cm).*

CARE AND CULTIVATION

SPRING
Protect young growths of the crambe against slugs. Clean up dead leaves and stems of geraniums. Remove dead flower stems from pulmonarias and mulch around the plants. Stake sedums if necessary.

SUMMER
Replace foxgloves after flowering with cleomes. Clip flowerheads from the senecio as they appear. Cut back flower stems of geraniums to encourage a second show and shear helianthemums after flowering. Deadhead all plants as necessary. Shear off straggly growths of violas in late summer.

FALL
Plant the pear in late fall or early winter, staking it firmly in position. Cut sedum flowers for drying.

WINTER
Cut down flowering stems of the crambe and cut back sedums.

Fragaria vesca **(Alpine strawberry)** *Perennial bearing small, sweetly flavored fruits. H 12in (30cm), S 18in (45cm).*

Pulmonaria saccharata **(Lungwort)** *Spring-flowering perennial with leaves blotched with silver. H 12in (30cm), S 2ft (60cm).*

Cleome hassleriana **'Colour Fountain' (Spider flower)** *Pink- or white-flowered annual. H 4ft (1.2m), S 18in (45cm).*

Viola **'Nellie Britton'** *Perennial with brownish mauve flowers in spring and summer. H and to S 6in (15cm).*

Pyrus communis **'Marguerite Marillat'** *Upright, deciduous tree with edible fruits. H 12–18ft (4–5.5m), S 10ft (3m).*

Digitalis purpurea **'Suttons Apricot' (Foxglove)** *Perennial grown as a biennial. H to 5ft (1.5m), S 2ft (60cm).*

Crambe cordifolia *Perennial with fragrant, white flowers in summer above large, crinkled leaves. H to 6ft (2m), S 4ft (1.2m).*

Geranium **'Johnson's Blue'** *Perennial with deep lavender-blue flowers borne through summer. H 12in (30cm), S 2ft (60cm).*

Senecio **'Sunshine'** *Evergreen, mound-forming shrub with gray leaves and clusters of yellow flowers. H 2½ft (75cm), S 5ft (1.5m).*

Saxifraga* x *urbium **(London pride)** *Evergreen perennial with small flowers in late spring. H 12in (30cm), S indefinite.*

Helianthemum **'Wisley Pink' (Rock rose)** *Evergreen shrub with pale pink summer flowers. H and S 12in (30cm) or more.*

ALTERING *the* PLANTING SCHEME

BULBS ARE WHAT YOU NEED to bring this bed to life in early spring, when only the pulmonarias will be in flower. Bulbs are the garden's buried treasure, and the best thing about them is that so often you forget you have planted them. Suddenly in spring, there they are, beaming and bountiful.

A PATCHWORK PLANTING OF BULBS

A good spring display requires forethought and a dedicated fall planting session. Bulbs should be put in after perennials, otherwise you are in danger of digging up the one while planting the other. Use daffodils around the pear tree, with crocuses around the crambe. The crocuses will be up, out, and over before the crambe even starts to heave itself out of its winter bed. Another patch of early crocuses can fill in between the violas and the geraniums, with De Caen Group anemones to fill in any other spaces. Use bulbs to boost the display at the end of the season, too, putting in galtonias and nerines for extra color in late summer and fall.

Anemone coronaria **De Caen Group** *Spring-flowering, tuberous perennial with white, blue, or red flowers, each surrounded by a neat, green ruff. H 6–12in (15–30cm).*

Crocus tommasinianus *Early spring-flowering corm with lilac-purple blooms. H to 4in (10cm), S 1–3in (2.5–8cm).*

Galtonia candicans **(Summer hyacinth)** *Late summer-flowering bulb with fleshy, strap-shaped leaves and spikes of hanging, white flowers. H to 4ft (1.2m), S 8in (20cm).*

***Narcissus* 'Pheasant's Eye'** **(Daffodil)** *Bulb bearing pure white flowers with stubby, orange-red trumpets in late spring. H 18in (45cm), S to 8in (20cm).*

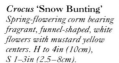

***Crocus* 'Snow Bunting'** *Spring-flowering corm bearing fragrant, funnel-shaped, white flowers with mustard yellow centers. H to 4in (10cm), S 1–3in (2.5–8cm).*

Nerine bowdenii *Fall-flowering bulb bearing a head of glistening pink flowers with frilled petals. It is a tender plant that will suffer in severe winters. H 18–24in (45–60cm), S 5–6in (12–15cm).*

A LOW-MAINTENANCE SCHEME

DECIDUOUS AZALEAS IN RICH SHADES of yellow and orange are the dominant feature of this bed, planned for plants that like acidic soil. These vibrant colors are set off by the cool tones of an evergreen rhododendron and the restrained foliage of a Korean fir. The fir is like a sober-suited chaperone, keeping an eye on a gaggle of artless ingenues, out in their new spring clothes.

SPRING SHOW
The glorious blooms of Rhododendron 'Frome' *bring a brilliant splash of fiery color to the bed in spring.*

DESIGN POINTS

ॐ

GOING WILD
An informal scheme perfect for a semiwild or wooded area.

ॐ

EASY CARE
Suitable for a site where access is awkward, such as a bank, since little maintenance is needed.

Schemes that are composed mainly of shrubs, as this one is, generally require a lot less maintenance than beds of mixed perennials. These plants do not need lifting or dividing. They do not need pruning. They are hardy and grow in sun or shade, although a site that gives them a bit of both is what they like best. In the wild, rhododendrons often grow in woodland; this informal bed would sit particularly well near the perimeter of a garden where there are trees beyond, echoing the rhododendrons' natural habitat.

COLOR FOR SPRING AND FALL

Spring will be the most eye-catching season for this bed, with a succession of flowers – yellow, orange, greenish white, and blue from the azaleas. The evergreen *Rhododendron hippophaeoides* will provide the first spring flowers in this scheme, appearing sometimes six weeks before the heavily scented blooms of *Rhododendron luteum*.

In fall, the gentian starts its searing display with flowers a more vivid blue than any artist would ever dare use. These will lap around the feet of the fir and make a brilliant pool in front of the maple, alight in its fall leaves. The yellow azaleas used in this bed are all deciduous. What you lose in winter you gain in fall, however: the leaves, before they drop, turn rich, burnished shades of bronze, red, and orange.

EVERGREEN CONTINUITY

For evergreen steadfastness you can depend on the fir, which grows slowly to make a broadly conical tree. This handsome conifer has the obliging habit of growing fir cones while it is still young. You can expect them on trees no more than 3ft (1m) high. The cones stand upright, like fat candles on a Christmas tree, borne usually along the topmost branches. They are an astonishing shade of violet blue, almost the same color as the blue azalea.

The arbutus is the chief, long-term landscape feature in this scheme. In the *really* long term, you may have to dispense with the fir. There will not be room for them both, but since both take a very long time to reach maturity, you need not lose sleep over this at the outset.

A WEALTH OF BRIGHT BLOOMS

In late spring, the bed is ablaze with the yellow and orange flowers of the azaleas. Cool contrasts are provided by the mass of the Korean fir and the pale green leaves of the maple.

POLYPODY
Polypodium vulgare provides ornamental ground cover with its deeply cut leaves.

JAPANESE MAPLE
Japanese maples, such as *Acer palmatum* 'Dissectum', are very slow-growing, eventually forming low mounds wider than they are high.

PLANTING PLAN

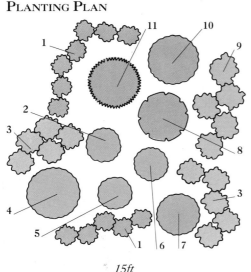
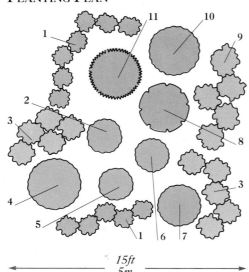

15ft
5m

15ft
5m

PLANT LIST

1 *Gentiana sino-ornata* (Gentian) x 12
2 *Rhododendron luteum* (Azalea) x 1
3 *Polypodium vulgare* (Polypody) x 10
4 *Acer palmatum* 'Dissectum' (Japanese maple) x 1
5 *Rhododendron* 'Frome' (Azalea) x 1
6 *Rhododendron* 'Narcissiflorum' (Azalea) x 1
7 *Rhododendron hippophaeoides* x 1
8 *Arbutus unedo* (Strawberry tree) x 1
9 *Hosta* 'Royal Standard' x 5
10 *Rhododendron* 'Palestrina' (Azalea) x 1
11 *Abies koreana* (Korean fir) x 1

FALL TINTS
The brilliant colors of the maple and the bronze tones of the deciduous azaleas give the scheme a second season of interest.

STRAWBERRY TREE
Arbutus unedo bears flowers and fruits together in early fall.

GENTIAN
Gentiana sino-ornata is covered in fall by azure blue trumpet flowers.

FRAGRANT AZALEA
The double, pale yellow flowers of *Rhododendron* 'Narcissiflorum' are sweetly scented and grow on a vigorous, upright bush.

Arbutus unedo

WHITE AZALEA
Rhododendron 'Palestrina' is a compact, evergreen azalea with funnel-shaped, white flowers.

HOSTA
Broad, heart-shaped leaves set off the late blooms of the fine *Hosta* 'Royal Standard'.

ORANGE AZALEA
Rhododendron 'Frome', a deciduous azalea of shrubby habit, bears orange-yellow flowers.

YELLOW AZALEA
The only European native azalea, *Rhododendron luteum* has yellow, sweetly scented flowers that appear before the leaves.

RHODODENDRON
Rhododendron hippophaeoides, one of the hardiest and most easily grown of the dwarf rhododendrons, bears flowers of a cool lavender-blue.

KOREAN FIR
The sparse, dark green leaves of *Abies koreana* have bright silvery undersides.

Gentiana sino-ornata

ACID-LOVING PLANTS *for* DAPPLED SHADE

IF YOU CHOOSE A SITUATION under trees for this scheme, it is a good idea to enrich the soil at planting time with leaf mold and bone meal. Ground in which trees are growing is often starved and, although none of these plants is outstandingly greedy, all will grow better with the benefit of special rations.

Do not be tempted to grow rhododendrons if your soil is very alkaline. However hard you try, it will be difficult to make them happy. The leaves will mope, becoming blotchy yellow instead of glossy green. Flowering will be sparse. The plants will look at you accusingly each time you pass, reminding you that they were made for a better kind of life than you will ever be able to give them.

Like most of its kind, the little polypody fern is happiest out of full sun; taller plants growing nearby can provide the necessary shade. Cut down the old fronds in spring so that you can take full advantage of the drama of the bright green new ones unfurling.

CARE AND CULTIVATION

SPRING
Plant the fir in midspring in a lightly shaded position that will give protection from late spring frosts. Choose a plant with a single, strong leading shoot; if a secondary shoot appears, prune it out flush with the trunk. In late spring, feed the fir and rhododendrons, and mulch. Arbutus needs no regular pruning, but cut straggly shoots flush with the main stem in midspring. Protect emerging shoots of hostas from slugs. Divide and replant congested clumps if necessary. Plant ferns, setting the rhizomes just beneath the soil surface; anchor them with small stones if necessary. Cut down old fronds of ferns.

SUMMER
Pinch out dead rhododendron flowers.

FALL
Plant the maple and arbutus in positions sheltered from wind. Plant gentians and hostas, enriching the soil with leaf mold. Plant rhododendrons.

WINTER
Protect young arbutus with leaves or straw. Clear dead leaves and flower stems of hostas.

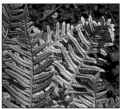

Gentiana sino-ornata (Gentian) *Evergreen perennial with rich blue flowers in fall. H 2in (5cm), S to 12in (30cm).*

Arbutus unedo (Strawberry tree) *Evergreen, spreading tree or shrub. White flowers appear in fall–winter as previous season's strawberry-like fruits ripen. H and S 22ft (7m).*

Rhododendron 'Palestrina' (Azalea) *Compact, evergreen shrub bearing white flowers. H and S to 4ft (1.2m).*

Polypodium vulgare (Polypody) *Evergreen fern with herringbone-like, narrow fronds. H and S 10–12in (25–30cm).*

Rhododendron luteum (Azalea) *Deciduous shrub with yellow flowers and richly colored fall leaves. H and S 5–8ft (1.5–2.5m).*

Abies koreana (Korean fir) *Slow-growing conifer with violet-blue cones. Needles have silver undersides. H to 30ft (10m), S 5ft (1.5m).*

Hosta 'Royal Standard' *Clump-forming perennial with broadly oval, pale green leaves. H 2ft (60cm), S 4ft (1.2m).*

Acer palmatum 'Dissectum' (Japanese maple) *Deciduous shrub with finely divided foliage. H 3ft (1m), S 5ft (1.5m).*

Rhododendron 'Frome' (Azalea) *Deciduous shrub with spring flowers and colorful fall foliage. H and S to 5ft (1.5m).*

Rhododendron 'Narcissiflorum' (Azalea) *Deciduous shrub with scented flowers. H and S 6ft (2m).*

Rhododendron hippophaeoides *Evergreen shrub with gray-green leaves and lavender-blue flowers in spring. H and S 1.5m (5ft).*

ALTERING *the* PLANTING SCHEME

THIS SCHEME SUBSTITUTES rich crimson, magenta, and pale pink shades for the bright yellow and slate blue of the original scheme. The two Kurume azaleas are more compact than the yellow ones they replace, and you may find that the scheme fits into a smaller planting space. These substitutes will change the character as well as the color of the bed.

The plants are lower, denser, less wild looking. Here, the emphasis is still on azaleas, but you could include a camellia instead of one of the azaleas in order to extend the season of interest. The camellia will bloom in early spring, two months ahead of the azaleas. A sturdy, weatherproof variety such as *Camellia* x *williamsii* 'Brigadoon' would be a good choice.

Eucryphia glutinosa
Deciduous tree with leaves that turn orange-red in fall and scented, white flowers in summer. H to 30ft (10m), S 20ft (6m).

COMPACT PLANTS IN PINK AND WHITE

These, of course, are acid-loving shrubs and must have lime-free soil to grow happily. The eucryphia likes the same kind of conditions as the arbutus, but it is deciduous and does not grow as big.

The Kurume azaleas flower most freely in warm, sunny areas. In wet regions, they sometimes become straggly and may need careful cutting back. *Rhododendron yakushimanum* can take any amount of rain, for its home is in the windy, sodden mountains of Yakushima Island in Japan. Its strength is its foliage. The leaves curve down slightly at the edges and are covered underneath with rich rust-colored felting. The new leaves are powdered with silver.

Rhododendron 'Strawberry Ice' (Azalea) *Deciduous, bushy shrub. In spring it bears deep pink buds that open to flesh pink blooms with yellow throats. H and S 5–8ft (1.5–2.5m).*

Rhododendron 'Hatsugiri' (Kurume azalea) *Compact, evergreen shrub that bears a mass of small, bright crimson-purple flowers in spring. H and S 2ft (60cm).*

Rhododendron 'Hinodegiri' (Kurume azalea) *Compact, evergreen shrub that bears abundant, small, funnel-shaped, bright crimson flowers in late spring. Thrives in sun or light shade. H and S 5ft (1.5m).*

Rhododendron yakushimanum Slow-growing, compact, evergreen shrub. Oval leaves are silvery at first, maturing to deep green. In late spring, pale pink flowers appear and gradually fade to white. H 3ft (1m), S 5ft (1.5m).

CORNER SITES

Corners provide special opportunities in gardens, whether open and sunny, dark and mysterious, or even awkward and narrow. Sometimes a sheltered corner will give just enough extra protection to a plant of borderline hardiness to see it through the winter. Some corners call for dramatic focal plants, placed to attract your attention. The positioning of these will depend on how you approach and view your corner.

TACTILE PLEASURE
It is hard to pass by the pleated, downy leaves of Alchemilla mollis, *lady's mantle, without reaching out to touch them. After a shower, raindrops cling to the leaves like beads of mercury.*

DESIGN POINTS

SURFACE CONTRASTS
Woolly willow contrasts with waxy euphorbia and the gleaming leaves of hebe.

BALANCED FORMS
Plants of differing habit are used to create balance and variety – softly rounded mounds of hostas and alchemillas are balanced by sternly upright irises and veratrums and fountain-like dieramas.

WATERY IMAGES
Wands of pink-flowered dierama arch over the water, creating intriguing reflections.

WATERSIDE TEXTURES

THE TEXTURE OF A PLANT'S LEAVES is one of those quiet pleasures that you take for granted, like the softness of wool or the shininess of a well-polished table. It is a less immediately eye-catching attribute than the leaf's color and shape, but leaves too may be woolly or smooth, shiny or matte. Their surfaces may be prickly or silky soft, crinkled or plain, waxy, sticky, or slippery as an ice cube.

Touching leaves is just like feeling different kinds of fabric: silk, satin, linen, angora, felt, wool. *Veratrum nigrum*, in this scheme grouped around a formal pool, has leaves like permanently pleated silk. Use it with mounds of alchemilla and domes of evergreen hebe. The form of these leaves differs markedly, which is a good reason for using them together, but the effect is enhanced by the contrasts in texture: pleated silk veratrum, alchemilla with the texture of brushed cotton, and dull satin hebe.

Often a plant's botanical name will give you a clue as to its outstanding characteristic. The *nigrum* of *Veratrum nigrum* refers to the purple-black flowers. A woolly texture is often signaled by the word *lanata*. The well-known lamb's ears, *Stachys lanata* (now renamed *Stachys byzantina*), sprawls over the apex of the corner. The woolly willow, *Salix lanata*, is set off by the iris and the waxy-textured leaves of a large hosta.

CONTRASTING FORMS
In a scheme where you want to see beyond the planting to another feature such as a pool, you need to keep most of the plants low, but the tall, swordlike leaves of iris and dierama will add vertical emphasis. The dieramas will surge dramatically out of the textured carpet but are airy enough to see through. The habit of the dierama is best explained by its common name, angel's fishing rod. Its wiry stems arch from the center of the clump, exploding into a shower of pink bells. The flowers are attached to the stems by a thread so fine they look as though they are suspended, magically, in space.

PLANT LIST
1 *Salvia argentea* x 2
2 *Dierama pulcherrimum* (Angel's fishing rod) x 2
3 *Hosta sieboldiana* var. *elegans* x 2
4 *Salix lanata* (Woolly willow) x 1
5 *Alchemilla mollis* (Lady's mantle) x 2
6 *Iris ensata* 'Alba' (Japanese iris) x 5
7 *Hebe albicans* x 2
8 *Euphorbia seguieriana* (Spurge) x 4
9 *Veratrum nigrum* (Black false hellebore) x 6
10 *Stachys byzantina* syn. *S. lanata* (Lamb's ears) x 1

PLANTING PLAN

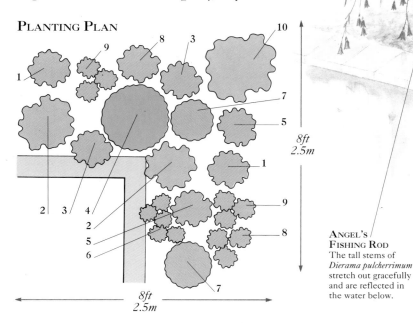

8ft
2.5m

8ft
2.5m

ANGEL'S FISHING ROD
The tall stems of *Dierama pulcherrimum* stretch out gracefully and are reflected in the water below.

SUMMER SENSATION
Late summer is the most dramatic time in this scheme – the extraordinary, dark flowers of the veratrums and the elegant sprays of the dieramas are set against a tapestry of contrasting leaves.

WOOLLY WILLOW
In spring, the yellow catkins of the woolly willow, *Salix lanata*, crawl like hairy caterpillars along the branches, contrasting with the woolly, young leaves.

COOL SHADES
In early summer, the overall effect is cool and restful with flowers in shades of greenish yellow and white, and abundant silver-gray and lush green foliage.

JAPANESE IRIS
Iris ensata has small flowers that are violet, blue, or – as here in the cultivar 'Alba' – white.

HEBE
Hebe albicans makes a compact dome of glaucous leaves, covered in early summer with short spikes of white flowers.

SPURGE
The narrow stems of *Euphorbia seguieriana* are set with whorls of equally narrow, glaucous leaves, topped in late spring with lime green flowers.

HOSTA
The leaves of *Hosta sieboldiana* var. *elegans* are the most sumptuous of all hosta leaves, broad and richly glaucous.

LAMB'S EARS
Stachys byzantina, or lamb's ears, makes good ground cover with its dense mats of felted, gray leaves, although it is unfortunately prone to mildew.

LADY'S MANTLE
The rounded leaves of *Alchemilla mollis*, lady's mantle, appear later than you would wish, but both the foliage and the greenish yellow flowers are excellent in schemes with white and purple flowers.

Iris ensata **'Alba'**

SALVIA
Given full sun and sharp drainage, *Salvia argentea* grows into a statuesque plant, the flowering stem rising from a basal clump of thick, woolly leaves.

BLACK FALSE HELLEBORE
Veratrum nigrum has been a treasured garden plant since the 16th century, appreciated then, as now, for its pleated, fanlike leaves as well as its plumes of dark flowers.

Euphorbia seguieriana

Hebe albicans

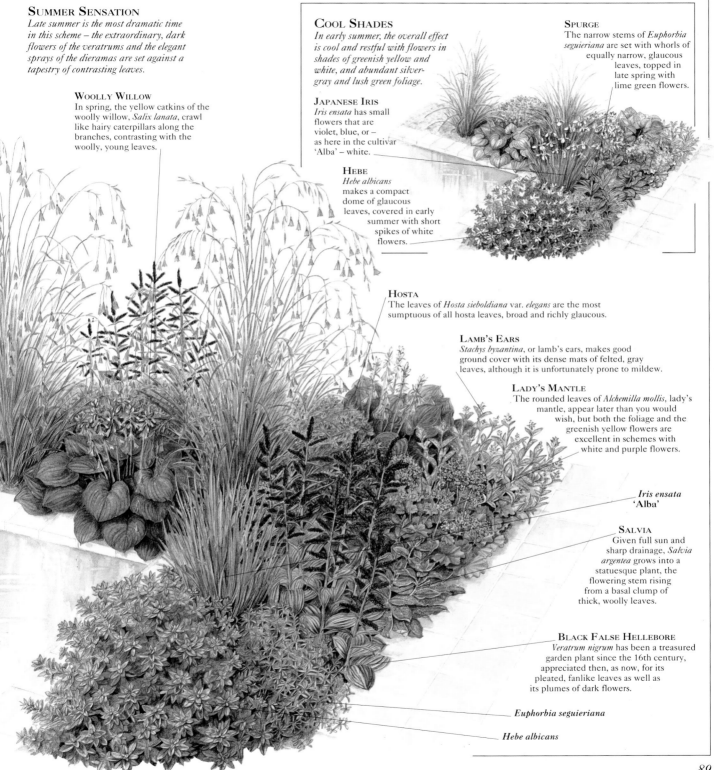

PLANTS *for* FOLIAGE EFFECTS

THE MASSIVE VARIATION IN THE TEXTURE of plants is not a show put on solely for our tactile delight, but is usually their response to a particular set of growing conditions or problems. For example, the hairs that give woolly plants their distinctive appearance protect them from the intense light of high altitudes and insulate them from extremes of temperature; many woolly plants grow in deserts or freezing upland steppes. The ones used in this planting scheme mostly do best in soil that never dries out.

The salvias need good drainage. They are best grown as biennials and so will need to be replaced every couple of years. The leaves of the first year – silvery, thickly furred rosettes – are very much better than the flowers of the second.

The veratrums do best in moist, light soil in a semishaded position. Applying a thick mulch in late spring will help to create the kind of conditions they most enjoy. Unfortunately, slugs love them, so – like the hostas – they must be well protected.

CARE AND CULTIVATION

SPRING
Plant dieramas, salvias, and stachys. Clear damaged leaves from plants before new growth starts. Protect hostas against slugs. Plant euphorbias and hebes. Hebes need no regular pruning, but cut back winter-damaged growth now. Do not let soil dry out around veratrums; mulch if necessary in late spring.

SUMMER
Deadhead hebes. Cut out flowered stems of euphorbias. Cut back stems of alchemillas as flowers fade and shear foliage to encourage fresh growth.

FALL
Plant hostas in soil enriched with compost or leaf mold. Plant veratrums and irises in a moist, slightly shaded position. Congested iris clumps will occasionally need to be divided. Plant alchemillas. Cut down stems of dieramas as flowers fade. In cold areas, lift corms and overwinter under cover.

WINTER
Cut down stems of veratrums.

Salvia argentea *Rosette-forming perennial with woolly, silver foliage, and white flowers in summer. H to 3ft (1m), S 18in (45cm).*

Euphorbia seguieriana (Spurge) *Perennial with narrow leaves and clusters of yellowish green flowers. H and S 18in (45cm).*

Hosta sieboldiana var. **elegans** *Clump-forming perennial with bluish gray, ribbed leaves. H 3ft (1m), S 5ft (1.5m).*

Stachys byzantina syn. **S. lanata (Lamb's ears)** *Perennial with woolly, gray foliage. H to 15in (38cm), S 2ft (60cm).*

Salix lanata (Woolly willow) *Slow-growing shrub with thickly textured, gray leaves. H and S to 4ft (1.2m).*

Hebe albicans *Dense, evergreen shrub with blue-gray foliage, and small, white flowers from early summer. H and S 5ft (1.5m).*

Dierama pulcherrimum (Angel's fishing rod) *Evergreen perennial with straplike leaves, and deep pink flowers in summer. H 5ft (1.5m), S 1ft (30cm).*

Alchemilla mollis (Lady's mantle) *Clump-forming perennial with downy leaves and greenish yellow flowers. H and S 20in (50cm).*

Iris ensata 'Alba' *Rhizomatous perennial with white flowers and leaves with a prominent midrib. H to 3ft (1m), S indefinite.*

Veratrum nigrum (Black false hellebore) *Erect perennial with oval leaves, and dark purple flowers from late summer. H 6ft (2m), S 2ft (60cm).*

ALTERING *the* PLANTING SCHEME

MANY EVERGREEN SHRUBS, SUCH AS HOLLY, choisya, fatsia, and camellia, have shiny foliage that provides an excellent foil for gray-leaved plants, but some could grow too large for this situation. Instead, increase the winter interest by using hart's-tongue ferns, with their highly polished fronds. Introduce extra spring color with carpets of low-growing species tulips.

Juniperus horizontalis **'Turquoise Spreader'** (**Juniper**) *Dwarf, evergreen conifer that spreads slowly to form a thick mat of glaucous, turquoise-green foliage. H to 20in (50cm), S 5ft (1.5m) or more.*

STRENGTHENING THE WINTER INTEREST

Evergreen hart's-tongue ferns, with a spreading, horizontal juniper, and clumps of cyclamen will all give this poolside more winter weight. Unlike the stachys, which it replaces, the juniper is as handsome in midwinter as it is in the more promising days of summer.

The cyclamen will liven up the juniper, providing a touch of frippery with its late summer or fall flowers. Its foliage echoes the tones of the juniper – both on the blue side of green. The cyclamen's leaves are more complex, marbled in silver in patterns as varied as fingerprints.

Phyllitis scolopendrium (**Hart's-tongue fern**) *Evergreen fern with bright green, leathery, tonguelike fronds. H 18–30in (45–75cm), S to 18in (45cm).*

Cyclamen hederifolium *Fall-flowering tuber. Silver-patterned leaves appear with or after pink flowers and last until spring. H to 4in (10cm), S 4–6in (10–15cm).*

A SWATH OF SPRING TULIPS

Increase the impact of spring which, apart from the upright catkins on the willow, is rather short of special effects, by filling the spaces between the other plants with species tulips. These are not as showy, nor as large, as the ordinary garden tulips, but are the original blueprints from which all garden varieties have been developed. They come into bloom earlier than the larger tulips and the scale of their flowers, used among low-growing plants, also seems more appropriate.

Tulipa turkestanica (**Species tulip**) *Early spring-flowering bulb, producing starry, white flowers with yolk yellow centers. H 4–12in (10–30cm), S to 8in (20cm).*

Tulipa tarda (**Species tulip**) *Bulb that bears yellow flowers in spring, with each pointed petal neatly tipped in white. H to 6in (15cm), S to 4in (10cm).*

Tulipa saxatilis (**Species tulip**) *Bulb bearing fragrant, lilac-pink flowers with yellow centers in early spring among shiny, pale green leaves. H 6–18in (15–45cm), S to 8in (20cm).*

COLORED FOLIAGE

GOLD FOLIAGE placed in a gloomy corner of the garden can instantly transform it from a pit of despair into a place of pilgrimage. A gold-leaved robinia lights up this group of shrubs that might fill an awkward corner. Although yellow is shunned by some extremely finely tuned gardeners, it is a cheerful color to have around. Purple foliage adds depth and density, while gray provides a cool contrast.

COLOR CHANGES
The young, golden leaves of
Robinia pseudoacacia
'Frisia' are suffused with green in summer, then turn a rich orange-yellow in fall.

DESIGN POINTS

FOLIAGE FEATURES
Gold, purple, and gray foliage are combined to create sharp color contrasts.

WINTER DISPLAY
Winter interest comes from euphorbia, phlomis, and senecio.

LOW-MAINTENANCE PLANTING
These plants need minimal maintenance, so are especially suitable for a corner that is hard to reach.

GLEAMS OF GOLD AND YELLOW

Color in this scheme comes mostly from leaves rather than flowers. The golden robinia is an outstanding foliage tree, the color clear and bright, the leaves like short strings of flat, yellow beads. If you can arrange a dark background for it, so much the better: a simple backing of ivy or pyracantha would be ideal. The branches of the robinia are rather brittle, so do not plant it where it will be exposed to high winds.

Gold and yellow foliage tends to be less stable than purple. The robinia starts with a fresh golden glow in spring, but is far less bright by fall. Its companion, the golden philadelphus, also fades as the season advances. Despite this,

PLANT LIST

1 *Robinia pseudoacacia* 'Frisia' (Black locust) x 1
2 *Berberis thunbergii* f. *atropurpurea* (Barberry) x 1
3 *Senecio* 'Sunshine' x 1
4 *Origanum vulgare* 'Aureum' (Golden marjoram) x 3
5 *Nepeta* 'Six Hills Giant' (Catmint) x 2

6 *Sedum spectabile* (Stonecrop) x 1
7 *Geranium cinereum* 'Ballerina' (Cranesbill) x 1
8 *Philadelphus coronarius* 'Aureus' (Mock orange) x 1
9 *Alchemilla mollis* (Lady's mantle) x 3
10 *Euphorbia characias* subsp. *wulfenii* (Spurge) x 1
11 *Phlomis fruticosa* (Jerusalem sage) x 1

PLANTING PLAN

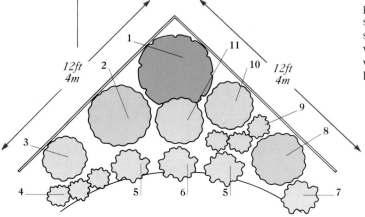

12ft
4m

12ft
4m

the philadelphus is a useful and easygoing shrub, and its cream flowers have the swooniest smell you could desire.

PATCHES OF PURPLE AND GRAY

Purple foliage may be more difficult to use in a garden than gold. It looks lovely in spring, but can sometimes seem heavy as summer wears on. This is more of a problem with large-leaved trees than with the neat berberis used here. Its leaves are the rich color of good port and, in fall, turn a blazing red before they drop.

By far the most restful of the three types of colored foliage included here is the gray – too restful if used all on its own, as it sometimes is. An unrelieved expanse of gray foliage has rather less allure than last week's laundry. Here, contrasted with the golden robinia and philadelpus and the rich, vinous tones of the berberis, it acts as a useful buffer.

Both senecio and phlomis bear yellow flowers in early summer, but the flowers are nowhere near as important as the leaves – the senecio's painted with palest silver on the undersides, those of the phlomis grayish green and roughly textured. Both have the advantage of staying on during winter. They continue to provide interest when the other shrubs are "resting," as actresses say. Similarly, the euphorbia, which constantly renews itself with fresh growth, never leaves a gap in the planting.

SENECIO
Senecio 'Sunshine' is a sprawling shrub wider than it is high, bearing branching heads of brilliant yellow, daisy flowers in early summer.

GOLDEN MARJORAM
The aromatic leaves of *Origanum vulgare* 'Aureum' are as useful for cooking as those of the plain green marjoram and make thick patches of color in the front of a bed.

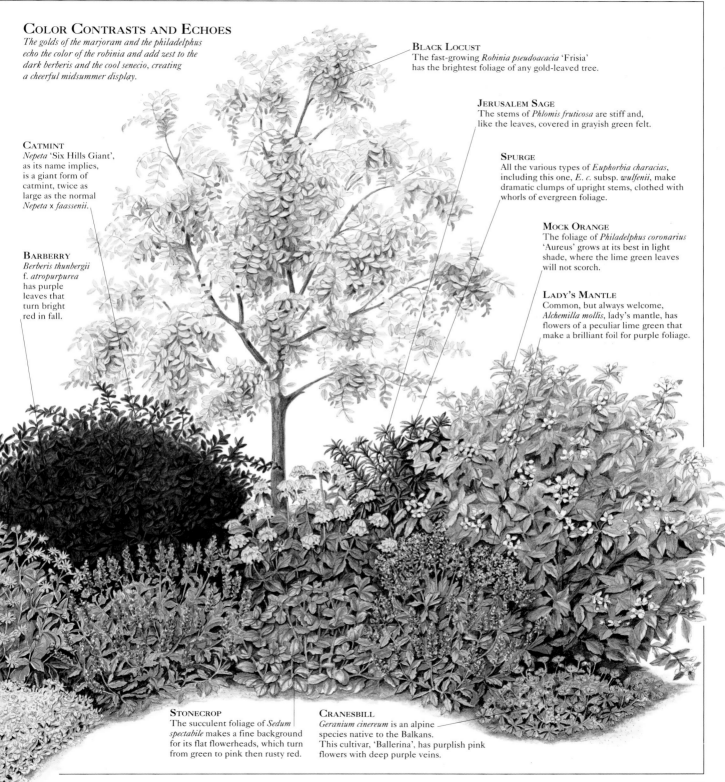

COLOR CONTRASTS AND ECHOES

The golds of the marjoram and the philadelphus echo the color of the robinia and add zest to the dark berberis and the cool senecio, creating a cheerful midsummer display.

BLACK LOCUST
The fast-growing *Robinia pseudoacacia* 'Frisia' has the brightest foliage of any gold-leaved tree.

JERUSALEM SAGE
The stems of *Phlomis fruticosa* are stiff and, like the leaves, covered in grayish green felt.

CATMINT
Nepeta 'Six Hills Giant', as its name implies, is a giant form of catmint, twice as large as the normal *Nepeta* x *faassenii*.

SPURGE
All the various types of *Euphorbia characias*, including this one, *E. c.* subsp. *wulfenii*, make dramatic clumps of upright stems, clothed with whorls of evergreen foliage.

BARBERRY
Berberis thunbergii f. *atropurpurea* has purple leaves that turn bright red in fall.

MOCK ORANGE
The foliage of *Philadelphus coronarius* 'Aureus' grows at its best in light shade, where the lime green leaves will not scorch.

LADY'S MANTLE
Common, but always welcome, *Alchemilla mollis*, lady's mantle, has flowers of a peculiar lime green that make a brilliant foil for purple foliage.

STONECROP
The succulent foliage of *Sedum spectabile* makes a fine background for its flat flowerheads, which turn from green to pink then rusty red.

CRANESBILL
Geranium cinereum is an alpine species native to the Balkans. This cultivar, 'Ballerina', has purplish pink flowers with deep purple veins.

CARE AND CULTIVATION

— ❧ —

SPRING

Plant marjorams, nepetas, and alchemillas, also the geranium and sedum. Cut down dead sedum flower stems before new growth begins.

— ❧ —

SUMMER

Deadhead the phlomis and senecio and shorten any overlong shoots. Thin out some old wood from the philadelphus after flowering. Cut down flowered stems of the euphorbia. Remove faded flowers of alchemillas to prevent self-seeding. Shear alchemillas and the geranium in late summer to produce fresh foliage.

— ❧ —

FALL

Plant the robinia, staking it until it is well rooted. Plant the berberis, phlomis, philadelphus, and senecio. Plant a small euphorbia specimen: large plants are difficult to establish. Cut back marjorams by two-thirds before plants die down in winter. Cut down nepetas.

— ❧ —

WINTER

Cut back straggly berberis growths in late winter. Rejuvenate old shrubs by cutting out some old stems at ground level.

PLANTS *for a* LOW-MAINTENANCE SCHEME

ONCE ESTABLISHED, the shrubs in this scheme will need little attention to keep them looking good. They will put up with thin, poor soil reasonably well, but will of course perform better if given a reasonable diet. The robinia needs sun, so do not consider this scheme for a position that is overhung by taller trees or in shade for most of the day.

The front ranks of herbaceous plants are mostly low growing and are unlikely to need propping up in any way. Only the sedum, as it increases in girth, may need a discreet corset of twigs and string to keep the heavy heads of its fall flowers upright. Leave the flowerheads on the plant during winter: they look spectacular when dusted with frost or snow.

Senecio 'Sunshine'
Summer-flowering shrub that forms a mound of evergreen foliage with silvery undersides. Leaves are silvery gray when young. H and S 3ft (1m).

Berberis thunbergii f. atropurpurea (Barberry) *Deciduous, arching shrub grown for its reddish purple foliage and fall berries. H to 6ft (2m), S 10ft (3m).*

Robinia pseudoacacia 'Frisia' (Black locust) *Fast-growing, deciduous tree with golden foliage that turns orange-yellow in fall. H to 50ft (15m), S to 25ft (7.5m).*

Philadelphus coronarius 'Aureus' (Mock orange) *Deciduous shrub bearing fragrant flowers in late spring and early summer. H 8ft (2.5m), S 5ft (1.5m).*

Nepeta 'Six Hills Giant' (Catmint) *Perennial with gray-green leaves and lavender-blue flowers in summer. H and S 2ft (60cm).*

Euphorbia characias subsp. *wulfenii* **(Spurge)** *Evergreen, architectural shrub with large heads of yellow-green flowers in spring. H and S 5ft (1.5m).*

Alchemilla mollis (Lady's mantle) *Perennial with velvety leaves, and greenish yellow flowers in summer. H and S 20in (50cm).*

Origanum vulgare 'Aureum' (Golden marjoram) *Perennial with aromatic, yellow leaves and tiny, mauve summer flowers. H 3–18in (8–45cm), S indefinite.*

Phlomis fruticosa (Jerusalem sage) *Evergreen shrub with yellow flowers in summer, amid sagelike, gray-green foliage. H and S 3ft (1m).*

Sedum spectabile (Stonecrop) *Fleshy-leaved, clump-forming perennial with flat heads of pink flowers in late summer–fall. H and S 18in (45cm).*

Geranium cinereum 'Ballerina' (Cranesbill) *Spreading perennial bearing pink flowers with purple veins in late spring and summer. H 4in (10cm), S 12in (30cm).*

ALTERING *the* PLANTING SCHEME

PURPLE AND YELLOW MAKE a strong contrast. If this is not to your taste, use a quieter shrub in place of the berberis. Choose one with good foliage – you can always add extra flowers by training clematis up one or two of the shrubs. Celebrate the arrival of spring by adding low bulbs in the foreground, letting them weave in and out of the alchemilla, nepeta, and geranium.

VARIEGATED FOLIAGE FOR A LIGHTER EFFECT

Using a pale-variegated shrub such as *Cornus alba* 'Elegantissima' instead of the berberis will lighten the whole effect. In winter, its bare stems will shine out like red neon strips, a brilliant contrast to the soft grays of the phlomis and senecio around it.

Let this variegation echo in the foreground of the scheme by using an astrantia with creamy yellow leaves instead of the plain, pink geranium. Replace the sedum with a different geranium, such as the blue-flowered *Geranium himalayense*. A straight swap between the astrantia and the sedum would put both variegated plants on the same side of the scheme, which might unbalance it.

A SWATH OF SPRING BULBS

Dwarf bulbs, such as crocuses, scillas, chionodoxas, and puschkinias, are ideal for filling bare spring ground that will be covered later by the spread of perennial plants. Bulbs are opportunists. They pop up and get their act over while everything else is hovering in the wings, wondering whether it is the right time to go on or not. Then, even more obligingly, they dive underground, sparing us the dreary sight of their foliage languishing for the rest of the year.

There is scarcely any dwarf crocus that is not a delight. They increase lavishly, too, if they are in a position where the sun can get at them to ripen the corms.

Cornus alba 'Elegantissima' (Dogwood) *Vigorous, deciduous shrub with white-margined leaves. The stems are bright red in winter. H and S to 6ft (2m).*

Astrantia major 'Sunningdale Variegated' (Masterwort) *Clump-forming perennial with deeply divided, variegated leaves. In summer, it bears greenish white flowers touched with pink. H 2ft (60cm), S 18in (45cm).*

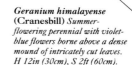

Geranium himalayense (Cranesbill) *Summer-flowering perennial with violet-blue flowers borne above a dense mound of intricately cut leaves. H 12in (30cm), S 2ft (60cm).*

Scilla siberica 'Atrocoerulea' *Early spring-flowering bulb that has nodding bells of startlingly clear blue flowers and strap-shaped, glossy leaves. H 4–6in (10–15cm), S 2in (5cm).*

Crocus 'E.A. Bowles' *Corm bearing scented, deep yellow flowers in spring. The petals are stained with bronze on the outside near the base. H 4in (10cm), S 2–3in (5–8cm).*

A Scheme *for* Scent

P OOLS OF AROMATIC THYME border this corner planting, placed so that you will tread on them, liberating the characteristic spicy perfume each time you pass up and down the paths on either side. Scent in the garden is an elusive delight, but a powerful one. This scheme uses a wide variety of plants noted for their perfume.

SWEET PERFUME
The madonna lily, Lilium candidum, *is crowned with graceful, pure white funnels, each one filled with heady fragrance.*

DESIGN POINTS

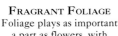

SCENTS FOR THE SUN
A richly perfumed medley of plants for a sunny corner site.

FRAGRANT FOLIAGE
Foliage plays as important a part as flowers, with scented-leaved pelargoniums, aromatic thymes, and rosemary.

Some plants, such as jonquils and Madonna lilies, release their scent uninhibitedly, pouring out great quantities of their perfume to intoxicate the world at large. Other plants are more reticent. You need to reach out and rub the foliage of the rosemary or the pelargonium to let loose their essential oils.

The daphne gives perfume early in the year, its small, waxy flowers sending out a smell strong enough to draw you in like a bloodhound. The evergreen species *Daphne odora* is the one to go for, especially the cultivar 'Aureomarginata', which has leathery leaves edged thinly in cream.

Spring- and summer-flowering bulbs add color to this scheme, but both are also richly scented. The jonquils are among the last of the daffodil family to flower, with brilliant yellow blooms among grassy foliage. What they lack in stature they more than make up for in smell. Madonna lilies are at their best when dusk falls in summer, sending out siren music to the moths from their wide, white trumpets.

AROMATIC HERBS

A spire of rosemary provides the centerpiece here. Choose a naturally upright variety, and clip and tie it in to make a neat column.

Lavender has been grown in gardens from late medieval times, and the essential oil used for perfumes. The oil is a powerful, natural antiseptic. Perhaps this is why the Romans used it in their baths; its name comes from the Latin verb *lavare*, meaning to wash. 'Hidcote' is a neat, compact, silver-leaved variety with particularly dark purple flowers.

Choose an upright thyme such as *Thymus* x *citriodorus*, which will release its lemony scent when you brush past it. Around the edges, plant low-growing thymes, such as *Thymus serpyllum*, that will creep across the paths to make scented mats under your feet. When the flowers are out, bumblebees roll around between them, drunk with the smell.

PLANTING PLAN

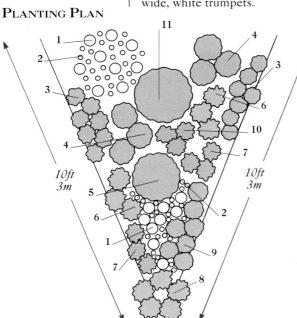

10ft 3m

10ft 3m

PLANT LIST
1 *Lilium candidum* (Madonna lily) x 18
2 *Narcissus jonquilla* (Jonquil) x 50
3 *Thymus* x *citriodorus* 'Silver Queen' (Lemon thyme) x 14
4 *Lavandula angustifolia* 'Hidcote' (Lavender) x 6
5 *Rosmarinus officinalis* 'Miss Jessopp's Upright' (Rosemary) x 1
6 *Pelargonium* 'Mabel Grey' x 6
7 *Iris graminea* syn. *I. colchica* x 6
8 *Dianthus* 'Prudence' (Pink) x 5
9 *Thymus serpyllum* (Wild thyme) x 7
10 *Hemerocallis citrina* (Daylily) x 3
11 *Daphne odora* 'Aureomarginata' x 1

COORDINATED COLORS
Undulating mats of pinks, irises, pelargoniums, and thymes merge together to create a wave of summer color in many shades of mauve, pink, and violet-blue. The accent plants are the madonna lilies, adding a distinctive splash of white.

LEMON THYME
The elegant, variegated *Thymus* x *citriodorus* 'Silver Queen' is more tender than the plain version but has the same tangy lemon scent.

PELARGONIUM
The scented leaves of pelargoniums such as 'Mabel Grey' add a distinctive aroma in a perfumed garden.

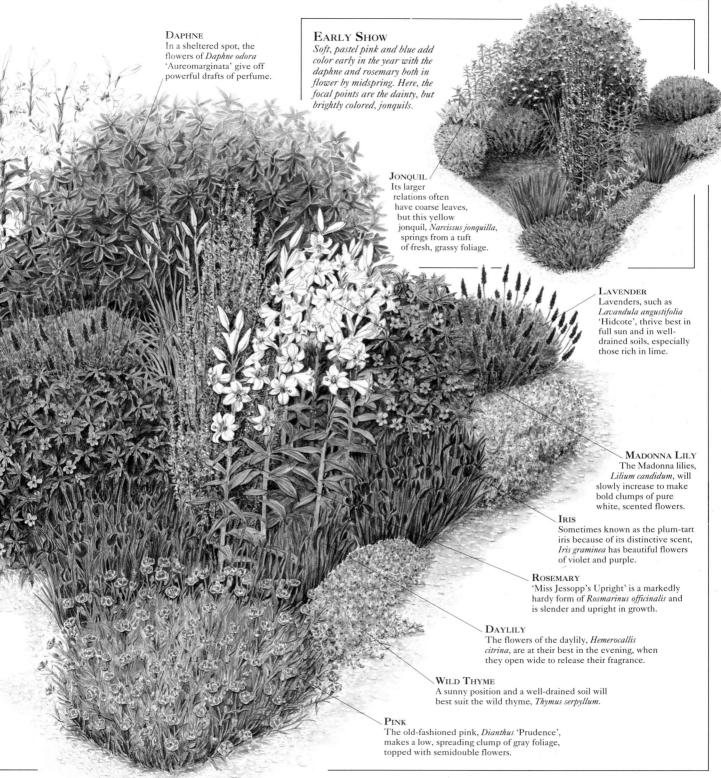

DAPHNE
In a sheltered spot, the flowers of *Daphne odora* 'Aureomarginata' give off powerful drafts of perfume.

EARLY SHOW
Soft, pastel pink and blue add color early in the year with the daphne and rosemary both in flower by midspring. Here, the focal points are the dainty, but brightly colored, jonquils.

JONQUIL
Its larger relations often have coarse leaves, but this yellow jonquil, *Narcissus jonquilla*, springs from a tuft of fresh, grassy foliage.

LAVENDER
Lavenders, such as *Lavandula angustifolia* 'Hidcote', thrive best in full sun and in well-drained soils, especially those rich in lime.

MADONNA LILY
The Madonna lilies, *Lilium candidum*, will slowly increase to make bold clumps of pure white, scented flowers.

IRIS
Sometimes known as the plum-tart iris because of its distinctive scent, *Iris graminea* has beautiful flowers of violet and purple.

ROSEMARY
'Miss Jessopp's Upright' is a markedly hardy form of *Rosmarinus officinalis* and is slender and upright in growth.

DAYLILY
The flowers of the daylily, *Hemerocallis citrina*, are at their best in the evening, when they open wide to release their fragrance.

WILD THYME
A sunny position and a well-drained soil will best suit the wild thyme, *Thymus serpyllum*.

PINK
The old-fashioned pink, *Dianthus* 'Prudence', makes a low, spreading clump of gray foliage, topped with semidouble flowers.

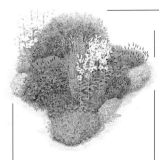

PLANTS *for a* WELL-DRAINED CORNER

ALL THE AROMATIC HERBS in this scheme need well-drained soil around their feet and plenty of sun on their heads. Winter dampness can be more of a problem than winter cold for Mediterranean plants. Dig in grit if necessary to ensure good drainage in heavy soils. Set the pinks and creeping thymes close to the edge of the bed so that they can disguise the edges of the paths.

Lavender is not by nature a very long-lived plant and will need replacing when it becomes woody and unproductive. Persuade it to produce plenty of new growth by cutting it back quite hard each spring. For more unusual flowers, arranged in two-tone plumes, choose the French lavender, *Lavandula stoechas*, but bear in mind that it is not as hardy as 'Hidcote'.

CARE AND CULTIVATION

SPRING
Plant the daphne, rosemary, thymes, and lavenders. Plant pelargoniums when all danger of frost has passed. Cut back straggly shoots of the daphne in early spring. Plant pinks, burying as little as possible of the stems. Mulch lilies with compost or leaf mold. Deadhead jonquils but leave stems and leaves to die down naturally.

SUMMER
Tie in growths of the rosemary to form a slim spire, and clip away ragged shoots. Shear off dead flowers of thymes and lavenders.

FALL
Plant lilies, setting bulbs just beneath the soil surface. Remove flower stems of lilies only when totally dry. Plant jonquils, daylilies, and irises. Lift pelargoniums before the first frost, cut them back, and overwinter in a frost-free place, or take cuttings for next year.

WINTER
Remove dead leaves and other debris from clumps of pinks and thymes.

***Thymus* x *citriodorus* 'Silver Queen' (Lemon thyme)** *Evergreen shrub with aromatic, silver-marked foliage. H and S 4–10in (10–25cm).*

***Pelargonium* 'Mabel Grey'** *Tender, evergreen perennial with diamond-shaped, lemon-scented leaves and small, mauve flowers. H to 2ft (60cm), S 12–18in (30–45cm).*

***Dianthus* 'Prudence' (Pink)** *Spreading perennial with mottled purple-pink and white flowers in midsummer. H 12–18in (30–45cm), S 12in (30cm).*

***Rosmarinus officinalis* 'Miss Jessopp's Upright' (Rosemary)** *Evergreen shrub with aromatic, needlelike leaves and small, blue flowers. H and S 6ft (2m).*

***Lilium candidum* (Madonna lily)** *Summer-flowering bulb bearing upright, elegant stems of white, funnel-shaped, scented blooms. H 3–6ft (1–2m), S 12in (30cm).*

***Daphne odora* 'Aureomarginata'** *Variegated, evergreen shrub with pink and white flowers in midwinter to spring. H and S 5ft (1.5m).*

***Hemerocallis citrina* (Daylily)** *Vigorous perennial with rich lemon yellow flowers, each lasting only a night, in midsummer. H and S 2½ft (75cm).*

***Thymus serpyllum* (Wild thyme)** *Low, creeping, evergreen shrub with small, scented leaves and mauve-pink flowers. H 3in (8cm), S indefinite.*

***Lavandula angustifolia* 'Hidcote' (Lavender)** *Evergreen shrub with dark purple flower spikes and aromatic, silver-gray leaves. H and S 2ft (60cm).*

Iris graminea* syn. *I. colchica *Rhizomatous iris with plum-scented, purple flowers that have heavily veined, violet-blue falls. H 8–16in (20–40cm), S indefinite.*

***Narcissus jonquilla* (Jonquil)** *Bulb with dark, shining leaves and, in spring, graceful, yellow flowers that have a fine fragrance. H 12in (30cm), S to 8in (20cm).*

ALTERING *the* PLANTING SCHEME

THERE ARE SEVERAL WAYS of increasing the flower power of this corner planting without sacrificing any of its capacity to please the nose. Roses are an obvious choice to replace the rosemary and the daphne, though none of them has much to offer in winter. Scented annuals and biennials will also introduce more color. You could use any combination of sweet williams, tobacco plants, heliotropes, sweet peas, night-scented stocks, verbenas, sweet sultans, and wallflowers.

BLOOMS FOR COLOR AND SCENT

Add an air of formality to this scheme by using a standard rose to replace the low-growing daphne. Standard roses always look as if they have wandered into the garden from a child's picture book, the flowers all perched in a rounded head balanced on top of a tall, clear stem. 'The Fairy' would be an excellent choice here. It is not the most heavily scented of roses, but it is one of the prettiest with large trusses of small flowers smothering a wide head of foliage.

A miniature cluster-flowered or patio rose mixes easily with the pelargoniums and thymes. Not all the new patio roses are well endowed with scent, so sniff before you choose. Pick a color that will blend in with the misty effect of the neighboring plants.

Although usually treated as annuals, wallflowers are short-lived perennials, and they acquire great character if you can persuade them to linger on for more than a year. Let them loll on their elbows over the path.

Sweet sultans provide a long show of flowers in shades of pink, white, purple, or a surprising lemon yellow, the same tone as the daylilies. Scatter the seed and sift some compost on top. Thin out seedlings growing too close together.

***Rosa* 'The Fairy'** *Dwarf, cluster-flowered bush rose, grown here as a standard, that bears pale pink, double blooms in late summer and fall. H 4–6ft (1.2–2m), S 2ft (60cm).*

***Centaurea moschata* (Sweet sultan)** *Annual with fragrant, fluffy flowerheads in pink, white, purple, or yellow, from summer to early fall, and grayish green leaves. H 18in (45cm), S 8in (20cm).*

***Cheiranthus* 'Bredon' (Wallflower)** *Short-lived, semi-evergreen perennial that produces spikes of bright mustard yellow flowers in late spring. H 12–18in (30–45cm), S 18in (45cm).*

***Rosa* 'Regensberg'** *Low-growing patio rose that bears fragrant, pale pink flowers with white centers for a long period in summer. H 18in (45cm), S 12in (30cm).*

PLANTING *by the* SEA

BLOSSOMS AND BERRIES
The hawthorn, Crataegus
laciniata, *provides a
showy explosion of spring
blossoms and bright
winter berries.*

DESIGN POINTS

— 🦋 —

YEAR-ROUND DISPLAY
Evergreen escallonias and
sculptural phormiums
continue to provide
interest in winter.

— 🦋 —

A FEAST OF FLOWERS
A long succession of
flowers comes from roses,
rock roses, and nicotianas.

— 🦋 —

FALL FRUITS
Fall brings tomato red
hips on one of the roses
and yellow-flushed
berries on the hawthorn.

W IND AND SALT are the chief difficulties of gardening near the sea, but there are blessings, too. The sea acts as a gigantic down comforter, keeping the temperature of coastal regions higher than those inland. Spring comes earlier, winter later. Choose plants that will be undaunted by the conditions; these will survive where many others would struggle – in an exposed corner of a seaside garden.

SHELTER AND SCREENING
The most important task is to create a first line of defense: a sacrificial offering of trees and shrubs to absorb the worst of the wind and shield the plants cowering behind. In large coastal gardens, Japanese black pine, Monterey pine, and Monterey cypress are good for screening. Plants with tough, leathery leaves, such as black jack oak, or minimal foliage, such as tamarisk, are also well adapted to the vagaries of seaside weather. Here, a hawthorn is used to protect the other plants in the group. As it grows, the hawthorn will probably take on the sculpted appearance of an overgrown bonsai tree, bent into a smooth curve by the prevailing wind.

Tough escallonias, hardy fuchsias, and Rugosa roses are arranged on either side of the hawthorn. Use a mixture of Rugosas so you can enjoy the best flowers ('Roseraie de l'Haÿ') and the best hips ('Frau Dagmar Hartopp').

An interference fence or some other filtering barrier around the corner will be a great help in protecting the plants while they are still finding their feet. Solid enclosures are less effective than perforated ones: when the wind bumps its nose against a solid wall, it drives turbulently over the top and creates extra mayhem on the other side. Slatted screens slow the wind down instead, and avoid inciting it to riot.

PLANTS FOR A SHIELDED SPOT
Once the artificial or natural barriers are in place, you can start filling in the protected space inside the shield. Low-growing shrubs, such as rock roses, are less at the mercy of the wind than tall ones. The rock roses, natives of hot, dry sites around the Mediterranean, also have tough foliage, naturally adapted to resist loss of water from the leaves. The papery flowers are not long lasting, but there are plenty of them, borne in succession through early summer.

Use two kinds of phormium, one a monster toward the back, the other a shorter type at the front, where you can admire the stripes of color down the leaves.

At the end of summer, the crinums send up stout stems crowned with trumpet flowers that smell like lilies. They flare open in succession to reveal a complex arrangement of stamens.

PLANTING PLAN

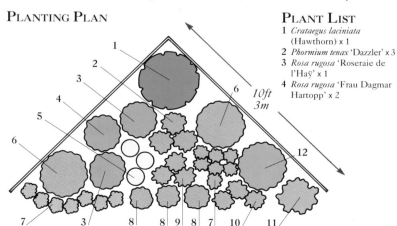

PLANT LIST
1. *Crataegus laciniata* (Hawthorn) x 1
2. *Phormium tenax* 'Dazzler' x 3
3. *Rosa rugosa* 'Roseraie de l'Haÿ' x 1
4. *Rosa rugosa* 'Frau Dagmar Hartopp' x 2

5. *Crinum* x *powellii* x 3
6. *Escallonia* 'Iveyi' x 2
7. *Nicotiana langsdorfii* x 14
8. *Cistus* x *corbariensis* (Rock rose) x 3
9. *Polygonum campanulatum* x 3
10. *Phormium tenax* 'Maori Sunrise' x 3
11. *Phlomis russeliana* x 1
12. *Fuchsia magellanica* 'Versicolor' x 1

10ft
3m

ESCALLONIA
The dark, glossy foliage of *Escallonia* 'Iveyi' provides an excellent backdrop to the large panicles of white flowers.

FLOWERS AND FOLIAGE

In midsummer, the roses take center stage, complemented by the striking sword leaves of the two phormiums. The nicotianas begin flowering in early summer and continue into the first few weeks of fall. Above their heads, the escallonias froth with white flowers.

FALL BOUNTY

In early fall, the hips on the hawthorn and one of the roses add warmth and color while the large phormium, the fuchsia, and the crinums provide striking flowers.

FUCHSIA
The crimson and purple flowers of *Fuchsia magellanica* 'Versicolor' are beautifully set off against the gray, green, and pink tones of the foliage.

CRINUM
The bold trumpet flowers of *Crinum* x *powellii* can be either white or pink.

PINK ROSE
The silver-pink flowers of *Rosa rugosa* 'Frau Dagmar Hartopp' appear on a bush that is usually wider than it is tall.

HAWTHORN
The deeply lobed leaves of *Crataegus laciniata* are often toothed at the tip, setting off the white spring blossoms and the red fall fruit.

CRIMSON ROSE
Rosa rugosa 'Roseraie de l'Haÿ' has scented, semidouble flowers of rich crimson-purple, but rarely produces hips.

DAZZLING PHORMIUM
Phormium tenax 'Dazzler' is aptly named for it has the brightest foliage of the entire genus.

POLYGONUM
The tiny, pink bell flowers of *Polygonum campanulatum* are set on elegant, branching heads.

NICOTIANA
The flowers of *Nicotiana langsdorfii* are smaller than those on other ornamental tobacco plants, but the color is an eye-catching lime green.

Fuchsia magellanica 'Versicolor'

ROCK ROSE
Cistus x *corbariensis* is one of the hardiest of the rock roses, bearing a long succession of white flowers in summer.

PHLOMIS
The rough leaves of *Phlomis russeliana* make excellent ground cover even when the whorls of soft, hooded flowers are not in evidence.

STRIPY PHORMIUM
Phormium tenax 'Maori Sunrise' has striped, sword-like leaves that grow slowly into a dramatic clump.

CARE AND CULTIVATION

SPRING

Mulch around shrubs and the hawthorn. Plant phormiums and the fuchsia. In cold areas, the fuchsia will be cut to the ground each year, but will sprout again from the base. Plant rock roses in full sun. Plant crinums, setting the bulbs 12in (30cm) deep. Sow nicotianas and plant out in late spring.

SUMMER

The hawthorn needs no regular pruning but may be trimmed to shape after flowering. Remove flowering shoots from escallonias as they fade.

FALL

Plant the hawthorn, phlomis, roses, and escallonias in late fall or early winter. Plant polygonums in light shade. The phlomis may become invasive: cut it back hard if necessary. Remove dead flower stems from phormiums.

WINTER

Rugosa roses need no regular pruning, but twiggy growths may be thinned out occasionally and old stems taken out at ground level. Cut down stems of polygonums and phlomis.

CARING *for* SEASIDE PLANTS

THE WINDS AND SALT SPRAY of a coastal location can be hard on even the toughest plants. Be patient with the plants in your scheme. It will take them a little time to settle in hostile conditions. Choose small plants – they will transplant more easily than large specimens. Planting in fall will give the hawthorn, roses, and escallonias time to find their feet before they need to think about flowering. Stout stakes, certainly for the hawthorn and possibly for the escallonias as well, will help to prevent wind rock. Mulching the ground at the base of trees and shrubs will help to conserve moisture in the soil around the roots. In cold areas, it will be necessary to protect early growth of phormiums and crinums against frost.

Crataegus laciniata **(Hawthorn)** *Deciduous tree with dark green, lobed leaves, and white flowers in spring or early summer. H and S 20ft (6m).*

Rosa rugosa **'Roseraie de l'Haÿ'** *Dense, vigorous rose with strongly scented, magenta flowers in summer–fall. H 6ft (2m), S 5ft (1.5m).*

Rosa rugosa **'Frau Dagmar Hartopp'** *Shrub rose with fragrant, single, pink flowers, then large, red hips in fall. H 5ft (1.5m), S 4ft (1.2m).*

Escallonia **'Iveyi'** *Evergreen shrub with dark green, glossy leaves, and fragrant, white flowers in mid- to late summer. H and S to 11ft (3.5m).*

Nicotiana langsdorfii *Erect perennial, grown as an annual, with hanging, pale green to yellow-green flowers in summer. H to 5ft (1.5m), S 12in (30cm).*

Crinum x ***powellii*** *Late-summer or fall-flowering bulb with fragrant, funnel-shaped, pink flowers. H to 3ft (1m), S 2ft (60cm).*

Cistus x ***corbariensis*** **(Rock rose)** *Evergreen, bushy shrub with masses of white flowers in late spring–summer. H 2½ft (75cm), S 4ft (1.2m).*

Polygonum campanulatum *Mat-forming perennial with oval leaves and bell-shaped, pink or white flowers in summer. H and S 3ft (1m).*

Phormium tenax **'Dazzler'** *Evergreen perennial with pointed leaves in tones of orange-red and bronze, and panicles of red flowers in summer. H to 6ft (2m), S 3ft (1m).*

Phormium tenax **'Maori Sunrise'** *Evergreen, upright perennial with stiff, pointed leaves margined with cream. H to 10ft (3m), S to 6ft (2m).*

Phlomis russeliana *Evergreen perennial with large, heart-shaped leaves. Butter yellow flowers appear on stout stems in summer. H 3ft (1m), S 2ft (60cm).*

Fuchsia magellanica **'Versicolor'** *Deciduous shrub with strikingly variegated foliage. Slender, red and purple flowers are borne in late summer. H 10ft (3m), S 6ft (2m).*

ALTERING *the* PLANTING SCHEME

THERE IS PLENTY OF OPPORTUNITY to juggle with different combinations of color in this group of plants. The hawthorn, roses, escallonias, fuchsia, rock roses, and crinum can all offer white flowers as well as a cornucopia of pink. This alternative scheme suggests ways that you can swing the color balance away from pink toward yellow, gray, and lime green. This is a more recessive, subtle combination of colors, which retains the white-flowering rock rose from the original scheme and builds on the acid green introduced by the nicotiana.

PALE COLORS FOR A COASTAL SPOT

In place of the escallonias and the fuchsia, spread the Rugosa roses all around the boundary to make an informal hedge. Use only white-flowered varieties such as 'Alba' and 'Blanc Double de Coubert'.

The homely hawthorn is replaced by a eucalyptus, which will change the whole character of the planting. This eucalyptus is a ghost tree, bark and foliage both bleached to phantom shades of gray.

Olearia replaces the phormium at the back, while the slow-growing dwarf pine is used instead of the one in the foreground. The tree lupine is covered all summer with yellow flowers that will scent this whole corner.

Eucalyptus coccifera (Tasmanian snow gum) *Evergreen tree with aromatic, gray-green leaves and blue-gray and white bark. H to 60ft (18m), S to 20ft (6m).*

Rosa rugosa 'Alba' *Vigorous rose with fragrant, white flowers in summer–fall, followed by large, tomato-shaped hips. H and S 3–6ft (1–2m).*

Lupinus arboreus (Tree lupine) *Semi-evergreen shrub with scented, yellow flowers above hairy, pale green leaves. H 3ft (1m), S 2½ft (75cm).*

Bupleurum fruticosum (Shrubby hare's ear) *Evergreen shrub bearing small, yellow flowers from summer to early fall. H and S 6ft (2m).*

Olearia x haastii (Daisy bush) *Bushy, evergreen shrub with small, oval, glossy leaves. In mid- to late summer it bears masses of scented, white, daisy-like flowers. The dense habit of this shrub makes it a good choice for hedging. H and S 6ft (2m).*

Pinus mugo 'Humpy' (Dwarf pine) *Low, spreading, shrubby conifer with needlelike leaves and egg-shaped cones. H 18in (45cm), S 2ft (60cm).*

SUNNY YELLOWS *and* BLUES

ROSES DO NOT HAVE TO BE CONSIGNED to beds on their own, like patients in an isolation ward. Shrub roses, particularly, make graceful centerpieces in a sunny corner site, surrounded by complementary shrubs, perennials, and bulbs. Here, a pale gold rose holds together a scheme of yellow and blue with a phlomis providing a cool mound of felted, gray foliage. Blue and white hyacinths sit stiffly between clumps of blue-flowered brunnera, echoing the crisp, clean effect of willow pattern china.

THE GLORY OF A GOLDEN ROSE

This scheme is suitable for a corner backed by a wall or fence, where you see the plants from the front only. Use a rose such as 'Frühlingsgold' that holds itself well. Large-flowered (Hybrid Tea) types would not be suitable: they are too stiff, too awkward. 'Frühlingsgold' has large, almost single flowers of clear yellow, fading to creamy primrose. The stamens are particularly beautiful, peppering the blooms with pointillist touches of gold and brown. It is vigorous and upright, rather than spreading, making it a friendly neighbor, and easy to plant under.

A HOST OF HANDSOME COMPANIONS

Roses are not generally endowed with good foliage, but you can compensate with other plants. The phlomis makes a rounded dome of evergray foliage, and so covers up the bare stems at the base of the rose. Daylilies and irises form vertical punctuation marks among the soft humps of the other plants. The irises' foliage spears through the ground in bright, fresh green. The daylilies also have good spring foliage – juicy enough to eat. They are often among the first herbaceous plants to poke through in those chill, late winter days when you are anxiously looking for signs of life. For this scheme use a yellow variety, rather than an orange or terracotta one. Look for 'Marion Vaughn', 'Cartwheels', or 'Hyperion'.

The ceratostigma comes into its own in late summer, when it is covered with brilliant blue flowers, and in fall, when the foliage is tinged with rich, lustrous red.

PLANTING PLAN

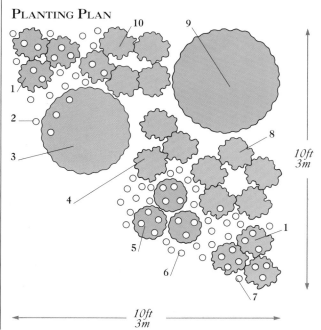

10ft
3m

10ft
3m

PLANT LIST
1 *Brunnera macrophylla* 'Hadspen Cream' x 6
2 *Hyacinthus orientalis* 'Delft Blue' and 'L'Innocence' (Hyacinths) x 25
3 *Phlomis fruticosa* (Jerusalem sage) x 1
4 *Hemerocallis* 'Marion Vaughn' (Daylily) x 3
5 *Ceratostigma willmottianum* x 3
6 *Tulipa* 'Candela' (Fosteriana tulip) x 25
7 *Tulipa* 'Bellona' (Single early tulip) x 25
8 *Campanula lactiflora* 'Prichard's Variety' x 5
9 *Rosa* 'Frühlingsgold' x 1
10 *Iris sibirica* x 5

SUMMERTIME BLUES

This border looks its best in early summer when the rose is in full bloom. It is complemented by Iris sibirica, *although you could use other blue irises instead. Additional blue comes from the forget-me-not flowers of* Brunnera macrophylla 'Hadspen Cream', *which has showy, variegated foliage.*

MIDSPRING SCHEME

The blue and yellow theme starts in spring when the tulips take center stage, sharing the limelight with blue and white hyacinths. The daylilies, more advanced, are showing spears of foliage about a foot high, matched by the bold, swordlike leaves of the irises.

JERUSALEM SAGE

Both stems and leaves of the Jerusalem sage, *Phlomis fruticosa*, are covered in gray-green felt, enlivened in summer with whorls of yellow flowers.

HYACINTHS

Hyacinthus orientalis 'Delft Blue' is a rich porcelain blue and early to come into flower. 'L'Innocence' has waxy, white flowers set loosely on each stem. Forced bulbs planted out after flowering indoors may take a season or two to recover, but will eventually give a good display.

TULIPS

The tulip 'Bellona' is a single early type, flowering usually in midspring with deep golden yellow flowers. 'Candela' may flower a couple of weeks earlier. It is slightly taller and an equally good color – clear, soft golden yellow.

ROSE

Rosa 'Frühlingsgold' has only one season of flowering, but it is both early and beautifully scented.

IRIS

Although it grows best in damp soil and full sun, *Iris sibirica* is an adaptable plant and will flourish in a wide variety of situations.

CAMPANULA

Campanula lactiflora 'Prichard's Variety' makes a magnificent companion for most shrub roses. It may need staking in a windy site.

DAYLILY

Daylilies are as useful for their early spears of foliage as they are for their flowers, which in the vigorous *Hemerocallis* 'Marion Vaughn' are clear lemon yellow.

CERATOSTIGMA

Although it may be cut to the ground in winter, the new growths of *Ceratostigma willmottianum* give a plentiful display of searingly blue flowers by late summer.

BRUNNERA

Forget-me-not flowers are carried in abundance on stems held above the variegated leaves of *Brunnera macrophylla* 'Hadspen Cream', which grows best where there is moisture and some shade.

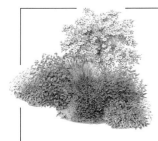

CARE AND CULTIVATION

SPRING

Plant phlomis and ceratostigmas. Deadhead tulips as they finish flowering but allow foliage to die down naturally. Top-dress irises with sifted compost. Mulch the rose. Cut out any brunnera foliage that reverts to plain green.

SUMMER

Spray the rose if necessary against mildew, aphids, and blackspot. Phlomis does not need regular pruning, but cut back straggly branches after flowering. Cut out old, flowered stems of daylilies and brunneras.

FALL

Plant campanulas, brunneras, and daylilies. Divide and replant established clumps if necessary. Plant irises, setting rhizomes no more than 1in (2.5cm) deep. Plant hyacinths and tulips. Cut down stems of campanulas when flowers have finished.

WINTER

Plant the rose, incorporating plenty of humus. In subsequent years, prune it lightly, taking out one or two old growths at the base.

COMPANION PLANTS *for a* SHRUB ROSE

Spring-flowering bulbs such as hyacinths and tulips are ideal for planting around a rose or other summer-flowering shrub. They provide another season of interest, before the perennials and shrubs have fully woken up and reached their stride, and you can alter the scheme with different varieties each year. Tulips do not always last well in the ground, so you may have to replace them every couple of years. This is not necessarily a disadvantage since it allows you to experiment with different kinds and colors. For example, a single early such as 'Bellona' can be preceded by an even earlier flush of a Fosteriana tulip such as 'Candela'. Plant them deep so that when you are working among the plants, or forking out weeds, you will not spear the bulbs accidentally on the end of your fork. There is no more mortifying experience.

If you want your tulips to flower reliably year after year, the best results come from lifting the bulbs at the end of each flowering season, drying them off, and storing them somewhere dry and mouseproof until the following planting season. This is the counsel of perfection. It is easier to think of tulips as annuals instead.

Rosa 'Frühlingsgold'
Shrub rose with scented, clear yellow flowers in early summer. H 7ft (2.1m), S 5ft (1.5m).

Hyacinthus orientalis 'L'Innocence' (Hyacinth) *Bulb with ivory-white flowers. H to 8in (20cm), S 4in (10cm).*

Phlomis fruticosa (Jerusalem sage)
Evergreen shrub forming a dome of woolly, gray leaves. H and S 2½ft (75cm).

Hemerocallis 'Marion Vaughn' (Daylily)
Perennial with yellow flowers in midsummer. H 3ft (1m), S 2ft (60cm).

Tulipa 'Candela' (Fosteriana tulip)
Bulb with yellow flowers in midspring. H 15in (40cm), S 8in (20cm).

Ceratostigma willmottianum *Deciduous shrub with a show of brilliant blue fall flowers. H and S 3ft (1m).*

Iris sibirica
Rhizomatous perennial with purplish blue flowers in late spring. H 3–4ft (1–1.2m), S indefinite.

Hyacinthus orientalis 'Delft Blue' (Hyacinth)
Bulb with rich blue flowers in spring. H to 8in (20cm), S 4in (10cm).

Tulipa 'Bellona' (Single early tulip) *Early spring-flowering bulb with golden flowers. H 15in (40cm), S to 8in (20cm).*

Campanula lactiflora 'Prichard's Variety'
Perennial with bell-shaped flowers in summer. H 4ft (1.2m), S 2ft (60cm).

Brunnera macrophylla 'Hadspen Cream'
Perennial with blue, forget-me-not flowers. H 18in (45cm), S 2ft (60cm).

ALTERING *the* PLANTING SCHEME

WHERE YOU HAVE A CORNER SITE that is really hot, dry, and sheltered, too hot and dry for the rose, you can substitute this more tender collection of plants for some of those in the original scheme. All the plants used here are adapted to survive summer droughts, but not harsh winter cold. Several have the gray foliage that is typical of drought-resistant plants.

PLANTS FOR A DRY, SHELTERED SPOT

Use the Cootamundra wattle for its finely cut foliage, more like bunches of glaucous blue feathers than leaves. It will grow larger than the rose, but its lightness and airiness stop it from ever becoming too dominant. The Russian sage – a native of Afghanistan and Tibet – is tougher, but it looks Mediterranean, with deeply cut leaves, grayish white on their undersides.

The tall, stately flowers of the verbascum rise from astonishing rosettes of white, felted leaves. The eryngium is from a family that does not have a single hanger-on in it. Its sturdy, blue stems are topped with extravagant, thistlelike flowers, each surrounded by a complicated ruff of the same steely blue. They drift into death, fading to a pale buff, but are almost as handsome then as they are in life.

Perovskia atriplicifolia **'Blue Spire' (Russian sage)** *Deciduous subshrub that has ghostly gray-green stems and leaves and a mass of spires of violet-blue flowers in late summer to midfall. H 4ft (1.2m), S 2½ft (75cm).*

Acacia baileyana **(Cootamundra wattle)** *Graceful, evergreen tree with arching branches covered in blue-gray leaves and, in winter–spring, small, fluffy, golden flowers. H 20ft (6m), S 15ft (5m).*

Verbascum olympicum **(Mullein)** *Biennial with large, gray, feltlike leaves and tall, downy stems that bear yellow flowers from mid- to late summer. H 6ft (2m), S to 3ft (1m).*

Eryngium alpinum **(Sea holly)** *Upright perennial with deeply toothed, glossy foliage above which rise stems of conical flowerheads surrounded by soft spines during summer. H 3ft (1m), S 2ft (60cm).*

Argyranthemum frutescens, syn. *Chrysanthemum frutescens,* 'Jamaica Primrose' *Bushy, evergreen perennial with fernlike leaves, and soft yellow flowers in summer. H and S to 3ft (1m).*

VERTICAL SPACES

❦

When you have used up all your horizontal planting space, send plants up to the sky, trained on trellises or wigwams, spread-eagled on a wall, or lolling against the arches of a pergola. It is vital to consider the scale and style of vertical features and how they will fit in with the rest of the garden. A grand processional way through a lushly planted pergola needs to lead somewhere more exciting than the compost heap.

PLANTS *for a* PERGOLA

RESCOES AT POMPEII, the Roman town spectacularly swallowed up in an eruption of Vesuvius, show that even as early as AD79 pergolas were popular garden features. Covered in climbers, a pergola makes a living tunnel for you to walk through. Swathe it in clematis, roses, and grapes, and use it to enclose a path or to link two separate areas of the garden.

In Pompeii, pergolas would probably have been covered with grapevines to provide a crop of fruit and also shade in the garden. In hot countries, shade is still an important function of a pergola, the plants making a living roof of greenery.

SITING AND MATERIALS
Place your pergola with a purpose. It needs to lead somewhere, not look as though it has just dropped at random from the undercarriage of a passing helicopter. If you are building your own pergola, make it strong. There is a surprising amount of weight in a grapevine when it is in full leaf and an extraordinary strength in the twisting trunk of a wisteria. It may be slower than a boa constrictor, but it is no less crushing. Wood, brick, stone, and iron can all be used to

construct pergolas, and the design will to a great extent depend on the materials you use. The most substantial are those with brick or stone pillars, connected by wooden beams across the top. Extremely pretty pergolas can be made from trellis work, which has an extra advantage for the plants: there are plenty of places for tendrils to get a hold and plenty of fixing points when you need to tie in stems. Use the sturdiest trellis you can find or make.

LEAFY COVERING
Clematis are popular plants for pergolas but can appear insubstantial if planted on their own. Think first of some handsome, leafy

GLORIOUS GRAPE
The leaves of Vitis coignetiae *can be as large as dinner plates. In fall, they become richly colored, earning the plant its common name, the crimson glory vine.*

DESIGN POINTS
— 🐌 —

HEAVEN SCENT
Roses and wisterias fill the air with fragrance, adding to the pleasure of sitting or walking beneath the pergola.

— 🐌 —

LUSH FOLIAGE
Plenty of leafy plants such as grapes create a feeling of luxuriant abundance.

— 🐌 —

A BLOOMING SUMMER
Clematis, wisterias, and roses provide a glorious show of flowers throughout late spring and summer.

PLANT LIST
1 *Wisteria sinensis* (Chinese wisteria) x 1
2 *Clematis viticella* 'Mme. Julia Correvon' x 1
3 *Rosa* 'Félicité Perpétue' x 1
4 *Solanum jasminoides* 'Album' x 1
5 *Vitis coignetiae* (Crimson glory vine) x 1
6 *Clematis* 'The President' x 1
7 *Rosa* 'Rambling Rector' x 1
8 *Clematis macropetala* x 1
9 *Clematis* 'Elsa Spath' x 1
10 *Vitis vinifera* 'Purpurea' x 1
11 *Wisteria floribunda* 'Alba' x 1
12 *Clematis viticella* 'Etoile Violette' x 1

PLANTING PLAN

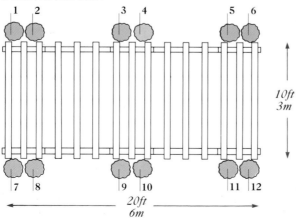

1 2 3 4 5 6

7 8 9 10 11 12

10ft
3m

20ft
6m

A CANOPY OF COLOR
In late spring and early summer, the wisterias are heavy with tassels of flowers in lilac and white. Some of the clematis are in bloom, too, threading their color through the backcloth of foliage.

CHINESE WISTERIA
The purple flowers of *Wisteria sinensis*, Chinese wisteria, grow in racemes sprouting from stems that twine counterclockwise. Hard pruning is necessary to encourage flowering.

CRIMSON CLEMATIS
Clematis viticella 'Mme. Julia Correvon' is one of the large group of viticella cultivars flowering in late summer, all of which can be hard pruned in late winter.

subjects to furnish the bare bones and add the clematis afterward, like decorations on a cake. Grapes are ideal. There are green- and purple-leaved versions; try *Vitis* 'Brant', *V. vinifera* 'Purpurea', or, for sweet grapes, *V.* 'Concord'.

Wisterias are also well suited to pergola life, their long racemes of blossoms hanging like bunches of grapes from the vine. For the roses,

choose cluster-flowered climbers such as 'Rambling Rector'; some, particularly those developed from large-flowered types, have too stiff a growth habit to look comfortable.

On a long stretch of pergola, use the same plants more than once but in different combinations. This will help to give a sense of unity and cohesion to the planting.

PALE PINK ROSE
The long, slender stems of *Rosa* 'Félicité Perpétue' are relatively easy to control on a pergola, and the double flowers are sweetly scented.

SOLANUM
The white flowers of *Solanum jasminoides* 'Album' are carried over a long period from summer to fall.

WHITE WISTERIA
The stems of *Wisteria floribunda* 'Alba' twine in a clockwise direction and need to be trained and well tied in as they grow.

CRIMSON GLORY VINE
This handsome species, *Vitis coignetiae*, is extremely vigorous with leaves that can be a foot across.

VIOLET CLEMATIS
Clematis 'The President' flowers in early summer, bearing masses of single, purple blooms with silver undersides.

PURPLE CLEMATIS
The viticella forms of clematis such as this dark purple *Clematis viticella* 'Etoile Violette' are hardy and rarely subject to wilt.

CREAM ROSE
The individual flowers of *Rosa* 'Rambling Rector' are tiny but are borne in such large clusters that the overall effect is luxurious.

BLUE CLEMATIS
An early-flowering species with pale, ferny foliage, *Clematis macropetala* has fine double flowers of violet-blue.

LAVENDER CLEMATIS
Clematis 'Elsa Spath' often blooms twice in a season, the deep lavender-blue flowers studded with centers of reddish purple anthers.

PURPLE GRAPE
Vitis vinifera 'Purpurea' is one of the best grapes for a pergola with superb purple foliage that erupts in a blaze of crimson during fall.

CLIMBERS *for a* PERGOLA

PATIENT TRAINING IS THE KEY to a well-furnished pergola. Little and often should be your motto, a job to be done on summer evenings while you are waiting for dinner to cook. Keep a pergola kit in a small basket – pruners, soft brown twine, plastic ties – and take it with you on your evening stroll. As the clematis shoots grow, train each one in a different direction, so that when the plants come into flower, their blooms will cover the largest possible area. Be ruthless with the wisterias. Pruning twice a year is the only way to get them to flower profusely.

CARE AND CULTIVATION

SPRING
Mulch wisterias, grapes, roses, and clematis. Tie in new growths of wisterias, grapes, and roses. Plant the solanum and tie in firmly. In subsequent years, thin out weak growths and cut back any shoots damaged by frost. Plant clematis. 'Elsa Spath' and 'The President' may be lightly pruned by removing old, dead stems. *C. macropetala* needs no regular pruning.

SUMMER
Train and tie in stems of wisterias as they grow. Shorten shoots that are not needed for the main framework, cutting them back by half.

FALL
Plant wisterias and grapes, tying them in securely to their supports. Prune roses after flowering, untying and cutting out some of the old flowering stems and tying in new, whippy growth.

WINTER
In late winter, prune wisterias hard and prune *Clematis viticella* varieties to within 18in (45cm) of the ground. Plant roses, cutting them back hard to produce strong, new growth.

Wisteria floribunda 'Alba' *Deciduous, twining climber with scented, white flowers in early summer. H to 28ft (9m).*

Rosa 'Rambling Rector' *Vigorous, rambling rose with clusters of fragrant, cream flowers in summer. H to 20ft (6m).*

Solanum jasminoides 'Album' *Semi-evergreen climber with star-shaped, white flowers in summer– fall. H to 20ft (6m).*

Rosa 'Félicité Perpétue' *Climbing rose with clusters of blush pink flowers in midsummer. H 15ft (5m), S 12ft (4m).*

Clematis viticella 'Mme. Julia Correvon' *Deciduous climber with red summer blooms. H 8–11ft (2.5–3.5), S 3ft (1m).*

Clematis macropetala *Deciduous climber with mauve-blue flowers in late spring and summer. H 10ft (3m), S 5ft (1.5m).*

Vitis vinifera 'Purpurea' *Deciduous, woody-stemmed, tendril climber with toothed, deeply lobed, purple leaves, and tiny purple grapes in late summer. H to 22ft (7m).*

Clematis 'The President' *Deciduous climber with purple blooms in early summer. H 6–10ft (2–3m), S 3ft (1m).*

Vitis coignetiae (Crimson glory vine) *Deciduous climber with large, matte leaves that color well in fall. H to 50ft (15m).*

Clematis 'Elsa Spath' *Deciduous, large-flowered climber with mauve-blue blooms during summer. H 6–10ft (2–3m), S 3ft (1m).*

Wisteria sinensis (Chinese wisteria) *Deciduous climber bearing lilac flowers in early summer. H to 100ft (30m).*

Clematis viticella 'Etoile Violette' *Deciduous climber with violet flowers. H 10–12ft (3–4m), S 5ft (1.5m).*

ALTERING *the* PLANTING SCHEME

LUXURIANT FOLIAGE should always be the prime requirement in covering a pergola. Since the grapes and wisterias will take time to cover their allotted space, gardeners in a hurry can use fast-growing climbers for quick results. If you want to spice up the soft colors of the scheme, include climbers such as eccremocarpus and campsis in cheerleader shades of orange and red.

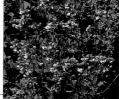

Lablab purpureus (Hyacinth bean) *Deciduous, twining climber with pink, purple, or white flowers in summer. H to 30ft (10m).*

CLIMBERS FOR INSTANT RESULTS

Use fast-growing, tender climbers on the same supports as the grapes to give instant cover. You will have to sacrifice the clematis, for their growths will become tangled, making it impossible to remove the tender climbers at the end of the season.

The cobaea and the lablab both grow vigorously. The convolvulus is more restrained and may be used instead of the solanum to twine its way through the rose. Its sky blue flowers are vivid, but short-lived, opening in the morning and fading in the afternoon.

Convolvulus tricolor 'Heavenly Blue' *Fast-growing, twining, annual climber that is covered in breathtaking, open blooms of purest blue from summer to early fall. H to 10ft (3m).*

Cobaea scandens (Cup-and-saucer vine) *Tender climber, often grown as an annual, with flowers that change from yellow-green to purple as they age. H 12–15ft (4–5m).*

Tropaeolum speciosum (Flame creeper) *Deciduous climber with scarlet flowers followed by bright blue fruits. H to 10ft (3m).*

A FEAST OF FIERY COLORS

These plants will set your pergola on fire in summer and fall, flames of tropaeolum licking up the supports among a mass of hand-shaped leaves. Use it to light up the grape and let the eccremocarpus flicker through the foliage of the wisteria. The campsis is worth growing only in areas with a warm to hot summer to tease out a good performance. Used instead of one of the roses, it will change the atmosphere of the pergola, making it strange and tropical.

Campsis x *tagliabuana* 'Mme. Galen' (Trumpet vine) *Deciduous climber with vivid orange flowers in late summer–fall. H to 30ft (10m).*

Eccremocarpus scaber (Chilean glory flower) *Climbing subshrub, often grown as an annual, with orange-red flowers in summer. H 6–10ft (2–3m).*

COLOR *for* FALL—WINTER

WALLS ARE OFTEN undressed of their clothes at the very time when they need them most, so this scheme suggests climbers and wall shrubs to keep a wall well covered throughout fall and winter. Fall color comes from the fiery tones of a parthenocissus. Pyracantha adds brilliant winter fruit, and jasmine defies winter weather with elegant sprays of bright yellow flowers.

LIVING GEMS
Thickly encrusting the stems like beads, the bright berries of Pyracantha 'Golden Charmer' are set off by evergreen leaves.

CARE AND CULTIVATION

SPRING
Plant *Jasminum humile*, the garrya, and the clematis. Mulch all shrubs well. Prune out some old wood from *J. nudiflorum* and tie in new stems.

SUMMER
Train the pyracantha as necessary. Train clematis stems through the garrya.

FALL
Plant the pyracantha, parthenocissus, and *J. nudiflorum*. Clip back parthenocissus as needed.

WINTER
Prune the pyracantha as necessary. In late winter, cut back clematis to within 18in (45cm) of the ground.

PLANTING PLAN

⟵ 30ft ⟶
10m

1   2   3   4   5   6

WARM COLORS FOR A COOL WALL
You could use these plants on a house wall, for houses particularly look sad and naked when all their summer accessories are stripped away by the onset of frost. Do not waste a precious sheltered, sunny wall on shrubs such as pyracantha. In all but the most exposed and chilly locations, the combination would be ideal for a cool or partly shaded wall or fence. The cheering yellows, oranges, and reds of this scheme will provide at least an illusion of warmth in a semishaded spot.

Only the *Jasminum humile* and the garrya will grizzle and sicken in intensely exposed situations. The others are made of stouter stuff. If you want to reproduce the scheme in a cold area, substitute a chaenomeles, the

A LIVING WALL
A formally trained pyracantha contrasts well with the leafy abundance of the other shrubs and climbers. The glowing colors of flowers, foliage, and berries enliven even the gloomiest of walls.

PLANT LIST
1 *Parthenocissus tricuspidata* 'Lowii' x 1
2 *Pyracantha* 'Golden Charmer' x 1
3 *Clematis tangutica* x 1
4 *Garrya elliptica* x 1
5 *Jasminum humile* (Yellow jasmine) x 1
6 *Jasminum nudiflorum* (Winter jasmine) x 1

herringbone-branched *Cotoneaster horizontalis*, or a forsythia for the two less hardy shrubs.

Pyracanthas look most interesting when they are carefully trained. The branches are long and straight and fall very easily into parallel lines, squares, or diamonds. Although they are thorny, they are not vicious and the growths are easy to handle. Train one horizontally below a window, or bring the main stem up beside a window and tie in the growths to create a mirror image, a green and growing window squared off in panes.

PARTHENOCISSUS
The flaming leaves of *Parthenocissus tricuspidata* 'Lowii' have strikingly jagged edges.

PYRACANTHA
Pyracantha 'Golden Charmer' is a vigorous cultivar with relatively upright growth and yellow fall berries.

SUCCESSIONAL INTEREST

In fall, the fiery berries of the pyracantha (yellow, orange, or red, depending on type) are complemented by the crimson leaves of the parthenocissus and the seedheads of the clematis. Garrya has extraordinary catkins of pale grayish green during late winter, but, exhausted by this bravura performance, it rests rather quietly for the rest of the year. Its foliage is evergreen, which is in its favor, but you can lend it jazzier summer clothes by allowing a clematis such as *Clematis tangutica* to thread through it. Choose your garrya with care; the catkins are less showy on female plants than they are on male. 'James Roof' is one of the best with extra-long catkins, the calyces tinted with purple.

Spring is not without its attractions, too: the evergreen yellow jasmine, *Jasminum humile*, picking up the flowering baton from its cousin the winter jasmine. For greater contrast, you could try the more upright *Piptanthus nepalensis* instead. It is covered in bright yellow, pealike blooms in spring and summer.

Parthenocissus tricuspidata 'Lowii'
Vigorous, deciduous climber with deeply cut, jagged leaves that turn brilliant crimson in fall. H to 70ft (20m).

Clematis tangutica
Late-flowering, deciduous climber with yellow lantern flowers in summer–early fall then fluffy, silvery seedheads. H to 20ft (6m), S 10ft (3m).

Jasminum humile (Yellow jasmine)
Evergreen shrub bearing bright yellow flowers on long, slender, green shoots from spring to summer. H 8ft (2.5m), S 7ft (2.2m).

Pyracantha 'Golden Charmer' *Evergreen shrub with glossy leaves. Its white summer flowers are followed by orange berries in early fall. H and S 10ft (3m).*

Garrya elliptica
Evergreen, bushy shrub with leathery leaves and, from midwinter to early spring, long, gray-green catkins. H 12ft (4m), S 10ft (3m).

Jasminum nudiflorum (Winter jasmine)
Deciduous shrub with dark green leaves and, from winter to early spring, yellow flowers on bare stems. H and S 10ft (3m).

CLEMATIS
The silky seedheads of *Clematis tangutica* are as valuable an ornament as its nodding flowers.

GARRYA
Because it is not reliably hardy, *Garrya elliptica* benefits greatly from the protection of a wall in winter.

YELLOW JASMINE
The bushy, evergreen *Jasminum humile* tends to sprawl, so it looks better when trained against a support, as here.

WINTER JASMINE
One of the most common winter-flowering shrubs, *Jasminum nudiflorum* is a cheering sight in the coldest months of the year.

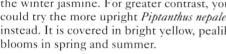

PALE PERFECTION
The blooms of Rosa 'Mme. Alfred Carrière', *have a heady perfume and a fine creamy color – flushed with the faintest blush of pink.*

DESIGN POINTS

DECORATIVE DIVISIONS
Screens covered in climbers may be used to divide a long, thin garden into more manageable, well-proportioned shapes.

PRECIOUS GOLD
Golden hops provide a glowing background for flowers of roses, honeysuckle, and clematis.

A SWATH OF SCENT
Summer scent comes from old-fashioned climbing roses, white jasmine, and swags of apricot-colored honeysuckle.

WOVEN COLORS
Climbers mingle to provide a changing tapestry of yellow, white, and blue.

SCREENING *the* GARDEN

USING A SCREEN to divide one part of the garden from another creates the illusion that you are entering a different world, but because it is not solid, you do not feel that the one world is entirely divorced from the other. A screen will always introduce an element of surprise, too, for there is nothing more intriguing in a garden than not being able to see it all at once.

The screen is a useful device for dividing up a long, thin garden. It gives you spaces that are easier to work with and also creates separate areas that can be commandeered for different purposes, such as growing fruit or herbs. You could use a screen to mark a change of style in a garden, dividing a formally planted area from a wilder, more informal layout with fruit trees growing in long grass. It could also signal a change of color combinations, perhaps marking a transition from cool to hot colors.

STYLE AND SUITABILITY
The style of the screen should be determined by the overall setting of the garden. For an informal effect, you can make a simple screen like a one-sided pergola, using cedar poles for uprights and horizontals, and bracing the joints with diagonal poles in between. This type of screen is relatively inexpensive and easy to cover with plants, but in town gardens the faintly rustic aura may be inappropriate. Here, especially in paved gardens, something more architectural may be called for.

FLOWER POWER
In early summer, the clematis, roses, and honeysuckle are at their peak, filling the screen with color and scent. The hops, with their handsome yellow leaves, provide a warm backdrop and contrast sharply with the dark-leaved jasmine.

DOUBLE-SHOW CLEMATIS
In most seasons, the clematis 'Lasurstern' will give two flower shows, one at each end of the summer.

COMMON JASMINE
Long cultivated in gardens, *Jasminum officinale* needs room to spread itself and some sun to ripen its wood if it is to flower freely.

GOLDEN HOP
The golden hop, *Humulus lupulus* 'Aureus', does not flower as freely as the plain green one, but the leaves are far superior in color.

OLD ROSE
Delicately colored and sweetly scented, *Rosa* 'Gloire de Dijon' is a beautiful old climbing rose.

This scheme has been put together with a fairly elaborate trellis structure in mind, swooping through the garden in a series of elegant curves. Stains are more practical than paints for outside woodwork, and either dark green or a grayish kind of blue would make a good background color for the plants.

A formal, productive division could be made by planting cordon fruit trees, slanting them in two directions to make a diamond pattern against taut wires and posts.

DRESSING THE SCREEN

The ratio of plants to structure needs to be considered carefully. Where you have an elaborate trellis screen, plants should be used only as set dressing. They should not completely swamp the underlying architecture. Where the screen itself is playing an entirely practical role, more vigorous plants will be needed as overall cover. Here, the golden hop, *Humulus lupulus* 'Aureus', is used as an anchor plant along the four panels of a decorative trellis screen. Its warm yellow leaves set the tone for the rest of the plants: creamy roses such as 'Gloire de Dijon' and 'Mme. Alfred Carrière', sweet-smelling honeysuckle, and clematis in varying shades of blue, yellow, and white.

PLANTING PLAN

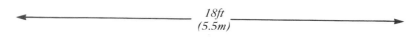

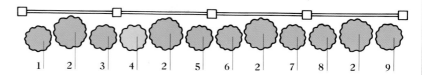

1   2   3   4   2   5   6   2   7   8   2   9

PLANT LIST

1 *Rosa* 'Gloire de Dijon' x 1
2 *Humulus lupulus* 'Aureus' (Golden hop) x 4
3 *Clematis* 'Lasurstern' x 1
4 *Jasminum officinale* (Common jasmine) x 1
5 *Clematis orientalis* 'Bill Mackenzie' x 1
6 *Rosa* 'Mme. Alfred Carrière' x 1
7 *Clematis* 'Perle d'Azur' x 1
8 *Lonicera* x *americana* (Honeysuckle) x 1
9 *Clematis* 'Henryi' x 1

YELLOW CLEMATIS
The vigorous *Clematis orientalis* 'Bill Mackenzie' has nodding flowers with thick, deep yellow petals.

LONG-LASTING ROSE
As well as being tolerant of shade, *Rosa* 'Mme. Alfred Carrière' flowers almost continuously through the summer, with white blooms lightly tinged with pink.

BLUE CLEMATIS
A useful late-flowering clematis, 'Perle d'Azur' has china blue flowers, the stamens tinged with green.

HONEYSUCKLE
The showy flowerheads of the honeysuckle, *Lonicera* x *americana*, have fortunately not sacrificed scent for the sake of size.

WHITE CLEMATIS
The most interesting clematis are usually those that, like *Clematis* 'Henryi', show a marked contrast between the color of the stamens and the petals, here chocolate brown on white.

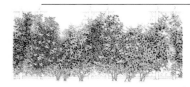

TRAINING *and* PRUNING PLANTS *on a* SCREEN

RELATIVELY FEW CLIMBERS are self-clinging, and all those pictured here need to be fixed securely to supports as they grow. As with all climbing plants, you need to take particular care with the initial training.

The hop dies down in winter, and its stems should be cut back then. When it begins to grow again, it does so with speed and you need to fan out the growths and tie them in. The leaves make a good background to show off the clematis, which rarely have much to boast about by way of foliage.

Climbing roses often flower better if you bend the long growths down toward the horizontal position, making a low, gentle arch of the stem. The hormonal effect this creates along the top of the stem produces more flowering side shoots than would show if you left the stems vertical.

Apart from the architectural qualities of the screen itself, there will be no winter interest in this scheme, but in many ways this is an advantage for it leaves the trellis structure relatively clear each season for maintenance. You can restain the wood when necessary without first having to unpick a forest of greenery.

CARE AND CULTIVATION

SPRING
Mulch all plants liberally. Train hop stems over the trellis, fanning them out as they grow and tying them in securely. Thin out shoots of jasmine and tie in growth as necessary. Plant clematis before growth is too far advanced.

SUMMER
Cut out some of the old stems of the climbing roses and tie in new growths. Spray if necessary against black-spot and mildew. Thin out the honeysuckle if necessary after flowering. Spray against aphids if these become troublesome. Tie in new clematis shoots.

FALL
Plant hops, jasmine, and honeysuckle.

WINTER
Cut down stems of hops. Plant roses in ground that has been well prepared with added organic matter. Check that all ties are secure. Prune *Clematis orientalis* in late winter, cutting stems down to within 18in (45cm) of the ground. The other types of clematis need only light pruning to tidy up some of the brittle, old stems.

Clematis 'Lasurstern'
Vigorous, deciduous climber with large, single, blue flowers in summer. H 6–10ft (2–3m), S 3ft (1m).

Rosa 'Gloire de Dijon'
Climbing tea rose with fragrant, cream-buff flowers in summer–fall. H 12ft (4m), S 8ft (2.5m).

Humulus lupulus 'Aureus' (Golden hop)
Herbaceous, twining climber with rough, hairy stems and golden yellow leaves. Greenish flower spikes are borne in hanging clusters in fall. H to 20ft (6m).

Jasminum officinale (Common jasmine)
Semi-evergreen climber with fragrant white flowers in summer. H to 40ft (12m).

Rosa 'Mme. Alfred Carrière' *Climbing rose with fragrant, cream flowers in summer–fall. H to 18ft (5.5m), S 10ft (3m).*

Clematis orientalis 'Bill Mackenzie' *Vigorous climber with yellow flowers in late summer. H 22ft (7m), S 10–12ft (3–4m).*

Clematis 'Perle d'Azur' *Twining climber with large, azure blue flowers in late summer. H 10ft (3m), S 3ft (1m).*

Lonicera x *americana* (Honeysuckle) *Woody, deciduous climber, with fragrant yellow flowers in summer. H to 22ft (7m).*

Clematis 'Henryi'
Climber bearing large, white blooms with chocolate brown anthers in summer. H 3m (10ft), S 1m (3ft).

ALTERING *the* PLANTING SCHEME

WHEN YOU ARE THINKING OF SUBSTITUTE PLANTS for a delicate trellis screen, avoid rampant climbers such as silver lace vine or passion flower that will smother the entire structure.

Self-clinging plants such as the climbing hydrangea and ivies are best avoided here, too, because they are difficult to remove and may force apart the wooden joinery.

SPLASH OUT FOR SUMMER

For a superabundant show, use the prolific rose 'Veilchenblau' in place of the hops on all four panels and replace the original roses with two leafy grapevines, either green or purple. The pretty parsley-leaved grape, *Vitis vinifera* 'Ciotat', would also work well here. Take out the yellow clematis and replace it with something redder such as 'Ville de Lyon' to tone with the new setting.

Vitis vinifera '**Purpurea**' *Deciduous, woody-stemmed, climbing vine, with purple-bronze foliage. Tiny, pale green flowers appear in summer followed by green or purple berries. H to 22ft (7m).*

Clematis '**Ville de Lyon**' *Deciduous climber covered in midsummer with single, bright carmine red flowers with yellow anthers and darker edged petals. H to 10ft (3m), S 3ft (1m).*

Rosa '**Veilchenblau**' *Vigorous, summer-flowering rambling rose. The violet-pink rosettes are streaked with white and have a fruity scent. H 12ft (4m), S 7ft (2.2m).*

PALE COLORS FOR A COOL EFFECT

By using another background plant to replace the hops, you can change the tone of the color scheme, making it louder or softer. Vertically trained white-variegated euonymus, used with different sweet peas, either annual or perennial, will give a very soft, cool effect, with no yellow.

Euonymus fortunei '**Silver Queen**' *Evergreen shrub with dark green leaves irregularly edged with a broad band of white. H 8ft (2.5m), S 5ft (1.5m).*

Lathyrus odoratus '**Lady Diana**' (**Sweet pea**) *Annual climber with fragrant, pale violet flowers in cool weather. H to 6ft (2m).*

Lathyrus odoratus '**Selana**' (**Sweet pea**) *Vigorous, annual climber with large, scented flowers flushed with pink. H to 6ft (2m).*

A Place *in the* Sun

NEVER WASTE A SHELTERED, sunny wall on rock-solid shrubs such as pyracantha or cotoneaster. You might as well feed caviar to a cart horse. Use the warmest wall in your garden to gamble with plants that are on the borderline of hardiness. Disasters may strike in particularly cold seasons, but the euphoria of the roller-coaster ride in between will more than compensate for any accidents.

TEXTURAL INTEREST
Both flowers and foliage of Acacia dealbata *have appealing textures – the leaves feathery and fernlike, the flowers in fluffy clusters of tiny balls.*

CARE AND CULTIVATION

SPRING
Plant the mimosa in late spring, and put in the eccremocarpus near the mimosa's base. Plant the campsis and cut it back to encourage basal growth.

SUMMER
Water the eccremocarpus in dry spells and remove seedheads as they appear. Tie in new growths of the ceanothus.

FALL
Plant the ceanothus, training the growths flat against the wall. Plant the clematis, setting it at a little distance from the base of the ceanothus.

WINTER
In late winter, cut back the eccremocarpus and prune the clematis. Hard prune established campsis.

CLIMBERS OF FLAMING COLORS
Hot places call for hot colors and this scheme is mostly composed of orange and yellow, with a soothing blue ceanothus to see you through late spring. This same ceanothus will later act as a prop for the scrambling yellow *Clematis tangutica*.

The display will be at its peak in late summer when the climbing trumpet vine, *Campsis* x *tagliabuana* 'Mme. Galen', has started to perform. "Flower" is too tame a word for the event. Its blooms are orange-red trumpets, loud, but not discordant, which hold themselves clear of the well-cut foliage. The buds are held in clusters and open in succession over a long period. Frost eventually snuffs them out. The trumpet vine is

self-clinging, but not in the sturdily tenacious way of ivy. Prudent gardeners should lash it to the wall at regular intervals, to nails or vine eyes, to prevent it from being forced loose by wind in winter.

Flowering at the same time is the clear yellow clematis, which you can allow to ramble at will over the ceanothus. Cut all the stems of the clematis almost to ground level in late winter each year. This will keep it in good condition and also allow the ceanothus to have its space to itself for a while.

Setting fire to the winter-flowering mimosa in summer is another scrambling plant, *Eccremocarpus scaber*, the Chilean glory flower.

BLAZE OF COLOR
In late summer, the star performer is the trumpet vine, its fiery color echoed by the Chilean glory flower and contrasting with the yellow lanterns of the clematis.

PLANT LIST
1 *Acacia dealbata* (Mimosa) x 1
2 *Eccremocarpus scaber* (Chilean glory flower) x 1
3 *Ceanothus impressus* x 1
4 *Clematis tangutica* x 1
5 *Campsis* x *tagliabuana* 'Mme. Galen' (Trumpet vine) x 1

MIMOSA
If the top-growth of *Acacia dealbata* is cut back during a harsh winter, it will often sprout with new growth from the base.

CHILEAN GLORY FLOWER
The usual type of *Eccremocarpus scaber* is orange, but there are also yellow and red forms, all having the same finely cut foliage.

PLANTING PLAN

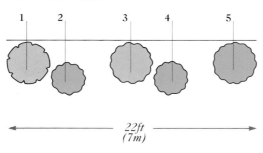

1   2   3   4   5

22ft
(7m)

This often dies back in winter, sprouting afresh from the woody base in spring. If it does not die back naturally, cut it back before the mimosa begins to flower, for nothing should get in the way of that brilliant outburst.

TENDER PLANTS FOR A WARM SPOT

Some varieties of mimosa are hardier than others. Suggested here is the relatively hardy common florists' mimosa, *Acacia dealbata*, but you could experiment equally well with less hardy types such as the Cootamundra wattle, *A. baileyana*, or the Ovens wattle, *A. pravissima*. All have the same key attributes: flowers the color of sunshine, a brave flowering season in late winter and early spring when little else is out, and finely divided, evergreen foliage that hovers on the grayish side of green.

If you have a conservatory rather than a sunny outside wall, you could grow these plants inside instead. The temptation then would be to experiment with even more tender subjects, substituting an ice blue plumbago for the ceanothus and the tender golden trumpet, *Allamanda cathartica*, which has flowers of a glorious butter yellow, for the hardy clematis.

Acacia dealbata **(Mimosa)** *Fast-growing, evergreen tree with feathery leaves and fragrant, yellow flowers in winter–spring. H 25ft (8m), S 6ft (2m).*

Eccremocarpus scaber **(Chilean glory flower)** *Climbing subshrub, often grown as an annual, with orange flowers in summer. H 10ft (3m), S 6ft (2m).*

***Campsis* x *tagliabuana* 'Mme. Galen' (Trumpet vine)** *Deciduous climber with orange flowers in late summer. H to 30ft (10m).*

Clematis tangutica *Climber with yellow flowers through summer and early fall. H 15ft (5m), S 8ft (2.5m).*

Ceanothus impressus *Evergreen shrub with masses of blue flowers from midspring to early summer. H and S 10ft (3m).*

CLEMATIS
The silky seedheads of *Clematis tangutica* are as valuable as its nodding, yellow flowers.

CEANOTHUS
Ceanothus impressus is one of the hardiest of this family, with dark green foliage and flowers of a particularly rich blue.

TRUMPET VINE
The flowering shoots of *Campsis* x *tagliabuana* 'Mme. Galen' hang from self-clinging growths. It needs a warm to hot summer to flower well.

SPIDER'S WEB
*The delicate threads
lacing between the leaf
tips of* Sempervivum
arachnoideum *account
for its unusual common
name of cobweb houseleek.*

CARE AND CULTIVATION

SPRING
Plant the thrift, erigerons,
sempervivums, and
the campanula. Shear
established erigerons
in early spring to tidy
them up before new
growth starts.

SUMMER
Removed faded thrift
and sedum flowerheads.
Cut back trailing growths
of the aubrieta by half.
Tease out dying
flowerheads and rosettes
of sempervivums
where necessary.

FALL
Plant the aubrieta and
sedum. Shear clumps
of campanula to clear
away dead flowers.

WINTER
Birds sometimes dislodge
plants such as sedum
while searching for
insects. Stretch cotton
thread over plants if
necessary to protect them.

A RETAINING WALL

ONLY MOUNTAINEERS CAN UNDERSTAND what it is like to hang spreadeagled on a vertical face of rock. Fortunately, there are more plants willing to adapt to this way of life than people. Aubrietas, thrifts, campanulas, sedums, drabas, lewisias, and arabis will all happily abandon the horizontal habit for the hanging, spilling their flowers over the rocks or stones.

Use a selection of these accommodating alpines to soften a retaining wall. You could also fit them into a boundary wall, or where a low wall runs along a driveway. This scheme could be combined with *Border of Miniatures* (pp.52–55), where alpines are used in a raised bed.

The wall has to be made in such a way that you can squeeze the plants in between the stones or bricks from which it is made. If you are constructing it yourself, leave gaps for planting or, in a dry-stone wall, position the plants as you go. In an existing wall, chip or scrape out mortar or soil to create a home for each plant. Choose small, young specimens for this type of planting. They will fit into smaller holes and will become established more easily than large, mature specimens. Trickle a little gritty soil mix around the roots as you plant.

NATURAL ALPINE PLANTING
Before you begin your planting, study the way nature arranges these things. Natural outcrops of limestone rock, even those as high as 3000m (8220ft), contain an astonishing range of wild alpine plants, trickling down vertical crevices, creeping along ledges. These habitats should be

PLANT LIST
1 *Erigeron karvinskianus*
(Spanish daisy) x 5
2 *Sedum spathulifolium*
'Cape Blanco' x 1
3 *Aubrieta deltoidea*
'Argenteo-variegata' x 1
4 *Sempervivum
arachnoideum* (Cobweb
houseleek) x 3
5 *Armeria maritima*
'Vindictive' (Thrift) x 1
6 *Campanula cochleariifolia*
(Fairy thimbles) x 1

AN UPRIGHT DISPLAY
*This sort of planting is particularly worth trying in a
small garden where horizontal space is in very short
supply. It is also a good way of softening the look of
an obtrusively new wall. The selection of plants used
here would suit a sunny position.*

your copybooks. Most of the plants suggested in this scheme will gradually spread to make large, natural-looking clumps. When you are placing the plants initially, try to avoid too mechanical an effect by varying the distances between the plants on the wall.

The Spanish daisy, *Erigeron karvinskianus*, flowers over a long period, unlike the alpines which tend to peak in spring. Its flowers gradually change color as they age, starting off clear white, then flushing to ever-deeper shades of pink before dropping. If you are lucky, it will begin to seed into the wall, cramming itself in the narrowest of cracks where you could never hope to plant it.

SPANISH DAISY
Although an only slightly refined
version of a lawn weed, *Erigeron
karvinskianus* is a charming wall plant.

EVERGREENS FOR WINTER COLOR

The sedum, sempervivum, aubrieta, and thrift are evergreen, so the wall will not look completely undressed in winter. They will all thrive on the excellent drainage provided by a vertical home. The thrift makes tight hummocks of needle-fine leaves, topped in summer with long-lasting, papery, pink flowers that are held out on fine stems.

Flowers are not such a blessing on the sempervivum for when a rosette flowers, it dies, bequeathing its space to the young baby sempervivums that cluster around the parent plant. The species suggested for this scheme, *Sempervivum arachnoideum*, has webs of fine hair around its leaves, as though it has been worked on by a hyperactive spider.

Aubrietas are one of the most common plants used in garden walls, and for good reason. They are adaptable and easy to grow. Colors range from pink through to a deep purple. The variety suggested for this scheme has variegated leaves and flowers of pinkish lavender.

Erigeron karvinskianus (Spanish daisy) *Spreading perennial with lance-shaped leaves and white flowerheads that turn pink as they age. H 4–6in (10–15cm), S indefinite.*

Sedum spathulifolium 'Cape Blanco' *Evergreen perennial with silvery green, fleshy leaf rosettes and small clusters of tiny, yellow flowers in summer. H 2in (5cm), S indefinite.*

Aubrieta deltoidea 'Argenteo-variegata' *Compact, evergreen perennial with trailing, variegated leaves, and pinkish lavender flowers in spring. H 2in (5cm), S 6in (15cm).*

Sempervivum arachnoideum (Cobweb houseleek) *Evergreen, mat-forming perennial covered with white hairs. H 2–5in (5–12cm), S to 4in (10cm).*

Armeria maritima 'Vindictive' (Thrift) *Evergreen, clump-forming perennial with grasslike leaves, and pink flowers in summer. H 4–6in (10–15cm), S 8in (20cm).*

Campanula cochleariifolia (Fairy thimbles) *Spreading perennial bearing clusters of white, lavender, or pale blue flowers in summer. H 3in (8cm), S indefinite.*

SEDUM
The waxy foliage of *Sedum spathulifolium* 'Cape Blanco' is a year-round asset, spreading slowly to make a dense mat.

AUBRIETA
The leaves of *Aubrieta deltoidea* 'Argenteo-variegata' are thickly splashed with cream.

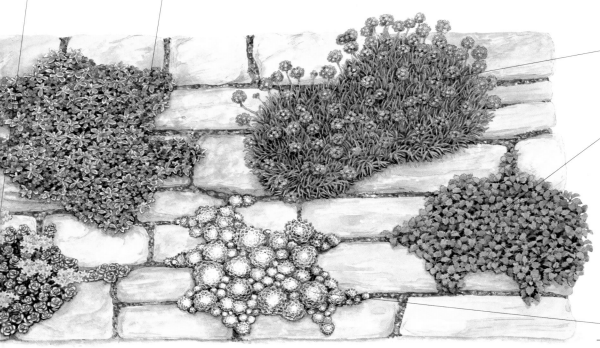

THRIFT
Full sun and good drainage are what this thrift, *Armeria maritima* 'Vindictive', needs to thrive.

FAIRY THIMBLES
Spreading by underground runners, *Campanula cochleariifolia* makes low mats of foliage topped by tiny, thimblelike flowers.

COBWEB HOUSELEEK
All the houseleeks make good wall plants, but *Sempervivum arachnoideum* is particularly intriguing with its web of fine filaments woven among the leaves.

CLIMBING FRAMES

A TRIPOD OR QUADRAPOD planted on its own, or incorporated into a bed or border, acts like a piece of sculpture in the garden. It provides a focal point. A vertical feature also breaks up the extent of a long, straight border in a useful way. Among the soft, humpy, rounded clumps of so many perennial plants, a well-planted tripod becomes a landmark, puncturing the hummocks like a lighthouse at sea.

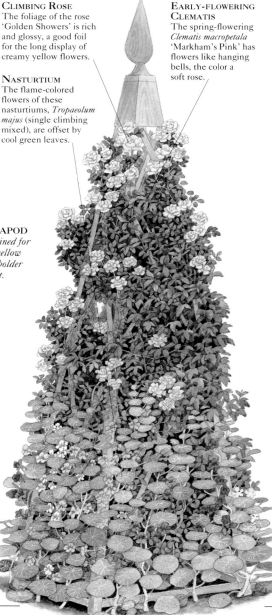

CROCK OF GOLD
With fragrant, yellow blooms that fade to cream, Rosa 'Golden Showers' flowers until late fall and tolerates partial shade.

CARE AND CULTIVATION

SPRING
Mulch all plants liberally. Tie in new growth of roses and honeysuckle. Plant clematis and fan out the shoots as they grow. Sow nasturtiums, raising seeds in pots and setting them out as plants, or sowing directly outside.

SUMMER
Deadhead roses and tie in new growth. Thin out wood on the honeysuckle after flowering. Spray against aphids if necessary.

FALL
Plant the honeysuckle. Prune roses when flowering has finished, untying and cutting out some old, flowered stems and tying in new growth.

WINTER
In late winter or early spring plant roses, cutting them back hard to produce new growth. Prune *Clematis* 'Ascotiensis' to within 18in (45cm) of the ground.

This type of structure draws the eye, perhaps masking something beyond your property line that you would rather not see. In a small space, it gives you extra room for planting. Horizontal spreads in a garden are quickly filled to bursting, but the vertical dimension is often underused.

The style of the structure, as with pergolas and screens, will depend on the style of the garden. In a rustic setting, lash three or four stout poles together and train plants up the poles. In a more formal scheme, use custom-designed structures, made from wrought iron or perhaps from trellis panels topped with decorative finials. Bamboo canes will not do; they look too temporary, too insubstantial.

***Rosa* 'Golden Showers'**
Upright climbing rose with fragrant, yellow blooms in summer–fall. H 6ft (2m), S 7ft (2.2m).

***Tropaeolum majus,* single climbing mixed (Nasturtium)** *Annual with trumpet flowers of red, yellow, or orange from early summer on. H 6ft (2m), S 4ft (1.2m).*

CLIMBERS FOR A QUADRAPOD
In summer, warm colors are combined for a cheering effect. The soft, buttery yellow of the rose is complemented by the bolder shades of the nasturtiums at its feet.

PLANT LIST
1 *Rosa* 'Golden Showers' x 1
2 *Clematis macropetala* 'Markham's Pink' x 1
3 *Tropaeolum majus,* single climbing mixed (Nasturtium) x 11

***Clematis macropetala* 'Markham's Pink'**
Early-flowering clematis with delicate, nodding, mauve-pink flowers in late spring– early summer. H 10ft (3m), S 5ft (1.5m).

CLIMBING ROSE
The foliage of the rose 'Golden Showers' is rich and glossy, a good foil for the long display of creamy yellow flowers.

NASTURTIUM
The flame-colored flowers of these nasturtiums, *Tropaeolum majus* (single climbing mixed), are offset by cool green leaves.

EARLY-FLOWERING CLEMATIS
The spring-flowering *Clematis macropetala* 'Markham's Pink' has flowers like hanging bells, the color a soft rose.

Wooden frames may be painted or, for a softer effect, stained so that the grain of the wood shows through. Frames are often painted black or white but this may look harsh; consider a gentler shade – gray, pale green, dark blue – instead.

LOFTY ASPIRATIONS

Use tripods and similar structures with restraint. Like exclamation marks and ultimatums, they quickly lose their effectiveness if overexploited. Make sure they deserve their prominence. Choose positions and planting with care. In terms of color, plants may either blend or contrast, but they must have the sort of habit that makes them look comfortable trained over a frame.

Old-fashioned rambling and climbing roses adapt well to tripod life. They have a yielding, relaxed habit of growth and many have abundant foliage, too. Steer clear of the stiffer large-flowered bush roses, such as Hybrid Teas and avoid bullies, such as the silver lace vine, and rampant climbing roses such as 'Kiftsgate', which would need a whole forest of tripods to contain it.

The planting for the quadrapod uses the climbing rose 'Golden Showers' with annual nasturtiums, which will continue to flower until the frosts. They are combined with the clematis 'Markham's Pink', an early-flowering variety that will provide spring interest. The tripod, planted in cooler colors, combines the semi-evergreen rose 'Albéric Barbier' with honeysuckle and the late-flowering clematis 'Ascotiensis'.

The fragrant climbing rose 'New Dawn' would make an equally good subject for a tripod, its pink flowers intertwined perhaps with a perennial sweet pea, or a later-flowering purple solanum. Clematis are naturals in this situation of course, but are always better used in company with other plants than on their own.

PLANTING UP A TRIPOD
The rich purple-blue flowers of the clematis make a sumptuous contrast with the creamy blooms of the rose. Fragrance comes from the rose and, in early summer, the honeysuckle. The rose's foliage is semi-evergreen and wonderfully glossy; it continues to provide bulk and textural interest long after its blowsy blooms have faded.

RAMBLING ROSE
Rosa 'Albéric Barbier', raised in France in 1900, is one of the best of the rambling roses with scrolled buds opening to small, creamy flowers.

HONEYSUCKLE
The scent of the early-flowering *Lonicera periclymenum* 'Belgica' is strongest in the evening, pulling in moths to pollinate the flowers.

LATE-FLOWERING CLEMATIS
The clear lavender-blue flowers of *Clematis* 'Ascotiensis' have a central boss of greenish stamens.

PLANT LIST
1 *Rosa* 'Albéric Barbier' × 1
2 *Clematis* 'Ascotiensis' × 1
3 *Lonicera periclymenum* 'Belgica' (Honeysuckle) × 1

Rosa 'Albéric Barbier'
Vigorous, semi-evergreen rambler. Glossy leaves make a foil for soft yellow buds that open to creamy white, scented blooms. H to 15ft (5m), S 10ft (3m).

Lonicera periclymenum 'Belgica' (Honeysuckle)
Deciduous, bushy climber with very fragrant flowers in early to midsummer. H to 22ft (7m).

Clematis 'Ascotiensis'
Late, large-flowered clematis that bears flat, purple-blue flowers in summer. H 10–12ft (3–4m), S 3ft (1m).

WALLS *without* SUN

SHADY WALLS AND FENCES can be clothed as elegantly as sunny ones, provided that the shade is caused by lack of sun, rather than lack of light. You may not get as colorful a display as you could create on a sunny wall, but foliage will grow luxuriantly and plants such as ivy will be far happier here than they would be exposed to the full glare of the sun.

Some walls receive no direct sun at all, though in summer a few slanting beams may drop in at the beginning and the end of the day. At least you know where you are with this kind of wall. Others are far more treacherous. Those that get sun in a burst at the beginning of the day can be fatal to plants frosted overnight: the rapid thaw may rupture the walls of the plant cells.

SERENE PLANTS FOR SHADE
Your star plant on a shady wall or fence will be the climbing hydrangea. Once established, it sticks itself to a wall in the same way as ivy. The leaves are a brilliant fresh green when they first come out and, in some falls, change to a fine clear yellow. It carries large, lacecap heads of creamy white flowers in midsummer.

COOL COLOR
In a partially shaded position, pale flowers such as those of Clematis 'Mrs. George Jackman' *gleam out from the gloom.*

CARE AND CULTIVATION

SPRING
Plant clematis. Deadhead hydrangeas and cut back growths that stray too far from their supports. Prune jasmines, taking out some of the old, flowered wood and tying in new stems that sprout from the base. Mulch all shrubs liberally.

SUMMER
Tie in growths of young hydrangeas. Train clematis through hydrangeas.

FALL
Plant hydrangeas, jasmines, and the ivy.

WINTER
In late winter or early spring, take out any dry stems of clematis that show no signs of breaking into bud. On a house wall, keep the ivy well away from gutters and roof tiles.

PLANT LIST
1 *Jasminum nudiflorum* (Winter jasmine) x 2
2 *Hydrangea anomala* subsp. *petiolaris* x 2
3 *Clematis* 'Mrs. George Jackman' x 1
4 *Hedera helix* 'Glacier' x 1
5 *Clematis* 'Nelly Moser' x 1

PLANTING PLAN

15ft
4.5m
1 2 3 4 5 2 1

SEASONAL CONTINUITY
At the start of summer, the clematis and hydrangeas will flower together but both clematis will continue to flower intermittently through the summer. Then you will have the hydrangeas' fall display followed by the winter flowers of the jasmine.

JASMINE
An indispensible shrub in gardens, *Jasminum nudiflorum* has bright yellow flowers that are particularly welcome in winter.

HYDRANGEA
The climbing *Hydrangea anomala* subsp. *petiolaris* needs moist, cool soil to do its best.

CREAM CLEMATIS
Flowering intermittently from early to late summer, *Clematis* 'Mrs. George Jackman' has creamy flowers with dark brown stamens.

The plant sometimes seems slow to get going; this is because it does not want to risk too much growth until it feels safely attached to something. Secure growths tightly to their supports and if they still will not cling, strain them upward with twine.

The winter-flowering jasmine, *Jasminum nudiflorum*, is common, but for a good reason. Little else chooses to start flowering at the onset of winter and, at that time of the year, its bright yellow flowers are particularly welcome. It cannot hold itself up without support, so is ideal growing in tandem with the hydrangea. This will be bare by the time the jasmine's display starts, and you can tuck the thin green shoots in and around the hydrangea's stouter branches.

Some clematis do well on shady walls; some even prefer them. All appreciate the coolness at their roots. A cultivar such as 'Nelly Moser' keeps its color better in shade than it does in sun. The pale tones of both types of clematis used here will show up far better in shade than would darker types.

IVY
Hedera helix 'Glacier' is a vigorous ivy handsomely variegated in gray-green and white.

PINK CLEMATIS
The early-flowering *Clematis* 'Nelly Moser' has a striking dark bar down the center of each lilac-rose petal.

***Jasminum nudiflorum* (Winter jasmine)** *Deciduous shrub that bears clear yellow flowers on leafless, whippy green shoots in winter and early spring. H and S to 10ft (3m).*

Hydrangea anomala* subsp. *petiolaris *Deciduous climber with frothy heads of white flowers in summer. H to 50ft (15m).*

***Clematis* 'Nelly Moser'** *Early, large-flowered clematis with rose-mauve flowers, each petal striped with dark pink. H to 11ft (3.5m), S 3ft (1m).*

***Hedera helix* 'Glacier' (Ivy)** *Variegated, evergreen climber covered in leaves patterned with gray-green and cream. H 10ft (3m), S 6ft (2m).*

***Clematis* 'Mrs. George Jackman'** *Early, large-flowered clematis that bears creamy white flowers in early summer. H 6–10ft (2–3m), S 3ft (1m).*

FORGOTTEN PLACES

＊

These are the orphans of the garden scene: the area around the garbage cans, the chilly little cliffs between stone steps, the tangle of drains and downspouts that you would like to disguise. Take heart. There are plenty of plants that actually prefer dark, dank corners to bright, sunny ones, and there are plants ample and generous enough to spread their foliage over the most unappetizing patches of your garden.

A POTTED DISGUISE

D RAIN COVERS AND DOWNSPOUTS are not what you want to see when you step out into your garden for a quick gulp of spiritual renewal. This exuberantly planted pot provides an excellent disguise for all kinds of necessary but ugly underpinnings of house and garden. Stand the pot on top of a drain cover or use it in a corner to camouflage a downspout and turn plumbing into paradise.

UNFURLING FANS
The leaves of Melianthus major *unfold from tightly pleated fans into sprays of jagged-edged leaflets. It is the most sumptuous plant ever invented.*

CARE AND CULTIVATION

SPRING
In midspring, plant up the pot using fresh soil mix. Harden off plants before setting the pot outside.

SUMMER
Deadhead the argyranthemum. Remove any dead leaves and nip back plants such as the helichrysum, which may try to swamp the others. Feed and water regularly.

FALL
Move the pot under cover before severe frosts set in. Overwinter mature plants or take cuttings each year and raise new ones. The phormium will last many years. The helichrysum, pelargonium, and argyranthemum are best raised fresh each spring.

WINTER
If retaining mature plants in the pot, keep them cool and make sure the soil mix is on the dry side.

This sort of gesture has to look as though you mean it. You do not want the pot to seem as though it has accidentally fallen off somebody else's delivery truck. Use a big container, 2ft (60cm) across at least, but remember that this display must remain a moveable feast: if your plumbing acts up, you may have to investigate.

PLANTS FOR SPECTACLE AND SUBSTANCE
For maximum value, you need plants that give width as well as height so that they can mask problems that are both fat and tall. This is why the melianthus, the phormium, and the helichrysum will be your three best friends. Use a dark-leaved phormium, not one of the six-foot monsters, but something compact like 'Bronze Baby' or 'Tom Thumb'. The other

ingredients should be equally bold and leafy. *Begonia fuchsioides* is a winner with dark, glossy leaves and red bell-flowers just like those of a fuchsia. Weaving between these you could use a pelargonium, perhaps a variegated one as here, or one with scented, dark foliage, such as 'Chocolate Peppermint', or both. Include at least one free-flowering plant among all this leafy bulk: a daisy-flowered argyranthemum would be ideal.

All these plants are tender. If you have a sheltered porch, a greenhouse, or a conservatory, plant the pot up in spring and keep it there until the danger of late frost has passed. Harden off the plants gradually, then, in early summer, you can stagger out with your pot already well furnished. In winter, you will have to put up with the sight of the drain covers, or design a different disguise.

Melianthus major (**Honeybush**) *Evergreen shrub with large, glaucous leaves and brownish red flowers. H and S to 6ft (2m).*

Argyranthemum gracile '**Chelsea Girl**' *Evergreen subshrub with gray-green foliage and daisy flowers. H and S to 2½ft (75cm).*

Pelargonium crispum '**Variegatum**'
Perennial with cream-variegated leaves. H 3ft (1m), S 18in (45cm).

Helichrysum petiolare
Evergreen shrub with trailing, silver stems and gray, felted leaves. H 12in (30cm), S to 5ft (1.5m).

Phormium tenax '**Bronze Baby**'
Perennial with stiff, bronze, swordlike leaves. H and S to 2ft (60cm).

Begonia fuchsioides
Evergreen, shrublike begonia with hanging, red flowers. H to 4ft (1.2m), S 12in (30cm).

Plant List

1 *Melianthus major* (Honeybush) x 1
2 *Argyranthemum gracile* 'Chelsea Girl' x 1
3 *Pelargonium crispum* 'Variegatum' x 1
4 *Helichrysum petiolare* x 1
5 *Phormium tenax* 'Bronze Baby' x 1
6 *Begonia fuchsioides* x 1

Small-scale Planting

A container scheme is like a bed in miniature, and the same design considerations of shape, color, and texture apply.

Begonia
Although not as showy as the large-flowered members of its family, *Begonia fuchsioides* is an elegant plant with hanging, fuchsialike flowers.

Phormium
The stiffly vertical habit of *Phormium tenax* 'Bronze Baby' provides an excellent contrast to low-growing mounds of pelargonium.

Helichrysum
One of the most widely used foliage plants in tubs and containers, *Helichrysum petiolare* spins a web of gray leaves around the other plants in the group.

Pelargonium
Pelargonium crispum 'Variegatum' is valued for its cream-marked leaves, which are more important than its small flowers.

Honeybush
Gray-green, deeply serrated leaves are the chief attraction of *Melianthus major*. Nothing else has foliage that can match it.

Argyranthemum
'Chelsea Girl' is a white-flowered cultivar of *Argyranthemum gracile* with particularly good foliage, gray-green and finely cut.

131

PATIO PLANTING

CARE AND CULTIVATION

SPRING
Set all the plants in pockets of good soil mix mixed with some grit to improve drainage. Thymes and phloxes do best in an open, sunny position. The acaena will tolerate partial shade as will the violas and the purple-leaved clover.

SUMMER
Shear off dead flowerheads of thymes to keep plants compact. Leave some seedheads on violas so that they can seed themselves randomly into cracks in the paving.

FALL
Clear away fallen leaves that lodge among the mats of foliage.

WINTER
No routine care is required.

PATIO IS A TERM USED BY SOME REAL ESTATE AGENTS to describe any collection of paving stones vaguely adjacent to a house. Builders like to include patios because they give an illusion of order to a new house. Less reputable ones may shove all the junk that should never be left behind into the area near the back door and then drop concrete slabs on top as they leave the site. A few low mats of plants growing in between the paving stones can go a long way toward softening a new and barren patio.

Growing plants in between paving is not everybody's idea of how such an area should be treated. Some people like to keep patios clear of all plants, so that they can be more easily swept and kept clean – and treated with weedkiller. If you are not one of those, read on. While you are reading, work out how you might fit the plants in between the slabs or stones. You will probably have to chip away a corner to make enough space. The builders may inadvertently have done this for you already. Treat it as a bonus rather than a black mark.

AROMATIC CREEPERS
The plants you choose should all have a low, spreading habit and should be able to survive the occasional shock of a foot crashing down on their heads. Choose colors that complement the background color of the patio paving, whether this is stone, brick, or concrete.

Aromatic plants such as creeping thymes are very useful in this context. Far from sulking when trodden on, they give you the extra bonus

PLANT LIST
1 *Thymus serpyllum* 'Coccineus' x 1
2 *Trifolium repens* 'Purpurascens' (Purple-leaved clover) x 1
3 *Acaena microphylla* (New Zealand bur) x 1
4 *Viola tricolor* (Heartsease) x 4
5 *Phlox douglasii* 'Boothman's Variety' x 1
6 *Thymus serpyllum* 'Snowdrift' x 1

SITING PATIO PLANTS
Before you decide where to place your plants, consider access points to the patio and where you are likely to position garden furniture or plants in urns or tubs. If the patio is large enough, you could remove one or two entire slabs to provide more planting space.

of scent. *Thymus serpyllum* is the most common form of creeping thyme, perfect for paving cracks. There is a particularly good variety called 'Pink Chintz', which has gray-green leaves spangled with tiny, pale pink flowers. You could, if you wished, create a whole scheme using only *T. serpyllum*, for there are ground-hugging varieties with white and deep red flowers as well as the pink. *Thymus caespititius* has a similar habit.

CRIMSON THYME
The creeping stems of *Thymus serpyllum* 'Coccineus' are spangled with deep pinkish red flowers.

Viola tricolor

COLORFUL CARPET

The little New Zealand bur, *Acaena microphylla*, has no noticeable scent but like the thyme is evergreen and comes into its own in fall and winter when decorative, tawny red burs develop from the summer flowers. Creeping alpine phloxes adapt well to life between paving stones and, like the thymes, come in a wide variety of colors – pinks, mauves, and white. One of the lowest growing is *Phlox douglasii* 'Boothman's Variety', which has pale lavender flowers in early summer. Each flower has a prominent eye, surrounded by blotches of a deeper violet-blue. For a fiercer splash of color, try *P. d.* 'Crackerjack', which has magenta flowers.

Plants cannot grow in the plastic sacks, ancient newspapers, and solidified cement powder that often seem to make up the foundations of patio. Excavate this detritus and substitute decent soil mix. A good start will see the plants through a great deal of subsequent neglect.

Thymus serpyllum **'Coccineus'** *Creeping shrub with scented, green leaves and crimson flowers. H 3in (8cm), S 8in (20cm).*

Trifolium repens **'Purpurascens' (Purple-leaved clover)** *Ground cover perennial. H 3in (8cm), S 12in (30cm).*

Acaena microphylla **(New Zealand bur)** *Mat-forming perennial with decorative fall burs. H 2in (5cm), S 6in (15cm).*

Viola tricolor **(Heartsease)** *Short-lived perennial or annual with flowers in combinations of white, yellow, and purple. H and S 2–6in (5–15cm).*

Phlox douglasii **'Boothman's Variety'** *Evergreen perennial with masses of pale lavender flowers. H to 2in (5cm), S 8in (20cm).*

Thymus serpyllum **'Snowdrift'** *Creeping shrub with small, faintly scented, bright green leaves and white flowers. H 3in (8cm), S 8in (20cm).*

PHLOX
The pretty flowers of *Phlox douglasii* 'Boothman's Variety' have prominent dark eyes.

PURPLE-LEAVED CLOVER
Each bronze clover leaf of *Trifolium repens* 'Purpurascens' is edged with brilliant green. Small pealike flowers are produced throughout summer.

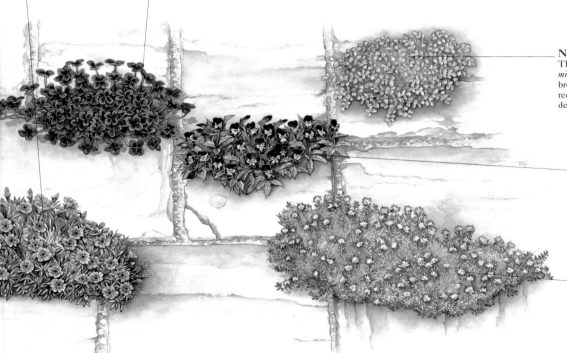

NEW ZEALAND BUR
The leaves of *Acaena microphylla* are tinged with bronze when young. It bears red summer bracts that develop into attractive burs.

HEARTSEASE
Equally easy in sun or part shade, the charming pansy flowers of *Viola tricolor* are produced over a long season.

WHITE THYME
Dwarf and delightfully aromatic, *Thymus serpyllum* 'Snowdrift' is covered all summer with white flowers.

WINTER WONDERS
The flower cups of winter aconites, Eranthis hyemalis, *form a golden carpet from late winter to early spring.*

CARE AND CULTIVATION

SPRING

Plant ferns, watering them in well. As new fronds unfurl, cut away old, tattered fronds. Plant crocosmias. In succeeding years, cut down dead foliage in early spring. Plant winter aconites "in the green" if available. Once the aconites have finished, plant pansies.

SUMMER

Clip boxwood to shape in late summer. Keep soil around ferns moist. Deadhead pansies regularly; shear over in late summer to rejuvenate foliage.

FALL

Plant boxwood now or in spring, adding bone meal to the soil. Plant cyclamen, barely covering the tubers, and winter aconites if unavailable in spring.

WINTER

No routine care is required.

A NARROW STRIP

EVERY TEXTBOOK ON GARDEN DESIGN warns against the problems of the too narrow border. You lose the balance between a border's width and its length. You lose the opportunity to build up contrasting groups of plants. Flowers look as if they have been lined up for the school photograph. Sometimes, however, it is narrow or nothing. When you have little room to maneuver, make a virtue out of necessity and exploit the linear possibilities of a thin strip of ground.

COMBINATIONS OF FORM

This scheme suggests a line of evergreen boxwood, cut into alternating cones and balls, which can march single file along the whole length of the border. Setting out a bold single row like this gets around the problem of trying to shoehorn tiers of plants into insufficient space.

The way that you fill in the spaces between the boxwood plants will depend on the amount of space you have to play with and whether the border is backed by a wall. This scheme would be ideal for a narrow strip of ground running between a path and a wall or fence. Shade will suit it even better than sun.

At the foot of a backing wall, try evergreen hart's-tongue ferns, *Phyllitis scolopendrium*, perhaps planted alternately with crocosmia. The shiny, strap-shaped leaves of the ferns contrast well with the boxwoods' fussy foliage and the dramatic, sword leaves of the crocosmia, which have deeply incised veins running from leaf tip to base. Some hart's tongues explode into bizarre forms, the fronds endlessly subdividing until they look like bunches of parsley.

Form in this border is more important than color, but there will be a brilliant explosion of red from the arching flower stems of the crocosmia in summer. Choose a cultivar such as 'Lucifer' that is both vigorous and pleasingly violent in its tone. There is nothing worse in a garden than an apologetic red.

COLOR WASHING

Use bulbs to provide washes of color at different seasons in any spaces left between the boxwood shapes. Start with aconites, because they are cheering in late winter and their clear, bright yellow flowers will contrast well with the somber bulwarks of the boxwood.

The plan here shows the aconites marching in a thin line in front of the boxwood, but they could equally well be used in blocks between the boxwood bushes. They die down completely by midspring so will not get in the way of later

PLANTING PLAN

| 1 | 4 | 6 | 4 | 5 | 4 | 6 | 4 | 5 | 1 |

| 2 | 3 | 1 | 2 | 3 | 1 | 2 | 3 | 1 | 2 | 3 | 1 | 2 | 3 | 1 | 2 | 3 |

15ft
5m

PLANT LIST

1 *Cyclamen hederifolium* var. *album* x 12
2 *Viola* Clear Crystals Series (Pansy) x 10
3 *Eranthis hyemalis* (Winter aconites) x 30
4 *Buxus sempervirens* (Boxwood) x 5
5 *Crocosmia* 'Lucifer' x 2
6 *Phyllitis scolopendrium*
   (Hart's-tongue fern) x 2

HART'S-TONGUE FERN
The broad, leathery, strap-shaped fronds of *Phyllitis scolopendrium* provide interest all year.

WINTER ACONITE
In the wild, *Eranthis hyemalis* grows in woods, so it is well adapted, if necessary, to shady positions in the garden.

bulb displays. Remember that aconites, if possible, should be planted "in the green," just after they have finished flowering. Dried bulbs, sold in late summer, do not establish so easily.

Snowdrops would be equally good for the first spring display, if you do not have them elsewhere. Like other white flowers, they look particularly cool and elegant with dark green foliage all around. Or you can wait for your white until early fall and plant blocks of white *Cyclamen hederifolium* between the boxwood bushes. The shuttlecock flowers are followed by intricately marbled leaves.

There remains only the choice of a flower to tide you over between the aconites and the cyclamen. Choose pansies or violas, but stick to a single shade. You are color washing between the boxwood bushes and need to keep the overall effect simple and clean.

Buxus sempervirens (Boxwood) *Dense evergreen shrub with small, glossy, dark green leaves. H and S to 4ft (1.2m).*

Crocosmia 'Lucifer' *Clump-forming corm with sword-shaped leaves and red flower spikes. H to 4ft (1.2m), S to 10in (25cm).*

Phyllitis scolopendrium (Hart's-tongue fern) *Evergreen fern with tonguelike fronds. H 2½ft (75cm), S 18in (45cm).*

Eranthis hyemalis (Winter aconite) *Tuber bearing yellow flowers, each with a rufflike bract. H and S to 4in (10cm).*

Cyclamen hederifolium var. **album** *Tuber with white flowers in fall and marbled leaves. H to 4in (10cm), S 6in (15cm).*

Viola Clear Crystals Series (Pansy) *Perennial, grown as an annual, with summer flowers. H 6–8in (15–20cm), S 8in (20cm).*

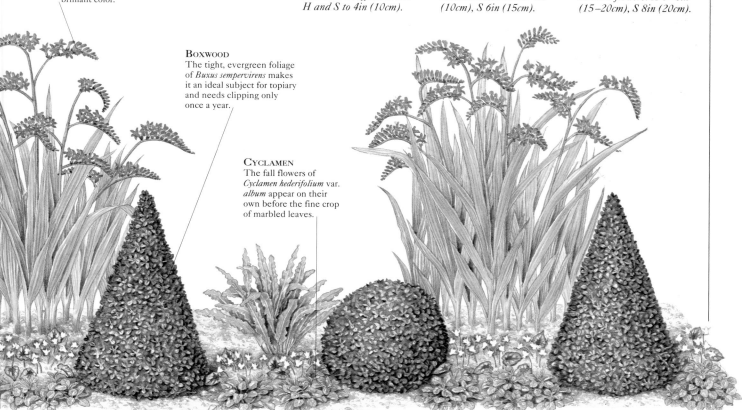

CROCOSMIA
The magnificent flowers of *Crocosmia* 'Lucifer' light up late summer with their brilliant color.

BOXWOOD
The tight, evergreen foliage of *Buxus sempervirens* makes it an ideal subject for topiary and needs clipping only once a year.

CYCLAMEN
The fall flowers of *Cyclamen hederifolium* var. *album* appear on their own before the fine crop of marbled leaves.

BETWEEN *the* STEPS

T HE NEAT-AND-TIDY, no-mess, no-rough-edges brigade will not want any plants to clutter up the carefully swept and weedkilled expanses of their steps and paths. Those with a more relaxed attitude to gardening may like to experiment with some of the plants suggested in this scheme for planting in the vertical spaces between the treads.

FLESHY FOLIAGE
The fleshy, spoon-shaped leaves of Sedum kamtschaticum *'Variegatum' have a subtle shine and are edged with a contrasting border of cream.*

CARE AND CULTIVATION

SPRING
Plant ferns in damp weather any time between midspring and early fall, incorporating leaf mold in the planting mix.

SUMMER
Cut out the faded flowerheads of the euphorbia, saxifrages, and sedums.

FALL
Plant the euphorbia, saxifrages, and sedums, incorporating grit if the soil is heavy and damp.

WINTER
Clear away any dead fern fronds in late winter before the new fronds emerge.

In some cases, of course, there are no spaces. Some steps are so firmly underpinned and anchored with cement and crushed stone, you would need a pickaxe to plant even a seed. These are probably best left alone. Other steps are more accommodating. You may be able to ease out a few bricks from the risers. There may be cracks already there that you can utilize.

The easiest steps to plant between are those that are laid directly on soil, with the soil left uncovered between the different levels. These are the sort of steps you might have on an informal path winding its way up a bank between flower borders on either side.

SELECTING LEAFY PLANTS
Only certain sorts of plant will do in this situation. They must not grow too big, so that they trip you up, or obscure the path. They must not be so invasive that they make takeover bids for the territory on either side of the steps, and they must be plants that can take advantage of the cool root run underneath the steps.

PLANT LIST
1 *Asplenium trichomanes* (Maidenhair spleenwort) x 4
2 *Euphorbia cyparissias* x 1
3 *Ceterach officinarum* (Rusty-back fern) x 3
4 *Saxifraga moschata* 'Cloth of Gold' (Saxifrage) x 2
5 *Sedum kamtschaticum* 'Variegatum' x 4
6 *Sedum obtusatum* x 2

PLANTING PLAN

Planting must be simple. Two different plants is the most that you should use on each riser. If you use more, the effect will be messy and the steps will look too busy and cluttered. Choose plants for their leaves rather than their flowers. There is nothing better than foliage to soften the hard corners of overaggressive masonry.

Small ferns are ideal and relish this kind of position where, even if they are in full sun, their roots are luxuriating in the cool, damp soil under the steps. The small rusty-back fern, *Ceterach officinarum*, would fit in well. So would the maidenhair spleenwort, *Asplenium trichomanes*, or, on acid soil, the parsley fern, *Cryptogramma crispa*.

SCULPTURAL STEPS
The hard, architectural lines of a flight of steps provide a sculptural setting for the lush fronds of ferns and the airy flower sprays of a euphorbia.

MAIDENHAIR SPLEENWORT
One of the most elegant ferns, *Asplenium trichomanes* enjoys the cool root run found beneath the treads of steps.

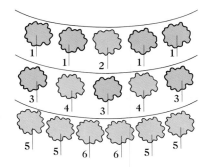

VARIEGATED SEDUM
The fleshy leaves of *Sedum kamtschaticum* 'Variegatum' are edged with cream.

SUN AND SHADE

If the steps lead from shade into sun, plant the ferns in the shade, which they will prefer. Try the rusty-back fern or a miniature polypody, such as *Polypodium polypodioides* or the taller but hardier *P. virginianum*, with one of the dwarf euphorbias, such as *Euphorbia cyparissias*. This euphorbia can be overenthusiastic, but is very easy to pull out if you see it pushing its nose where it is not wanted. The feathery plumes of leaves are joined by brilliant lime green flowers in late spring. Use the spleenwort alongside a soft, mossy saxifrage. *Saxifraga moschata* 'Cloth of Gold' has rosettes of fine, golden foliage and, like the ferns, prefers some shade.

If planting in a sunnier set of steps, use a couple of sedums, choosing between low, fleshy kinds, such as *Sedum kamtschaticum* 'Variegatum', or *S. spathulifolium* 'Cape Blanco', which has neat rosettes that are gray-green, sometimes suffused with purple. *S. obtusatum* has fat leaves that turn a lustrous bronze-red in summer. Sempervivums such as *Sempervivum arachnoideum*, which is covered in a cobweb of fine white hairs, would be equally suitable companions.

Asplenium trichomanes (Maidenhair spleenwort) *Semi-evergreen fern. H 6in (15cm), S to 12in (30cm).*

Euphorbia cyparissias *Leafy perennial with a mass of slender, gray-green leaves and lime green flowers. H and S 12in (30cm).*

Ceterach officinarum (Rusty-back fern) *Semi-evergreen fern with lance-shaped, dark green fronds. H and S 6in (15cm).*

Saxifraga moschata 'Cloth of Gold' (Saxifrage) *Evergreen with white flowers. H 6in (15cm), S 12in (30cm).*

Sedum kamtschaticum 'Variegatum' *Semi-evergreen perennial with orange-yellow flowers. H to 3in (8cm), S 8in (20cm).*

Sedum obtusatum *Evergreen perennial with small, succulent leaves that turn bronze-red in summer. H 2in (5cm), S 6in (15cm).*

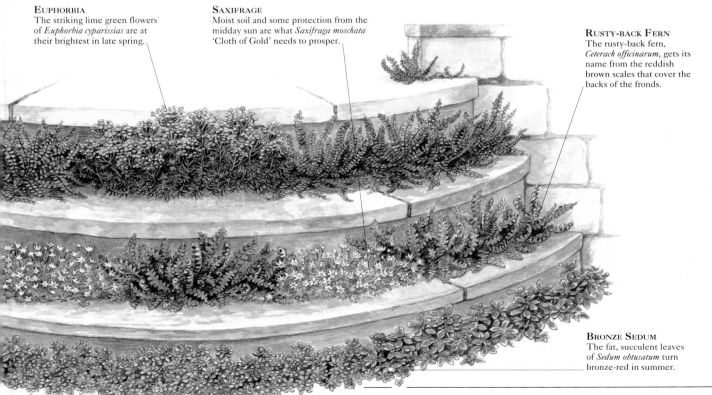

EUPHORBIA
The striking lime green flowers of *Euphorbia cyparissias* are at their brightest in late spring.

SAXIFRAGE
Moist soil and some protection from the midday sun are what *Saxifraga moschata* 'Cloth of Gold' needs to prosper.

RUSTY-BACK FERN
The rusty-back fern, *Ceterach officinarum*, gets its name from the reddish brown scales that cover the backs of the fronds.

BRONZE SEDUM
The fat, succulent leaves of *Sedum obtusatum* turn bronze-red in summer.

A STONY PATCH

THERE ARE TWO THINGS you can do with a dry, stony patch in your garden: set about removing all the stones by hand (the sort of job you usually find a good reason never to finish) or accept what fate has thrown at you and fill the area with plants that eat stone for breakfast. If you take the latter course, you will save yourself a great deal of backbreaking work and can also congratulate yourself on your ecological correctness.

IDEAL FOR CUTTING
The single, yellow blooms of Chrysanthemum segetum, *which appear in summer and early fall, make excellent cut flowers.*

CARE AND CULTIVATION

SPRING
Plant the artemisia, rosemary, and ceratostigma. In subsequent years, prune out leggy or frosted growths where necessary. Sow chrysanthemum seed in trays under cover and, later, prick out seedlings. Plant out as soon as all danger of frost has passed.

SUMMER
Deadhead plants as necessary.

FALL
Remove faded flower stems from the artemisia in early fall. Plant asphodels and Welsh poppies.

WINTER
Cut back seedheads of asphodels in late winter.

There are plenty of plants that will positively enjoy this kind of well-drained billet, however unpromising it may look to you. They are the ones that you might find growing on the hillsides of the Mediterranean, or covering the slopes of the mountains of Eastern Turkey. Like these natural habitats, the site for this scheme needs to be open and sunny.

Soil that is packed with pebbles and stones will be very free draining. The most difficult period for the plants introduced here will be the initial one, immediately after planting. You will need to mulch and water assiduously until they are established and have sent their roots running deep underground in search of food and drink.

Do not try to make a formal edge to a patch such as this. The edges should be irregular and blend gently with the adjoining land. It should look like a small piece of mountainside, come to rest in your back yard. Enhance the effect by adding more gravel and pebbles, making a complete top-dressing of stone.

PLANT LIST
1 *Ceratostigma plumbaginoides* x 1
2 *Artemisia abrotanum* (Southernwood) x 1
3 *Chrysanthemum segetum* x 22
4 *Meconopsis cambrica* (Welsh poppy) x 22
5 *Rosmarinus officinalis* 'Severn Sea' (Rosemary) x 2
6 *Asphodeline lutea* (Yellow asphodel) x 5

A DISPLAY FOR DRY GROUND
A piece of dry, stony ground is transformed from an eyesore into an eye-catching display with hot-colored flowers complemented by cool blues and gray.

WELSH POPPY
Though a determined self-seeder, *Meconopsis cambrica* bears welcome poppy flowers of sharp lemon or brilliant orange.

SPLASHES OF SUNNY YELLOWS
The bulk of this small scheme is provided by three plants: feathery artemisia, which makes an ever-gray mound of foliage; aromatic rosemary, studded with blue flowers; and the blue-flowered *Ceratostigma plumbaginoides*, which peaks at the end of summer. Lavender, with its aromatic foliage and flowers, would be equally suitable.

CERATOSTIGMA
The bushy *Ceratostigma plumbaginoides* has blue flowers and leaves that turn red in fall.

Under this low canopy, you can spread carpets of yellow. Use the Welsh poppy, *Meconopsis cambrica*, for its long season of silky flowers. It seeds itself about with abandon, but in a rough site such as this, you will be glad of anything that is so willing to do its best.

Add height with spires of asphodel, which has grassy, blue-gray leaves and, in late spring, is covered with starry, yellow flowers. The seed spikes remain a feature long after the flowers have finished – leave them on the plants to add interest in winter.

To fill in at the end of the summer season, try a late-flowering annual, such as *Chrysanthemum segetum*, which will get into its stride as the poppies are finishing. This has small, bright yellow, daisy flowers on neat bushes, the flowers held on stout, stiff stems. There is little by way of foliage, but you will still have the poppy and the asphodel lending their leaves, as well as the foliage and flowers of the shrubs.

SOUTHERNWOOD
The stiff, erect stems of *Artemisia abrotanum* are clothed with lacy, aromatic foliage, which is unfortunately not evergreen.

Ceratostigma plumbaginoides Bushy perennial with blue flowers on reddish stems. H 12in (30cm), S 18in (45cm).

Artemisia abrotanum (Southernwood) Semi-evergreen shrub with yellow flowers and aromatic leaves. H and S 2½ft (75cm).

Chrysanthemum segetum Erect annual bearing daisylike, yellow flowers. H 18in (45cm), S 12–18in (30–45cm).

Meconopsis cambrica (Welsh poppy) Perennial with yellow-orange blooms and fernlike foliage. H to 18in (45cm), S 12in (30cm).

Rosmarinus officinalis 'Severn Sea' (Rosemary) Evergreen shrub with blue flowers. H to 12in (30cm), S 4ft (1.1m).

Asphodeline lutea (Yellow asphodel) Neat perennial that bears star-shaped, yellow flowers. H to 4ft (1.2m), S to 3ft (1m).

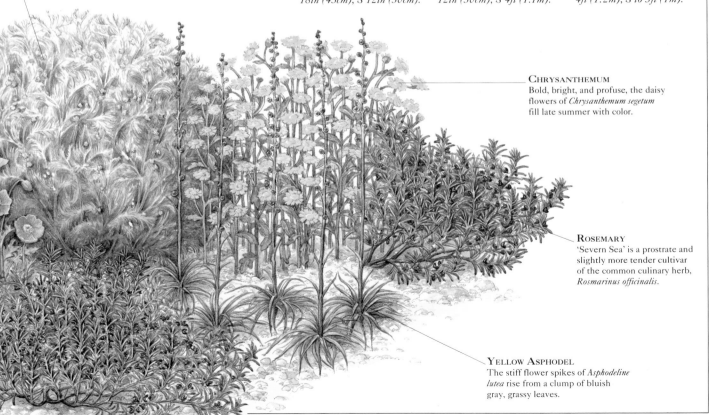

CHRYSANTHEMUM
Bold, bright, and profuse, the daisy flowers of *Chrysanthemum segetum* fill late summer with color.

ROSEMARY
'Severn Sea' is a prostrate and slightly more tender cultivar of the common culinary herb, *Rosmarinus officinalis*.

YELLOW ASPHODEL
The stiff flower spikes of *Asphodeline lutea* rise from a clump of bluish gray, grassy leaves.

OCCASIONAL POTS

ASPHALT AND CONCRETE have a disagreeable way of commandeering important places in a garden where we would much prefer to see flowers and foliage: directly outside the kitchen window, along the side of the garage, around a garden seat. In these situations, where there is little or no soil, pots and other containers packed with plants are your greatest allies.

WELL CONTAINED
Spectacular in the border, lilies also make striking container plants. Lilium 'Enchantment' *will grow in sun or partial shade.*

CARE AND CULTIVATION

SPRING
Set out pelargoniums and the aeonium once all risk of frost has passed. Sow nasturtiums in the pot in which they will grow outside. Plant pittosporum; trim any straggly shoots as needed in late spring.

SUMMER
Deadhead pelargoniums. Keep lilies well fed and watered.

FALL
Lift pelargoniums, cut them back, and overwinter in a frost-free greenhouse or shed. Or overwinter cuttings instead. Plant lilies as soon as available, setting them well down in the pots. Keep under cover until top-growth appears in spring.

WINTER
Overwinter the aeonium on a cool windowsill indoors. Do not overwater.

In *A Potted Disguise* (pp.130–131) half a dozen plants are used all together in one large pot to conceal downspouts and covers. Here, groups are built up by using plants in individual pots. You can mix and match the plants as you like to suit the time of year and the available space.

The advantage of growing plants in this way is that it is flexible and you can move particular ones out of the scheme when they are past their best. When the lilies' performance is over, for example, trundle them off to die down away from the limelight and move in another potted performer to take their place.

TAILOR-MADE PLANTING
Using collections of pots means that you can arrange them to fit any kind of space, whatever its shape. In a deep, narrow corner, you might use a potted evergreen to provide a backdrop to lilies and pelargoniums. By the front door, keep an ever-changing array of plants to reflect the seasons: camellias and early crocus giving way to scented-leaved pelargoniums, summer-flowering annuals, then neat winter evergreens.

Planting should always be adapted to suit a particular situation. Some plants, such as the golden Japanese maple, *Acer japonicum* 'Aureum', scorch in full sun. Use this as the backdrop to pots of scented, white regal lilies and lime *Alchemilla mollis* in a shady spot. White is always most effective when glowing from dark, shady corners.

This scheme uses brilliant flowers to sing out from a bare, concreted space, perhaps along the garage. Hot colors suit hot spots and here there are bold orange lilies, rising behind pots of the dark-leaved pelargonium 'Mme. Fournier'. This is a compact cultivar with clear red flowers, but any red pelargonium with dark foliage would be effective. If you want to use a pink type such as 'The Boar', which also has fine leaves, sharply zoned with a dark, central blotch, use different lilies: white or perhaps dark-flowered ones such as the crimson 'Empress of India'. Do not use

the tallest kinds, which would need staking in a pot. In a separate container, grow nasturtiums or pot marigolds, *Calendula officinalis*.

An evergreen gives substance to the group. This could be a clipped cone or sphere of boxwood, or a shrub such as osmanthus, variegated euonymus, or pittosporum. If planted in the open ground these may become large shrubs. In pots, growth will be curtailed, and you can clip and snip to keep them in shape.

YELLOW LILY
Lilium 'Destiny' somtimes bears as many as ten flowers on a stem, each with petals curling back at the tip.

NASTURTIUM
Tropaeolum majus 'Alaska' is an unusual nasturtium, its leaves heavily marbled with white.

HARMONIOUS GROUP

When grouping containers, combine plants of contrasting form and habit to create a balanced display. Use upright plants for vertical emphasis and trailing plants for an informal, relaxed effect and to soften the hard lines of the pots.

PITTOSPORUM

The black stems of *Pittosporum tenuifolium* contrast well with the light green, wavy leaves.

AEONIUM

Aeonium arboreum 'Schwarzkopf' is a lustrous dark succulent, but it is tender.

ORANGE LILY

The bright orange-red flowers of *Lilium* 'Enchantment' appear in early summer.

PLANT LIST

1 *Lilium* 'Enchantment' (Lily) x 9
2 *Tropaeolum majus* 'Alaska' (Nasturtium) x 15
3 *Pittosporum tenuifolium* x 1
4 *Pelargonium* 'Mme. Fournier' x 5
5 *Lilium* 'Destiny' (Lily) x 9
6 *Aeonium arboreum* 'Schwarzkopf' x 1

PELARGONIUM

Pelargonium 'Mme. Fournier' is a zonal pelargonium with brilliant scarlet flowers offset by dark leaves.

Lilium 'Enchantment' (Lily) *Early summer-flowering bulb that bears upward-facing, orange-red flowers with black-spotted throats. H 3ft (1m), S to 12in (30cm).*

Tropaeolum majus 'Alaska' (Nasturtium) *Annual with variegated leaves and trumpet-shaped, orange or yellow flowers in summer and early fall. H and S 12in (30cm).*

Pittosporum tenuifolium *Evergreen shrub with wavy-edged, oval, glossy, mid-green leaves, bearing honey-scented, purple flowers in late spring. H and S 4ft (1.2m).*

Pelargonium 'Mme. Fournier' *Tender perennial with almost black leaves and small, single, scarlet flowers. H 6–8in (15–20cm), S 4in (10cm).*

Lilium 'Destiny' (Lily) *Early summer-flowering bulb that bears upward-facing, cup-shaped, yellow flowers spotted with brown. H 3–4ft (1–1.2m), S to 12in (30cm).*

Aeonium arboreum 'Schwarzkopf' *Bushy, perennial succulent with stems each crowned by a rosette of long, spoon-shaped leaves of blackish purple. H to 2ft (60cm), S 3ft (1m).*

SPLENDOR *in the* GRASS

GRASS IN A GARDEN DOES NOT HAVE TO BE CUT every week. Once you grasp hold of this revolutionary notion, new possibilities open up on every side. Instead of toiling with a mower to shave grass off steep banks and awkward, tree-bound corners, allow the grass to grow tall. In orchards, or at the edge of a lawn where it meets countryside beyond, let the herbage grow under your feet. Mow wide paths through it. Contrast areas of mown and unmown turf.

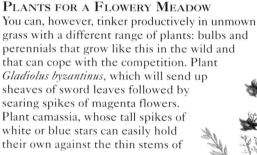

Do not suppose, however, that you can persuade poppies and cornflowers to flutter beguilingly among the feathery grasses of your backyard meadow. Poppies and cornflowers will leap up brightly in the first year if sown on freshly prepared bare soil, but they are annuals, lasting only one year, and they favor newly disturbed ground. This is why they like cornfields, where, after a neck-and-neck race with the corn, they seed themselves, ready to bob up after the next round of plowing. Where grass is permanently established, as in an orchard, poppies die out.

PLANTS FOR A FLOWERY MEADOW

You can, however, tinker productively in unmown grass with a different range of plants: bulbs and perennials that grow like this in the wild and that can cope with the competition. Plant *Gladiolus byzantinus*, which will send up sheaves of sword leaves followed by searing spikes of magenta flowers. Plant camassia, whose tall spikes of white or blue stars can easily hold their own against the thin stems of

grasses. Both of these will establish more easily if you put them in as growing plants (if available) rather than dry bulbs. Take out a square spadeful of sod and settle the plants in the bare soil so that they briefly have the space to themselves before their neighbors start jostling in.

Columbines can be used in the same way and look particularly pretty growing in grass. Transplant evening primroses into the wild grass areas in fall, using plants grown from seed. All these are plants that peak in the first half of

FIELD OF BLOOMS
The color scheme here is gloriously unrestrained in keeping with the wild look of the planting. Bright dabs of color are seen through a feathery haze of grasses.

PLANT LIST
1 *Gladiolus byzantinus* x 3
2 *Geranium phaeum*
   (Mourning widow) x 2
3 *Aquilegia vulgaris* (Columbine) x 5
4 *Oenothera biennis*
   (Evening primrose) x 3
5 *Camassia leichtlinii* (Quamash) x 5

GLADIOLUS
In light soils, *Gladiolus byzantinus* will spread rapidly, throwing up sheaves of magenta flowers in early summer.

MOURNING WIDOW
Flourishing even in deep shade, *Geranium phaeum* has dark purple flowers that appear in late spring.

EVENING SCENT
The flowers of the evening primrose, Oenothera biennis, *have the heaviest perfume when they open in the evening. Each flower lasts only a day, but there is a long succession of blooms.*

CARE AND CULTIVATION

SPRING
Plant gladioli in holes cut into the turf. Add bone meal to the underlying soil. Sow seed of evening primroses in late spring.

SUMMER
Toward the end of the summer, give the meadow grass its first cut. Transplant evening primrose seedlings in rows outside to grow on until fall.

FALL
Cut the grass several more times during fall so that at the end of the growing season it has been reduced to a close-mown sward. Plant camassias, geraniums, columbines, and evening primroses in holes cut into the turf.

WINTER
No routine care is required in winter.

summer, because the meadow should be cut toward the end of the summer. If you have later-flowering plants, you will behead them as you mow. After the first late summer cut, fit in perhaps three more cuts before late fall. Then you will start off in spring with a close-mown sward against which plants such as primroses, fritillaries, and cowslips can display themselves to advantage.

Cranesbills, such as *Geranium pratense* 'Plenum Violaceum' and other reasonably tall-growing, herbaceous geraniums such as 'Kashmir Purple', 'Mrs. Kendall Clarke', and *Geranium psilostemon*, will be equally willing to supply splendor in the grass. Cut after the first crop of flowers. You may be lucky and get another, later show.

Any plant that includes the word "meadow" in its common name – meadow rue (*Thalictrum*), meadowsweet (*Filipendula*) – will be likely to have the right qualifications. Do not overdo the introductions, or you will lose the meadow and find yourself with another herbaceous border.

Geranium phaeum (Mourning widow) *Clump-forming perennial with maroon-purple flowers in late spring. H 2½ft (75cm), S 18in (45cm).*

Aquilegia vulgaris (Columbine) *Leafy perennial bearing pink, purple, or white flowers in early summer. H 3ft (1m), S 20in (50cm).*

Gladiolus byzantinus *Corm with upright spikes of deep pink flowers in summer. H 15–30in (38–75cm), S 2½in (6cm).*

Oenothera biennis (Evening primrose) *Erect biennial with pale yellow, fragant flowers in summer to fall. H 3ft (1m), S 12in (30cm).*

Camassia leichtlinii (Quamash) *Bulb with erect leaves and star-shaped, bluish violet or white flowers in summer. H 3–5ft (1–1.5m), S 12in (30cm).*

QUAMASH
Long spikes of starry flowers, which range from white through to a rich, deep blue, rise from the bulbs of *Camassia leichtlinii* in early summer.

EVENING PRIMROSE
As its species name suggests, *Oenothera biennis* is a biennial, the tall flowering spike arising from the basal rosette in the second season, giving a long succession of silky yellow flowers.

COLUMBINE
The dumpy, short-spurred flowers of *Aquilegia vulgaris* are held above elegantly divided foliage.

PLANTER'S GUIDE

If you want to extend or adapt a planting scheme, use this planter's guide to help you. Plants featured in the book are grouped according to their suitability for particular sites or their characteristics, making it easy to find plants for any part of the garden. Use the lists to supplement any of the schemes: add plants to expand a design for a larger site, substitute plants to tailor a scheme to suit your taste or the growing conditions in your garden, or combine plants to create entirely new schemes.

PLANTS FOR SHADY SITES

Acer palmatum 'Dissectum'
Arum italicum 'Pictum'
Asplenium trichomanes
Astilbe x *arendsii*
Brunnera macrophylla
   'Hadspen Cream'
Camellia x *williamsii*
   'Brigadoon'
Carex elata 'Aurea'
Ceterach officinarum
Convallaria majalis
Cornus alba 'Elegantissima'
Crataegus laciniata
Cyclamen hederifolium
Decaisnea fargesii
Galanthus nivalis
Hamamelis x *intermedia*
   'Arnold Promise'

Helleborus orientalis

Helleborus
Hosta
Hydrangea
Ligularia przewalskii
Mentha x *gentilis* 'Variegata'
Pernettya mucronata
   'Mulberry Wine'
Phyllitis scolopendrium
Pieris 'Forest Flame'
Polygonatum x *hybridum*
Polygonum campanulatum
Polypodium
Polystichum setiferum
Rhododendron

Tellima grandiflora 'Purpurea'
Tiarella wherryi
Viburnum opulus
   'Compactum'
Viburnum plicatum 'Mariesii'

PLANTS THAT TOLERATE DRY SHADE

Ajuga reptans 'Atropurpurea'
Alchemilla mollis
Berberis thunbergii
   f. *atropurpurea*
Bergenia ciliata
Brunnera macrophylla
   'Hadspen Cream'
Buxus sempervirens
Cortaderia selloana
   'Sunningdale Silver'
Cotoneaster horizontalis
Epimedium perralderianum
Euonymus fortunei
   'Silver Queen'
Hedera helix
Iris foetidissima
Lamium maculatum
   'White Nancy'
Mahonia x *media* 'Charity'
Pittosporum tenuifolium
Pulmonaria saccharata
Salvia officinalis
   'Purpurascens'
Saxifraga x *urbium*
Vinca minor
   'Argenteovariegata'

PLANTS FOR LIGHT, SANDY SOILS

Acacia dealbata
Aeonium arboreum
   'Schwarzkopf'
Agave
Antirrhinum majus
Brachycome iberidifolia

Chrysanthemum segetum
Cistus x *corbariensis*
Cleome hassleriana
Crocus
Echeveria
Foeniculum vulgare
   'Purpureum'
Helianthemum 'Wisley Pink'
Iris (except *I. laevigata* and
   I. pseudacorus)
Juniperus
Lavandula
Linaria maroccana
   'Fairy Lights'
Nepeta 'Six Hills Giant'
Origanum vulgare 'Aureum'
Papaver orientale
Pelargonium
Pennisetum villosum
Pernettya mucronata
   'Mulberry Wine'
Rosmarinus
Scilla siberica 'Atrocoerulea'
Sedum
Sempervivum
Verbena
Vitis vinifera 'Purpurea'

Sempervivum tectorum

PLANTS FOR HEAVY, CLAY SOILS

Berberis thunbergii
   f. *atropurpurea*
Choisya ternata
Cornus alba 'Elegantissima'
Cotoneaster horizontalis
Crataegus laciniata
Eucalyptus gunnii
Eucalyptus niphophila
Filipendula

Hedera helix
Humulus lupulus 'Aureus'
Iris laevigata 'Variegata'

Lysichiton americanus

Lysichiton americanus
Malus
Matteuccia struthiopteris
Osmunda regalis
Philadelphus
Primula florindae
Primula japonica
Prunus 'Tai Haku'
Pyracantha
Pyrus communis
   'Marguerite Marillat'
Rosa filipes 'Kiftsgate'
Salix lanata
Sorbus
Viburnum
Vitis coignetiae

PLANTS THAT PREFER ACID SOIL

Abies koreana
Camellia x *williamsii*
   'Brigadoon'
Erica x *darleyensis*
   'Ghost Hills'
Gentiana sino-ornata
Hamamelis x *intermedia*
   'Arnold Promise'
Lithodora diffusa
   'Heavenly Blue'
Magnolia x *soulangeana*
Osmunda regalis
Pernettya mucronata
   'Mulberry Wine'
Pieris 'Forest Flame'
Pinus pumila 'Globe'
Rhododendron

PLANTS FOR BOGGY SITES

Astilbe x arendsii
Carex elata 'Aurea'
Cimicifuga simplex
Cornus alba 'Elegantissima'
Eupatorium ligustrinum
Eupatorium rugosum
Filipendula
Hemerocallis citrina
Iris laevigata 'Variegata'
Iris pseudacorus 'Variegata'
Iris sibirica
Ligularia przewalskii
Lobelia syphilitica
Lysichiton americanus
Matteuccia struthiopteris
Osmunda regalis
Polygonum campanulatum
Primula florindae
Primula japonica
Rodgersia
Zantedeschia aethiopica 'Crowborough'

PLANTS FOR WINDY AND COASTAL SITES

✦=salt-tolerant plants
Antirrhinum majus
Arbutus unedo ✦
Bupleurum fruticosum
Calendula officinalis
Crinum x powellii
Eccremocarpus scaber
Erigeron karvinskianus ✦

Eryngium x oliverianum

Eryngium x oliverianum
Eschscholzia californica
Eucalyptus coccifera ✦
Eucalyptus gunnii ✦
Euonymus fortunei 'Silver Queen' ✦
Euphorbia characias subsp. *wulfenii*

Felicia amelloides 'Santa Anita'
Galtonia candicans
Hyacinthus orientalis
Ilex aquifolium 'Argentea Marginata' ✦

Kniphofia caulescens

Kniphofia caulescens
Kniphofia 'Percy's Pride'
Laurus nobilis
Lavandula angustifolia 'Hidcote'
Matthiola
Narcissus
Nerine bowdenii
Phormium tenax ✦
Pulsatilla vulgaris
Pyracantha
Rosmarinus
Salvia argentea
Scilla siberica 'Atrocoerulea'
Sedum spathulifolium 'Cape Blanco'
Sempervivum arachnoideum
Senecio maritima 'Silver Dust' ✦
Senecio 'Sunshine' ✦
Viola cornuta
Wisteria sinensis

PLANTS FOR HEDGES AND WINDBREAKS

Arbutus unedo
Buxus sempervirens
Choisya ternata

Arbutus unedo

Cortaderia selloana 'Sunningdale Silver'
Crataegus laciniata
Ilex aquifolium
Laurus nobilis
Lavandula
Phormium tenax
Pittosporum tenuifolium
Pyracantha x wateri
Rosa 'Felicia'
Rosa 'Penelope'
Rosa rugosa
Rosmarinus officinalis

PLANTS FOR PAVING AND CREVICES

Acaena microphylla
Armeria maritima
Aubrieta deltoidea
Campanula carpatica
Campanula cochleariifolia
Erigeron karvinskianus
Helianthemum 'Wisley Pink'
Lithodora diffusa 'Heavenly Blue'
Lobelia erinus
Phlox douglasii
Sedum spathulifolium
Sempervivum
Thymus praecox
Thymus serpyllum
Trifolium repens 'Purpurascens'
Viola tricolor

PLANTS WITH SCENTED FLOWERS

Acacia dealbata
Cheiranthus 'Bredon'
Choisya ternata
Daphne x burkwoodii 'Somerset'
Daphne odora 'Aureomarginata'
Dianthus
Galium odoratum

Hamamelis x intermedia 'Arnold Promise'
Hyacinthoides hispanica
Hyacinthus
Iris graminea
Jasminum officinale
Lathyrus odoratus
Lavandula
Lilium
Lonicera
Mahonia x media 'Charity'
Malus floribunda
Narcissus
Nicotiana sylvestris
Oenothera biennis
Pelargonium (some)
Philadelphus
Pittosporum tenuifolium
Rhododendron luteum

Robinia pseudoacacia 'Frisia'

Robinia pseudoacacia
Rosa
Viburnum x bodnantense 'Dawn'
Wisteria

PLANTS WITH AROMATIC FOLIAGE

Artemisia abrotanum
Calendula officinalis
Coriandrum sativum
Eucalyptus
Foeniculum vulgare 'Purpureum'
Laurus nobilis
Mentha x gentilis 'Variegata'
Myrrhis odorata
Nepeta 'Six Hills Giant'
Origanum vulgare 'Aureum'
Pelargonium
Rosmarinus
Salvia officinalis 'Purpurascens'
Thymus

CARE AND CULTIVATION

PLANTS WILL MOSTLY TRY TO GROW, whatever you do to them. Sometimes they will also die, even if you are the world's acknowledged expert on their care. But there is a lot you can do to help, rather than hinder, their passage through life; this section is a practical guide that shows you how to keep your planting schemes looking their best.

The ideal way to learn about plants is by watching the way that they grow in your garden. The more time you spend with your plants, the more attuned you will become to their needs. Like people, some have quite specific requirements, and it is foolish to ignore them. Work with the prevailing conditions in your garden, not against them.

PREPARING *the* SOIL *and* PLANTING

Soil is a mixture of organic matter, water, and small pieces of rock. The size of the rock particles and the amount of organic matter determine whether the soil is heavy or light, fertile or infertile. Adding manure, leaf mold, or compost helps improve soil structure. The extra humus closes up the spaces in sandy soil, making it capable of holding more water. In clay soils, humus opens up the spaces, and so helps drainage. You can certainly improve your soil, but do not attempt to alter its basic type. You will be fighting a losing battle if you try to make an alkaline soil acidic. If you want a garden filled with rhododendrons and azaleas, move to an area with acidic soil.

The perfect soil is loam, which is what good gardeners get when they go to Heaven. Loam is neither too wet nor too dry, neither sticky nor sandy. It contains an ideal blend of clay, sand, and humus, with just the right amount of mineral seasoning. If you work hard at the humus, you may get your loam in the here and now rather than the hereafter.

SITE PREPARATION AND PLANTING

You cannot altogether avoid digging when preparing beds, but only a masochist will make this chore loom large in the gardening calendar. On heavy ground, digging exposes clods of soil that can then be broken up by frost. You also dig to get air into the soil and to bury weeds or other organic material. On light soils, you may not need to dig at all; forking over is often enough. A mulch of mushroom compost or other weed-free material may be spread thickly over the surface to prevent weed seeds from germinating and will eventually be pulled down

PLANTING IN OPEN GROUND

1 *Dig a hole about twice the width of the plant's root ball. Mix the soil you have taken out with some compost or bone meal. Fork over the base of the hole. Place one hand over the soil mix in the pot and tip the pot over to ease out the plant. Gently tease out any tightly coiled roots. Settle the plant into the prepared hole.*

2 *Use a stake to check that the soil on top of the root ball is level with the ground around it. Adjust the depth if necessary by adding or removing soil underneath the plant. If planting a tree, drive in a supporting stake alongside, clear of the root ball (see p.148). Fill around the plant with the soil and compost mixture.*

3 *Firm the soil around the plant in stages to make sure there are no spaces between the roots, using your heel or knuckles. Water thoroughly and, for shrubs, trees, and moisture-loving perennials, spread a deep mulch of well-rotted compost or ground bark around the plant in a circle 12–18in (30–45cm) wide.*

4 *Your new plant may not need shaping or pruning at the outset, but if you can see diseased or damaged stems or wood, cut back to fresh, healthy growth. On a tree or shrub, prune out any stems growing toward the center of the bush. Also remove any long, weak, or straggly stems that look as though they may spoil the balanced framework.*

by worms to enrich the earth. This is a lot easier than doing it yourself.

Where there are persistent weeds, use a nonresidual weedkiller to clear the ground before using a mulch. Once the weeds have died down, you can plant direct into the ground without disturbing it any further. Tackle heavy clay soils at the beginning of winter, but leave light soils until late spring. The best time to plant trees, shrubs, and perennials is in spring or fall. Most should be planted so that the surrounding soil is at the same level as the top of the root ball. However, some perennials, such as irises, are best planted slightly above the surface of the soil, while moisture-loving plants, such as hostas, prefer to be slightly below ground level.

PLANTS IN CONTAINERS

You may want to create planting schemes using ornamental containers. Choose a container with drainage holes and add a layer of drainage material such as broken clay pots in the base. Cover this with fibrous material such as sphagnum moss or upside-down sod. Set plants at the correct depth (see above) in a suitable soil mix, firming them in well, and water thoroughly.

If you are growing plants in a bed, and they are too tender to overwinter outdoors, plunge them in the ground in pots. They can then be lifted easily when necessary and brought under cover until the following season.

PLANTING LEVELS

STANDARD PLANTING
(Aster)

SUNKEN PLANTING
(Hosta)

BULBS

Bulbs need to be planted as soon as you can get hold of them. Most are sold in a dried-off state but your success rate with the earliest flowering kinds, such as snowdrops and aconites, will improve significantly if you can plant them "in the green," lifting them just after flowering, while still in full leaf. Plant these at the same depth as before, shown by the color change near the base of the leaves. Unless you are using them in bold blocks for formal bedding, all bulbs are best planted in random clumps or drifts, particularly if in a semiwild setting, under trees or in grass. In general, light soils are kinder to bulbs than heavy ones. They warm up more quickly in spring and they are usually better drained.

PLANTING DEPTHS

The ideal planting depth depends on the size of the bulb. Use the length of the bulb as a rough guide and plant each bulb at two to five times its own depth.

PLANTING IN A WALL CREVICE

Before planting in a wall (or in the crevices of paving), chip out some mortar if necessary so you can add soil mix to support the plants. Choose plants such as sedums, saxifrages, and sempervivums that naturally grow in situations such as these.

1 *Ease the roots of the plant into a crevice, using a widger, teaspoon, or the tip of a small trowel. Firm the plants in place with your fingers, trickling in more soil mix if necessary.*

2 *When all the plants are in position, water them from the top of the wall, or mist them with a hand sprayer. Keep them moist until well established. Refirm any plants that become loose.*

WALL SHRUBS AND CLIMBERS

Before planting, secure any support such as vine eyes and wires or a trellis (hinged so it can be lowered and the wall painted when necessary). The bottom of a wall is a dry place, so the most important thing when planting a wall shrub or climber is to set the plant at least 18in (45cm) away from the base of the wall. After that, regular training and tying in (see pp.150–151) are the keys to success. Keep climbers close to the wall, or they will crowd out other plants growing beneath.

TRELLIS SUPPORT

Fix trellis at top with hook and vine eye.

Fix hinge at base.

1 *Dig a hole larger than the plant's root ball. Loosen the soil in the hole. Soak the root ball, then settle the plant in the hole, leaning it at 45°. Spread out the roots away from the wall.*

2 *Fill in around the plant, firming in stages. Untie the plant from its stake and cut back any weak, damaged, or outward-growing stems. Spread out and tie in remaining shoots.*

CARING *for* PLANTS

In the wild, plants find their own lodging and they choose what suits them best. In a garden, they have to make the best of what we give them. If you take the trouble to learn what requirements each plant has, you will be amply rewarded.

FEEDING AND WATERING

Food and drink are as necessary to plants as they are to people. It is the gardener's duty to see that each plant has enough of both. Food means more than inorganic, or "chemical," fertilizers. These work fast, but they drain out of the soil quickly and can displace other nutrients, upsetting the soil's delicate chemical balance. Inorganic fertilizers offer a limited range of major nutrients (nitrogen, phosphorus, and potassium) and are often deficient or lacking in minor nutrients that are just as essential.

Soil well supplied with organic matter, such as compost and leaf mold, and treated with organic fertilizers, such as seaweed and bone meal, will provide the correct amounts of nutrients for most plants over a long period. Organic fertilizers, if used properly, foster healthy populations of microbes and larger creatures, such as worms and ants, that help keep the soil alive and in good heart.

MULCHING AND WEEDING

Adding bulky organic matter to the soil will enhance its fertility and structure. The simplest way to do this is with a thick mulch. This also helps to retain moisture and control weeds. Different mulches provide different benefits. Gravel, for instance, will not do anything by way of feeding, but is excellent around alpines or Mediterranean herbs, which are used to thin rations. It prevents mud from splashing onto low leaves or flowers and provides drainage.

Weeds compete with your ornamental plants for food and water and may even smother their growth. Mulching helps to keep weeds in check but will not remove the need for weeding altogether. Take care to remove weeds while still young and certainly before they flower and set seed. Use a hoe, fork, or trowel to remove weeds or treat them with a weedkiller such as glyphosate that does not persist in the soil.

MULCHING
When mulching, spread the material around the plant to the same extent as its top-growth, keeping clear of the plant's stem. A mulch should be 2–4in (5–10cm) thick if it is to keep down weeds.

STAKES AND TIES

The best answer to staking is to use plants that do not need it, for it is a difficult job to do well. The mechanics should not show, nor should the stake rule the plant, giving it the air of a patient in a neck brace. Some plants, such as delphiniums, you stake as a matter of course, for they have been bred far beyond the point where they can hold themselves up in a crisis. But to stake a foxglove is like caging a gazelle. You take away its soul. Any support you give a plant must be in keeping with its natural habit. Brushwood, either bent over and woven into an approximation of a lobster pot, or pushed in to make a stockade around a plant, provides the maximum support with the minimum interference. It is also attractive to look at before it is disguised by the plant's growth. That matters.

SINGLE STAKE
Tie single-stemmed plants such as gladiolus to a bamboo stake before they are about 12in (30cm) tall. When flower buds begin to form, tie the stem to the stake just below the buds to provide support.

LINK STAKES
Use link stakes for clump-forming or multistemmed plants that need support. Push the stakes deep into the soil when the plant is still young, and raise them gradually as it grows.

ANGLED STAKE
A low, angled stake such as this allows a tree to move naturally in the wind. Drive it into the ground clear of the roots at a 45° angle so that it leans into the prevailing wind. Secure the tree to the stake with a buckle-and-spacer tie. Pull the tie taut, without damaging the bark, and adjust it as the tree grows.

CUTTING BACK AND DIVIDING

Many plants, including roses and some perennials, produce more flowers if the old, dying blooms are cut off (see right). Shrubs grown for their variegated foliage should have any plain shoots removed. A number of perennials and bulbs benefit from being divided and replanted if they are no longer flowering well and have become overcrowded (see p.152).

Herbaceous perennials may be cut down at the end of the season. As well as looking tidier, this helps prevent problems caused by diseased or decaying material.

PEST AND DISEASE CONTROL

If plants are growing well, as they will if you take care to give them what they need, they will be far less vulnerable to pests and diseases. The problem with using insecticides is that you wipe out the good guys along with the bad. There are plenty of good insects, but they seem slower on the uptake than the bad. Ladybirds, for instance, are good because they eat prodigious numbers of aphids. Encourage ichneumon flies, which prey on caterpillars, by planting goldenrod and fennel. Centipedes and black ground beetles are both fond of slug breakfasts.

Weather conditions have a great influence on some diseases. There are good and bad years for mildew, rust, blackspot, and blight. Fungicides help, but only if you doggedly apply them at the correct intervals. Help yourself by choosing varieties of plants that are resistant to disease.

DEADHEADING
The purpose of deadheading, that is removing faded flowers, is to stimulate the earliest possible development of new, young shoots and further blooms throughout the flowering season. On a cluster-flowered bush rose such as this, cut out the central bloom first to stimulate the other buds into flower. When all the flowers have faded, remove the whole cluster, cutting back to an emerging bud or a fully formed shoot.

REMOVING REVERTED SHOOTS
Many variegated shrubs are propagated from green-leaved plants that have produced mutated branches, known as sports. Sometimes branches of these variegated shrubs revert to the foliage of the parent. Since these branches have more chlorophyll and so are more vigorous, they may swamp the variegated growth. Cut them out as soon as you notice them.

PROTECTING PLANTS FROM COLD AND WIND

In general, you should garden with your climate, rather than against it, but all adventurous gardeners are constantly trying to extend the boundaries of what is possible in their patch. Plants that are on the borderline of hardiness in your area should be protected from the worst of winter, particularly while they are young and at their most vulnerable. Surround a tree or shrub with an insulating barrier of straw or leaves, for example, held in place with a cage of wire netting. Even if their top-growth has been cut to the ground by cold in winter, many shrubs will sprout again from the base once they have a well-established network of roots. Leafy plants such as palms and cordylines can be protected by having their leaves bound and wrapped in burlap. For small plants and seedlings, use glass or plastic cloches, low polytunnels, or fleecy, floating row covers. Another solution is to pot up plants, then bring them under cover before the first frosts and overwinter them indoors.

BURLAP
To protect leafy plants against frost, tie in the leaves, then wrap them in burlap. Pack the base of the plant with straw.

DOUBLE NETTING
Protect vulnerable plants from wind with a barrier to diffuse the wind's strength. Most effective are permeable barriers such as this flexible netting which makes a temporary shelter for plants while they become established.

CLOCHE
Use a cloche to protect seedlings, tender herbaceous plants, or young shrubs. Cover the open ends with glass or plastic to stop wind from blowing through. Water plants if necessary. Remove the cloches by day as the temperature warms up.

MOUNDING UP SOIL
In cold areas, protect tender bush roses or plants such as agapanthus from cold damage by mounding up soil around the crown to a depth of about 5in (12cm).

PRUNING *and* TRAINING

Pruning is the gardener's way of enhancing the performance of a particular plant and encouraging it to produce better flowers, foliage, or fruit. It is something we do for our benefit rather than theirs. Shrubs do not die if they are left unpruned, as anyone who has taken over a neglected garden knows only too well. They just get bigger.

AIMS OF PRUNING

Good pruning is a matter of working with rather than against the natural habit and inclinations of a plant. If it flowers on new wood, as buddleia and perovskia do, then it is in your interests to persuade it to produce as much of this as possible by pruning hard each season. Shrubs such as dogwoods with decorative winter bark also benefit from hard pruning or coppicing (see opposite), since the bark color is always brighter on new wood than old. Compensate for the extra work you are giving such shrubs by feeding them liberally.

Many trees, shrubs, roses, and climbers benefit from pruning to remove dead, unproductive, congested, or spindly growth, but do not look upon pruners as offensive weapons to brandish around all your plants. Abutilon, acer (maples), camellia, cotoneaster, magnolia, and rhododendron do not need regular pruning. All you need to do with these is remove dead shoots and occasionally thin out overcrowded or crossing branches.

If you use shears on shrubs, you run the risk of reducing them all to the same barbered, bunlike shape. When pruning, do not cut back all branches by the same amount. Remove some stems entirely, cutting them back to the base or at the junction with another branch. In this way, you will be more certain of retaining the shrub's natural outline. If pruning stems partially, cut back to an outward-facing bud or shoot.

Before you make any cut, have its purpose clearly in mind. Some shrubs such as cotinus, forsythia, winter jasmine, spiraea, philadelphus, and weigela are best treated in a three-year

WHERE TO CUT
When pruning, cut back to just above a healthy bud or shoot or pair of buds or shoots.

Strong pair of buds

Make a straight cut on plants with opposite buds.

Angle the cut on plants with alternate buds.

Cut back to an outward-facing bud.

OLD WOOD
Periodically remove wood that is very old and no longer flowering well. Use pruners or, for very thick stems, pruning loppers to remove a proportion of the oldest stems, cutting them back to within 2–3in (5–8cm) of the ground. On established suckering shrubs, cut back up to half the old wood to the base after flowering, and prune the remainder by half.

PRUNING ROSES

Prune roses when dormant, between fall leaf drop and spring bud break. Large-flowered bush roses (Hybrid Teas) need the hardest pruning. Surprisingly, trials at the Royal National Rose Society's grounds in England showed that a quick haircut with a hedgetrimmer can yield better results than more traditional methods. Old shrub and species roses flower on old wood rather than new and so must be pruned more lightly. Most roses should be hard pruned after planting to stimulate vigorous growth.

REMOVING OLD STEMS
On mature roses, occasionally remove old, unproductive wood at the base to encourage the shrub to produce young, new growth.

SHORTENING SIDE SHOOTS
Some shrub roses, such as the Gallicas, have an overabundance of twiggy side shoots. Shorten these after flowering, cutting them back by about two-thirds.

DEAD WOOD
All shrubs at some stage in their lives have shoots or whole branches that die back, due to age, disease, or some kind of damage. This wood should be cut back to a healthy pair of buds, leaves, or shoots.

THIN STEMS
Prune back weak, twiggy, or straggly stems to just above soil level. Aim to create a balanced-looking shrub with an open center. Prune very thin growth hard, but strong growth only lightly.

COPPICING

This is a useful technique for dogwoods and other plants grown for their winter bark because it stimulates the growth of new stems, which have a much brighter color than the old. Cut down all the stems to the base in spring before new growth begins. After this hard pruning, mulch around the plants and feed well.

rotation. Each year after the shrub has flowered, you remove one-third of the oldest shoots to encourage fresh, young growth to sprout from the base. After three years of this treatment, you will have rejuvenated the entire bush.

Pinching out, or stopping, is a form of micro-pruning often used on argyranthemums and chrysanthemums to force plants to make more growth or flower buds. It is best done when plants are growing quickly in spring and summer.

WHEN TO PRUNE

In the most general terms, shrubs that flower in winter, spring, or early summer do so on growth made in the previous year. These can be pruned after flowering. Shrubs that flower in summer or fall bear their flowers on the new wood they have made earlier in the growing season. These are best left until early spring the following year.

Pruning kicks a shrub into top growing gear, causing it to pump energy into dormant growth buds to replace what it feels it has lost. If you prune a buddleia or caryopteris in late summer when it has just finished flowering, the resultant new growth will coincide fatally with the first frosts. For this reason these plants, as well as deciduous ceanothus, ceratostigma, lavatera, and perovskia, should be left until spring.

TRAINING

For wall shrubs and climbers, training and tying in is as important as pruning. Relatively few plants come complete with their own adhesive. The Virginia creepers and ivies have good self-sticking sucker pads. So does the climbing hydrangea, but most wall shrubs need careful attention in the early years while you build up a basic framework of branches and secure them strongly to their support. Once you have established this well tied-in framework, it is much clearer what can be pruned and what should be left alone.

Walls can provide shelter for relatively tender shrubs, such as ceanothus. If a shrub sticks its nose out too far from the shelter of its wall, it is far more likely to be damaged by wind and frost. Keep it spread-eagled flat for its own protection. If you tie in wall shrubs well, rather than letting them loll where they will, you create extra growing space under and around them, and by tying in branches, you stop them from lashing around and smashing themselves in high winds. For a formal effect, train shrubs on parallel wires, strung through vine eyes fixed to the wall.

PRUNING CLEMATIS

Clematis can be divided into three separate pruning groups. The first group, mostly early-flowering species such as *Clematis alpina* and *C. macropetala*, need little or no pruning. The second group includes early, large-flowered cultivars such as 'Henryi' and 'Niobe' and needs only light pruning in early spring. The late-flowering types need the hardest pruning: those such as 'Perle d'Azur' and 'Jackmanii' should be cut back hard to within 18in (45cm) of the ground in late winter or early spring.

EARLY, LARGE-FLOWERED CLEMATIS
When pruning clematis in the second group, cut back old stems to a strong pair of buds to stimulate new, flowering wood.

LATE-FLOWERING CLEMATIS
In early spring, hard prune all stems just above the lowest pair of strong buds, about 6–18in (15–45cm) above the ground.

CLIMBERS ON PERGOLAS AND ARCHES

Little and often is the key to training plants on a pergola or arch. Stems should be tied in throughout the growing season. Spread them out to cover as much of the structure as possible. Train the stems of twining species around their supports, making sure that the shoots are going in the right direction. Some climbers grow clockwise, some counterclockwise. When flowering is over, take out any dead or diseased shoots and prune the plants as necessary.

TYING IN
Tie in stray side shoots to the support in their natural direction of growth. Encourage scramblers by wrapping wire netting around the posts to provide support.

CUTTING BACK
In late summer, cut back all the leading stems by one-third to promote lateral growth. Untie rambling roses, cut out old growth, and tie in new stems.

PROPAGATING PLANTS

Propagation is the catchall phrase for the various means by which gardeners can increase their plant stock. Plants, being superbly profligate by nature, usually offer more than one means of doing this. Only annual plants, which complete their life cycle within a year, reproduce themselves solely by seed. Many other plants also set seed that can be germinated fairly easily, although many perennials and some bulbs may also be split and divided. Shrubs are usually propagated by vegetative methods such as taking cuttings or rooting layers.

GROWING PLANTS FROM CUTTINGS

Propagation can easily become an obsession. There is no more wildly parental feeling than watching your first successful cutting turn into a grown-up bush. If you are a beginner, start with pelargoniums. They are least likely to let you down, are always useful, and are expensive to buy. They may be difficult to overwinter unless you live in a frost-free area. Cuttings provide your insurance policy.

For your cuttings, look for healthy, new, bright green shoots without flowers. The reason for choosing shoots without flowers is that the cuttings can put all their effort into producing roots, without having to bother about what is happening on top. Take and prepare the cuttings (see above right) and push them into a soil mix that is easy for the roots to infiltrate. A mixture of peat and sand is traditional, but a mix of vermiculite and a fibrous medium such as sphagnum moss is just as good.

Many cuttings root most easily in a moist, enclosed atmosphere and should be kept covered with a plastic bag or in a propagator. Pelargonium cuttings do not. Stand the pot in a light, airy place and keep the soil mix moist, but not sopping wet. The cuttings should root within ten days.

TAKING CUTTINGS

Take cuttings about 3–5in (7–12cm) long from the tips of strong, healthy shoots. Trim each just below a leaf joint and remove the lowest leaves. Push cuttings around the edge of a pot of soil mix, then water. Cover with a plastic bag, making sure it does not touch the cuttings. When the cuttings have rooted, set them in small pots.

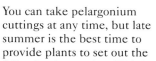

You can take pelargonium cuttings at any time, but late summer is the best time to provide plants to set out the following late spring. This is also the best season to take cuttings of other tender perennials, such as osteospermums, argyranthemums, and penstemons. For a number of shrubs such as fuchsias, cuttings are best taken in spring.

Pelargoniums can also be propagated in early spring, but you need to overwinter the mother plants in a frost-free place. Force the overwintered plants into growth to provide plenty of juicy new cutting material by cutting them back and watering and feeding them generously in late winter.

DIVIDING PLANTS

Many perennials and some suckering shrubs that produce plenty of shoots from the base can be increased by division. This also allows you to discard old or unproductive parts and so helps rejuvenate the plant. The best time to divide plants is when they are dormant, between fall and early spring, avoiding very cold, wet, or dry spells.

PROPAGATION BY DIVISION

2 Carefully pull these new, small segments away from the old clump, checking that each piece has several fresh, new shoots and good roots. Take care at all times to avoid any damage to the roots.

1 Perennials such as helianthus are most easily propagated by dividing mature clumps. The best and most vigorous pieces are usually at the edges of the clump. Lift the plant with a fork and chop off these sections with a spade.

3 Cut back any long stems that remain on the new plants and replant them at the same depth as before in soil enriched with compost or bone meal. Firm them in and then water well. Keep them moist until well established.

RAISING PLANTS FROM SEED

1 *There are various ways of ensuring that seed is sown thinly and evenly over the surface of the soil mix. You can scatter it from a folded piece of paper, as here, or sprinkle it with your finger and thumb. Cover with a fine layer of sieved soil mix or vermiculite.*

2 *Cover the pot with a pane of glass or with plastic wrap to retain moisture. Check whether it needs to be kept in the dark or the light. A warm cupboard makes a good germination chamber for seed that needs darkness to germinate. An indoor windowsill is ideal for others.*

3 *Germination times vary widely, so check the pots frequently and uncover them as soon as the seedlings emerge. When they have developed their first true leaves, prick them out into a larger container – either a seed tray or individual pots.*

4 *Plants need to grow on without check, so regular watering is essential. Gradually harden off the plants, putting the trays or pots out on warm days and bringing them in at night. When this hardening off is complete, you can set out your plants.*

SOWING SEED

To the uninitiated, seed sowing is the impenetrable rite of passage that separates the novice from the seasoned gardener. But it is not as difficult as experts would have you believe, nor do you need batteries of equipment. A heated propagator speeds up the germination process, but is not vital. At some stage seedlings have to face real life. The tougher they are raised, the better they will cope.

If you are a beginner, avoid sowing seeds that have complicated germination mechanisms. Some seeds need cold, or alternating periods of cold and heat, before they germinate. These conditions usually mirror the circumstances that occur in their natural habitats. Most just need warmth and moisture.

Not all need light. Nemesia, pansy, and verbena, for example, germinate best in total darkness. Ageratum, alyssum, snapdragon, lobelia, mimulus, impatiens, nicotiana, and petunia, on the other hand, all need light.

The basic routine for seed sowing is simple. Use a clean plastic pot or seed tray for the initial sowing. Fill it with soil mix and firm it down gently. Scatter the seed over the surface of the soil mix, then cover it with a thin layer of soil mix or vermiculite. The latter drains quickly and you do not have to worry about the exact depth of the covering, as you must if you are using soil mix. Water the pot thoroughly before covering it with a sheet of glass or plastic or piece of plastic wrap. Remove the cover once the seedlings are visible.

OVERCROWDED BULBS

If bulbs are happy, they will increase, each bulb gradually building up into a large clump. This is a joy, of course, but if they get too congested, you may get fewer flowers. Then you need to split them up and replant them, discarding any that have dried up.

1 *When the bulbs are dormant and the foliage has died down, lift the entire clump from the ground and sort through the bulbs, discarding any that seem unsound.*

2 *Gently pull the bulbs apart. Early-flowering bulbs such as snowdrops and aconites are best split "in the green" just as they have finished flowering.*

DIVIDING RHIZOMATOUS PERENNIALS

Rhizomatous plants such as bearded iris can also be propagated by splitting congested clumps. The best pieces are usually on the edges of the clump. Replant the rhizomes, each with plump roots, level with or just above the soil surface.

1 *Lift a clump of iris and split it into pieces, each with a single fan of leaves. Discard any unproductive rhizomes with old, dark roots and no leaves.*

2 *Trim the rhizomes with a sharp knife, cutting back any very long roots. Shorten the foliage and replant the rhizomes about 5in (12cm) apart.*

INDEX

Page numbers for plant entries that appear in **bold** refer to a plant featured in a main scheme or supplementary planting. Page numbers given in normal type direct you to text on a plant or topic, while those in *italic* indicate that there is a picture and caption.

ACKNOWLEDGMENTS

AUTHOR'S ACKNOWLEDGMENTS

Most of the schemes in this book have no direct provenance, often arising out of experiments in my own garden. Some, however, do and I would like to thank Mr. and Mrs. Paice of Bourton House, whose garden was the inspiration for the large planted pot on pp.130–31, and the superb gardeners at Kingston Maurward, Dorset, England's college of agriculture, where I first saw the border that was adapted for the tropical scheme on pp.32–5.

A book such as this is made by a large team – writing is only the first step – and I am grateful to Dorling Kindersley for providing such superb support. I would particularly like to thank Claire Calman, Jill Andrews, and Melanie Tham for their tenacity, good humor, and exemplary attention to detail.

Dorling Kindersley would like to thank: Jackie Bennett, Marion Boddy-Evans, Diana Craig, Eleanor Hoffman, Kate Swainson for editorial assistance; Joanna Chisholm for the index; Karen Ward, Karen Mackley, Suzanne Stevenson for design and DTP assistance; Sarah Fuller and Hilary Stephens for production; Cooling Brown for typesetting.

ILLUSTRATORS
Sharon Beeden pp.24–5, pp.28–9, pp.32–3, pp.36–7, pp.44–5, pp.48–9, pp.52–3, pp.58–9, pp.66–7, pp.78–9
Martine Collings pp.40–41, pp.62–3, pp.70–71, pp.74–5, pp.82–3, pp.88–9, pp.92–3, pp.96–7, pp.100–101, pp.104–105
Catharine Slade pp.110–11, pp.114–15, pp.116–17, pp.126–7
Vanessa Luff pp.120–21, pp.132–3, pp.134–5, pp.138–9
Ann Winterbottom pp.122–3, pp.124–5
Gill Tomblin pp.136–7, pp.140–41, pp.142–3
David Ashby pp.130–31
Karen Cochrane all planting plans
Additional illustrators Sally Hynard, Will Giles, Liz Pepperell, Sandra Pond, Michael Shoebridge, Ross Watton

PHOTOGRAPHY CREDITS

tl=top left; tr=top right; tcl=top center left; tc=top center; tcr=top center right; ul=upper left; ur=upper right; ucl=upper center left; ucr=upper center right; lcl=lower center left; lc=lower center; lcr=lower center right; bl=bottom left; br=bottom right; bc=bottom center; bcl=bottom center left; bcr=bottom center right.

CREATIVE PLANTING
p.10 Eric Crichton: bl; Steven Wooster: cr.
p.11 Will Giles: br.
p.12 Stephen Robson: tl; Steven Wooster: tr; Will Giles: bc.
p.13 Steven Wooster: tr, bl.
p.14 Eric Crichton: bl; Steven Wooster: tc.
p.15 Steven Wooster: tl; Eric Crichton: br.
p.16 Steven Wooster: bl; Stephen Robson: tr, br.
p.17 Stephen Robson: bl; Steven Wooster: tr.
p.18 Steven Wooster: tr; Stephen Robson: bl.
p.19 Stephen Robson: tr, br; Steven Wooster: bl.
p.20 Steven Wooster: tc; Will Giles: br.
p.21 Steven Wooster: main pic.

MIXED BORDERS
Cool Colors for Damp Shade
p.26 Harry Smith: cr; Will Giles: bcr, br.
p.27 Eric Crichton: ucl; Will Giles: ucr; Gillian Andrews: br.
Pretty Pastels
p.30 A–Z Botanical Collection: tcl, br; Andrew Lawson: tr.
p.31 Guernsey Clematis Nursery Ltd: bl.
A Tropical Summer Border
p.34 Harry Smith: cl, tr.
p.35 The Garden Picture Library: bcr.
A Lush Poolside
p.38 Neil Holmes: ucl; Harry Smith: tl, tcr.

Bright Berries for Fall
p.42 Harry Smith: ucl; Will Giles: tr.
p.43 Harry Smith: tl.
Cottage-garden Border
p.46 Harry Smith: bl; Pat Brindley: lcl; Will Giles: tr; Harry Smith: br.
p.47 Pat Brindley: bcl.
A Display for Fall and Winter
p.51 Harry Smith: br, bl; The Garden Picture Library: tl.
Border of Miniatures
p.54 Harry Smith: ul; Gillian Beckett: bcl; Will Giles: ur; Gillian Beckett: bcr; Eric Crichton: tr.

ISLAND BEDS
A Bed of Roses
p.61 Pat Brindley: br, bl; Eric Crichton: bc.
A Bold Desert Bed
p.64 Gillian Beckett: br; Harry Smith: ucl.
p.65 Will Giles: bcl; Harry Smith: tl.
Instant Flowers
p.68 Will Giles: ucr; Harry Smith: br; Pat Brindley: tr.
p.69 Derek Gould: bc.
A Formal Herb Design
p.76 Harry Smith: bl.
Flowers and Fruits
p.80 Will Giles: ucl; A–Z Botanical Collection: lcl; Harry Smith: bcr; Brogdale Slide Library: lc.
A Low-maintenance Scheme
p.84 Harry Smith: tl.
p.85 Christopher Brickell: br.

CORNER SITES
Waterside Textures
p.90 Diana Grenfell: tcr.
p.91 Harry Smith: bl.

Colored Foliage
p.95 Harry Smith: tr.
A Scheme for Scent
p.98 Harry Smith: cr.
p.99 Photos Horticultural: bl; Harry Smith: br.
Planting by the Sea
p.102 Eric Crichton: bcr; Will Giles: bcl.
p.103 Hazel le Rougetel/Biofotos: cl; Will Giles: bl.
Sunny Yellows and Blues
p.106 Harry Smith: lcl, tl, lcr, bl; Pat Brindley: tr.
p.107 Harry Smith: lcl, bl.

VERTICAL SPACES
Planting up a Pergola
p.112 Hazel le Rougetel/Biofotos: ul; Harry Smith: lc.
p.113 Harry Smith: bl; Pat Brindley: ucr.
Screening the Garden
p.118 Harry Smith: bl.
p.119 Harry Smith: bl, br, ur.
A Place in the Sun
p.121 Harry Smith: tl, tc, tr.
Climbing Frames
p.124 Suttons Seeds: bl.
Walls without Sun
p.127 Pat Brindley: br.

FORGOTTEN PLACES
A Potted Disguise
p.130 Will Giles: tr, bl.
A Stony Patch
p.139 Harry Smith: tl, bc.
Occasional Pots
p.141 Harry Smith: bl.
Splendor in the Grass
p.143 Harry Smith: tl.